PHEEP!
AND WE'RE OFF! HERE, BUSTER...
...RUN WITH IT!

KR-RUNCH!
GAAAA!
I'LL TAKE THAT

FOUL!
NONSENSE, GONAD... I WAS GOING FOR THE BALLS... ARF!

SEE MR BULLCRUSHER
HEIR 18-YARD BOX...
GOOD PASS!

SNATCH!!
BAH!
NICE TACKLE, TOMMY!
THAT'S A DETENTION FOR YOU, BOY

THROUGH BALL, TOMMY... I'M IN SPACE!
RIGHT-HO, BUSTER
THANKS
PUNT!

PHEEEP!
EH!?

HUNH!? WHERE DID THE BALL GO...!?!

IN THE BACK OF THE NET... THANKS TO GONAD'S GENITALS!
HO! HO!
OOER!
ONE NIL TO US, I BELIEVE

YOUR MASSIVE PODS UNSIGHTED THE KEEPER!
YEAH, BIG NUTS!
NOW WE'RE ONE-NILL DOWN, WITH FIVE MINUTES TO GO

EP!

THUNDER!!
OUT OF MY WAY!

TRIP!
PHEEP!
KNACKER OBSTRUCTION

FREE KICK TO THE TEACHERS
OH, WELL DONE BUSTER... BULLCRUSHER NEVER MISSES FROM THIS RANGE
HE'S GOT THE HARDEST SHOT IN THE STAFFROOM!

M!!
GAAAA!!
THUK!

SPROING!
IT'S IN!! IT'S IN OFF BUSTER'S KNACKERS
BAH!
PHEEP!
BOYS WIN 2-1 .... BAH!

THREE CHEERS FOR BUSTER'S PODS...
HIP! HIP!
HUSSAH!!

OH LORDY! IT'S
THE FAT SLAGS

ONE DAY...

'ERE, TRAY... COME AN' LOOK AT THIS!
HMM!..

WHAT?
LOOK AT THAT, TRAY... WHADYA RECKON T' THAT, EH?
I 'OPE YOU 'AVEN'T DRAGGED ME UP 'ERE JUST T' LOOK AT BAZ'S COCK, SAN

NO! I WAS JUST GIVIN' 'IM A NOSH AN' I NOTICED HIS HELMET WAS THE EXACT COLOUR I WANT ON ME BEDROOM WALL...

LOOK... IT GOES SMASHIN' WITH THE CURTAINS

C'MON, BAZ. PUT YER TROLLIES ON. LET'S GO!
HOMEBASE
EH?.. WHERE?
THEY'VE GOT A MACHINE THAT SCANS STUFF AN' MAKES PAINT THAT COLOUR

SHORTLY...
HOMEBASE

COLOUR SCAN
'ERE, MISTER. CAN I 'AVE TWO LITRES OF EMULSION THE SAME COLOUR AS HIS LID

COME ON, BAZ... DROP YER TROLLIES. ME AN' TRAY'LL GO AN' GET SOME ROLLERS.
COLOUR SCAN
HOME BASE

QUICK AS Y'CAN, MATE!
COLOUR SCAN

TEN MINUTES LATER...
ALL DONE, LADIES.

BACK HOME...
RIGHT, TRAY...
LET'S GET GOIN'

OOH, TRAY... THAT DON'T LOOK RIGHT... THAT'S NEVER PURPLE
NO... THAT'S MORE OF A GREENY- PINKY- GREY!

EEH! IT MAKES Y'FEEL SICK T'LOOK AT IT
HEY! THERE'S NOWT WRONG WI THAT!
LET'S SEE Y' COCK AGAIN, BAZ

AYE! IT'S THE SAME ALRIGHT
WELL IT WEREN'T THAT COLOUR EARLIER ON
THAT'S COS IT WAS ON THE BLOODY BONK EARLIER ON

WHAT? IT WERE ON THE SOFT WHEN HE SCANNED IT?
AYE!

BUT IT LOOKS ALRIGHT! I THINK IT'S A NICE RESTFUL COLOUR, TRAY. I LIKE IT. IT'S A SORT OF... PINKY OCHRE.

FUCK PINKY OCHRE! BONKED UP BELL END PURPLE WE WANTED, 'AN BONKED UP BELL END PURPLE WE'RE GOIN' TO 'AVE!
GET YER FUCKIN' COAT ON

NO... NO... IT'S TOO CERISE! IT STILL NEEDS T' BE MORE PURPLE!
PASS ANOTHER RAZZLE, SAN!

THE BUTCHER'S DUSTBIN

A MAGGOT-INFESTED HEAP CONTAINING THE GUTS OF ISSUES 122~131

SIRLOIN STEAKS:
Alex Collier, Chris Donald, Simon Donald, Robert Doyle, Graham Dury, Simon Ecob & Guy Campbell, Wayne Gamble, Stevie Glover, Barney Farmer & Lee Healey, Ray Fury, Robin Halstead, Jason Hazeley, Alex Morris & Joel Morris, Davey Jones, Paul Palmer, G. Ravishankar, Lew Stringer, Cat Sullivan, Simon Thorp, Nick Tolson, Biscuit Tin and Brian Walker

COCKTAIL SAUSAGE:
Will Watt

Published by Dennis Publishing (Family Butchers since 1932)
The Sausage Factory, 30 Cleveland Street, London W1T 4JD
Telephone: 0207 907 6000

ISBN: 075 222 8110
First Printing Autumn 2005

Viz Comic is cooked on a barbecue until it's charred on both sides yet still frozen in the middle ten times a year by Dennis Publishing wearing one of those comedy pinnies with women's tits on. To subscribe call 0845 126 1053 or go to www.viz.co.uk

Prininited in Geat Birtain

JOKES BEST BEFORE
END NOV 1979

EEH, LUV. THAT WOH TH'LUVVLIEST F-FF-FFUCKIN' XMUSS DINNEH A EVEH 'AD. IT WOH F-FF-FFUCKIN' TOP.

M-FFFUCKIN'-WAH! THEM MICROCHIPS WAS DUN TER A F-FFUCKIN' TURN. AN' THAT'S NOT AALL...
...A FUND ONE FORTEH NINE IN ME PUDDIN'.

WELL, EIGHT. WOT ARE WE GUNNEH DO WI TH'REST OF US DAY? TH'BBAIRNS IS ALL SAFELEH TUCKED UP IN CARE... AN' THEH'S A ROARIN' BAR ON'T FIRE...

A-HEM! FANCEH CUMMIN' UPSTAIRS FERRABIT OF A CHRISSMUSS CUDDLE?
HEH HEH.

HURREH UP, EIGHT.
AYE LUV.
A'LL BE REYT WI' YER.

YOO GET IN BED AN' TEK YER KNICKEHS OFF, LUV. A'LL JUSS BE TOO F-FFUCKIN' MINNITS WHILE A 'AVE A NICE PISS.

...EIGHT! EIGHT! 'URREH UP! A'M WAITIN' FOH YER!
BLAM! BLAM!

BLAM! BLAM!
Z-ZZ_ Z-ZZ...
CUM ON, EIGHT! FUCKIN' URREH UP! A AN'T GOT AALL FFUCKIN' DAY!

BLAM! BLAM!
..ZZ-ZZ ZZZ... HUNH!?
EIGHT! GERRUP NOW! YER USELESS FUCKIN' BASTOD!

JESUS... ME F-FF-FFUCKIN' 'EAD!
WORRISSIT, LUV?

SHALL A CUM IN AN' GIVE Y'AN 'AND WRAPPIN' UP T'BBAIRNS'S PLAYSTATIONS?
NO. A WANT SUM NICE CHRISSMUSS LIGHTS LIKE THEM NEXT DOOR'S GOT.

THEH'VE GORREM ON SPECIAL OFFEH AT ONE FORTEH-NINE STRETCHEH.

NOW, EIGHT. YOO SPEND THIS MUNNY ON LIGHTS AN' NOT ACE, AN' A'LL LET YER CUM IN TH'OUSE FOH YER CHRISSMUSS DINNEH... FER REAL!

DUN'T WURREH. A'LL NOT LET YER DAHN. A'M SPENDIN' THIS ONE FORTEH NINE ON LIGHTS AN' F-FFUCKIN' NOWT ELSE. YOO JUSS SEE IF A DUN'T.

...CHRISSMUSS LIGHTS... NOT ACE... CHRISSMUSS LIGHTS... NOT ACE... LIGHTS NOT ACE... F-FFUCKIN NOT ACE... NOT THE ACE... NO.. LIGHTS.
A WAIN'T LET 'ER DAHN THIS TIME...

SO...
EEH, LUV. THAT WOH TH' LUVVLIEST FFUCKIN' XMUSS DINNEH A EVEH 'AD. IT WOH F-FF-FFUCKIN' TOP.

..ZZ... M-FFUCKIN'-WAH... MUMBLE..ZZ.. THEM MICROCHIPS WAS DUN TER A F-FF... MUMBLE... ZZZ ....ZZ... A FUND ONE FORTEH... ZZ-ZZ... NINE IN ME PUDDIN... Z-ZZZ...

SID the SEXIST
TITS OOT!
TYNESIDE'S SILVER-TONGUED CAVALIER

IN THE PUB...
...AN' SHE SAYS TIV US, "YE SMELL NICE, WHAT HAVE YE GOT ON?" I SEZ, "I'VE GOT A HARD ON, BUT I DIDN'T KNAA YE COULD SMELL IT!"
HA! HA! HA! HA! HA!
IS PORFUME NOT JUST FOR LASSES AN' POOFS, THOUGH, LADS?
SID MAN, YER BEHIND THE TIMES. IT'S CAALLED MALE GROOMIN', MAN. AALL THE LASSES LOVE IT.

AYE. Y'SEE, THE THING IS NOW, LASSES LOVE LADS WHAT ARE AALL A BIT POOFY AN' THAT. YE'VE GORRA BE AALL LASSY IF YE WANT TODAY'S MURST CLASSEST BORDS.

AYE. THEY AANLY GAN FOR LADS WHAT PUT AALL GOOEY SHITE IN THEIR HAIR AN' THAT, AN' RUB SALAD CREAM STUFF AALL AWA THEIR FACES, MAN.
AYE, THE' LOVE LADS WHAT DEE POOFY STUFF. AS LANG AS THEY'RE BUTCH, LIKE.
WILL PORFUME PULL THE BORDS, LIKE?
AFTA SHAVE, SID. AFTA SHAVE.
GET THE SMELLIES HOYED ON, AN' BELIEVE ME, SID... FANNY MAGNET-GUARANTEED.
SO...
WHAT I'M AFTA PET, IS SUMMIK REALLY STINKY, WHAT SNAPS LASSES KNICKER ELASTIC, Y'KNAA... ERM... NOT THAT I NEED ANY HELP, LIKE.
SALE
OF COURSE, SIR. I CAN HIGHLY RECOMMEND 'PLOOP! POUR L'HOMME'. IT'S IRRESISTIBLE TO WOMEN AND IS ON A SPECIAL FIFTY PERCENT DISCOUNT TODAY.

AYE. SOONDS CANNY. I'LL TEK ONE O'THEM.
...AN'... ERM... D'YU LIKE CHRISTMAS?... SUCK ME TORKEY, IT'S... NAH... ERM, GOBBLE... I'LL GOBBLE... NAH... ERM... STUFFIN'... AYE! I'LL STUFF YER TORKEY... NAH... ERM... I'VE GOT A CHIPOLATA... THAT CANNAT BE REET...
THAT'LL BE £75-99.

GUMPH!
SWOON!
WOOOSH!
SALE
STOTT!

SHORTLY...
HAS THIS MAG GOT FREE PORFUME ON ONE O'THEM PAPER FLAPS?
GQ
FHM
loaded
BEANO
DANDY
MAN STUFF
AYE. FAWA-TWENTY.

SO...
HERE GANS FAWA POOND TWENTY.
BAR
RUB! RUB! RUB!

INSIDE...
HOO PETAL. YE SMELL LUSH. I'LL SUCK YER COCK OOTSIDE.
GUMPH!

MIND YE, I WANNA SUCK IT, NOT EAT IT ON A CRACKER, SO YE CAN GAN IN THE BOGS AN' WASH THE FUCKER!
G.G.GUMPH!

AND...
FUCKIN' HELL! THE SINKS IS AALL BUST! ... I KNAA... I'LL RUB PORFUME ON ME LID!
OUT OF ORDER

RUB! RUB! SLIT!
UNH?

ACGH! ACGH! ACGH!
ACGH! ACGH! ACGH!

IN HOSPITAL...
WELL, MR. SMUTT, THIS IS THE WORST PENILE PAPER-CUT WE HAVE EVER SEEN. THE AFTER-SHAVE INDUCED STINGING SHOULD SUBSIDE BY AROUND EASTER.
HA! HA!
HA! HA!
GUMPH!
HA! HA! HA!
WITH PROPER CARE, YOU MAY BE ABLE TO TOUCH IT AGAIN BY CHRISTMAS NEXT YEAR.
GUMPH!

Letterbocks

It's the page that spent the night coughing, and found a big grey pube in its throat this morning

Letterbocks
Viz Comic
PO Box 1PT
Newcastle NE99 1PT

In this space age you can electromail your letters and tips to letterbocks@viz.co.uk

★★Star Letter★★

I WOULD just like to say what a load of bollocks these hygiene laws are. I have been a baker for nearly 12 years now, and not once have I washed my hands after having a shit. So far, no one has complained.

F. U. Bowen, Essex

• **My heart** goes out to young Gareth Gates having to suffer the unwanted sexual attentions of breast model Jordan. Women must learn that sexual harrassment cuts both ways, and when a man says n.. n... nnnn... nn.. n... nnn... no, he *means* n.. n... nnnn... nn.. n... nnn... no.

Sam Bismuth
Leeds

• **I was** sitting watching the football on the BBC last night, and it said you could get 'interactive' by pressing the red button on the remote. I pressed mine and the telly went off.

Ken Topping
e-mail

Chip off the old block

• **If any** of your readers are toying with the idea of marrying Jennifer Lopez, perhaps they ought to have a look of this picture of her grandmother from the Christmas issue of Hello. If that's what the future has in store for her face, just think what her arse is going to look like. It's put me right off, I can tell you.

John Antimony
Barnstaple

• **The** government recently announced that first-time burglars will no longer receive a custodial sentence, but will be given community service instead. With that in mind, I am looking for three other law-abiding citizens to have a crack at nicking the Crown Jewels from the Tower of London. The rewards are untold wealth, and the worst that can happen is that you would have to spend thirty days picking up crisp packets. Any takers?

Gary Beard
e-mail

• **Last** summer my local vicar knocked on the door and asked me to contribute to funds to repair the church roof. As we live in a tight-knit community with the church at its centre, I happily made a donation. It would have been nice if the vicar himself had shown a similar sense of community spirit when my gutters needed replacing last week. I knocked on his door to see if he would go halfers and the bastard didn't want to know.

Percival Mercury
Wales

• **Cilla** Black advised ITV to axe Blind Date after she left, telling them that she was irreplaceable. In fact she believed herself to be a 'sacred cow' and I must say, I half agree with her.

Stig Blomqvist
Friskiforskin

• **When** the Liverpool dockers were on strike, The PM's father-in-law and former scouse git Tony Booth was very vocal in support of them. Yet we have heard little from him during the current firefighters' dispute. Perhaps this is an example of self interest taking over, as he feels that they need to be on hand 24 hours a day in case he sets fire to himself again.

Andrew Dunn
e-mail

• **Is it** me, or does actess Lesley Ash now look like Herr Lipp from the League of Gentleman? Perhaps she walked into a door in the Homebase advert.

Glenn Pickersgill
Howden

• **I was** recently convicted for a string of armed robberies and was sentenced to be detained at Her Majesty's pleasure. I know I've done wrong, but the thought of the Queen sitting in a palace, smirking at my plight really galls me.

T. Francis
HMP Durham

• **I just** went for a shit and it smelt exactly the same as the Chicken Jalfrezi I had last night - absolutely gorgeous.

Ed Bowden
Bromley

• **I was** heartened by the actions of a Millwall FC supporter who came into my local pub last Saturday, took two balls from the pool table, slipped them into a sock and left looking for "Northern cunt Preston fans". Imagine our surprise when he returned a few minutes later, set the balls back on the table and apologised for the disruption to our game. His conduct was a credit to Millwall FC. What a pity certain other of their supporters don't behave in such a courteous manner.

P Pugnano
Preston

• **How** come every time I buy a bongo mag, the newsagent looks at me like I'm a dirty bastard? He's the one profiteering from such filth.

Joel Young
Middlesbrough

• **Could** Fru T Bunn knock me up one of his gingerbread sex dolls? The tits on the one he made for Christmas...*MMMMMMMM-MM!*

Jimmy Insoleyo
West London

You Ask, We Answer

with Naylor Hammond, BSc

Dear Naylor,

WHY do women's nipples stick out when it's cold, whilst men's dicks shrink to nothing?

Mrs JP
Grangemouth

** The answer to this question is simple. The effect is all down to the nature of the material involved. Certain substances, such as mercury in thermometers and penises get **smaller** as the temperature drops. Inversely, there are many substances which get **larger** under the same conditions, such as ladies' nipples and the cream in bottles of milk. All things freeze at 0° centigrade, or absolute zero, as scientists call it. To convert degrees centigrade to Farenheit, multiply by 1.8 and add 32.*

That's all for this time

Naylor Hammond BSc.

FALLOPIAN TUBES JOKE

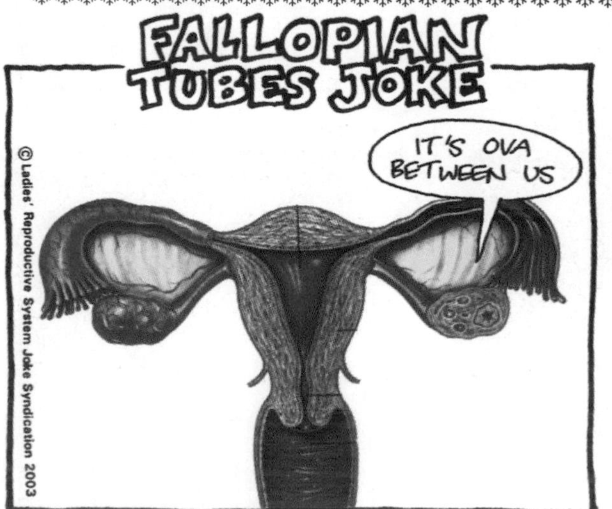

I noticed that a local PFI hospital is being built in my town, and the developers are offering members of the public the chance to 'buy a brick' for £40. They must be going to the wrong builders' merchants. Our local B&Q does them for about 20p each.

Thor Odin
Barnsley

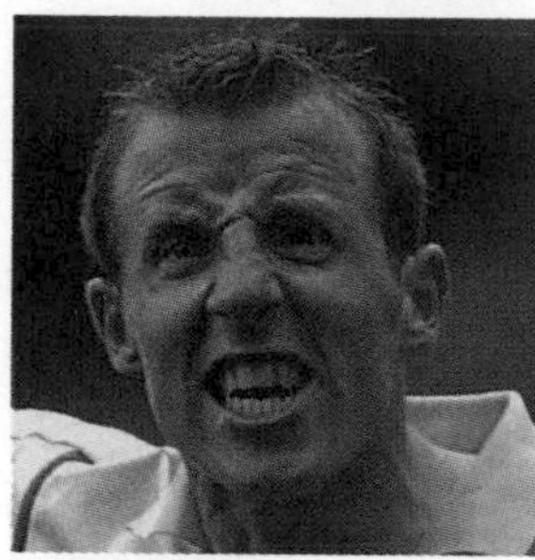

• **I wonder** if any readers could help me. I've just bought the new FIFA PlayStation game, and I can't work out which button makes Lee Bowyer stamp on people's heads.

Tim Woods
e-mail

Coogan's muff

• **So much** for top comedian Steve Coogan's claim that any woman can be 'laughed into bed'. I tried this recently with disastrous consequences, and was subsequently convicted of aggravated rape. I have also been placed on the sex offenders register for life. Nice one, Steve.

G Dyme
HMP Wakefield

• **The** Queen's Birthday Honours list was set up to recognise people who have provided an invaluable service to their country. How about an MBE or something for the spiritualist who told Cilla Black to quit TV?

Terry Yclept
Basildon

• **Congratulations** to Crimewatch for staging a reconstruction of the horrifying tiara theft at the Scottish home of the late Princess of Wales's mother Mrs Shand-Kydd. It's heartening to know that interest is being taken in property crime perpetrated against elderly ladies. Doubtless the BBC will soon be popping round to my Granny's flat in the West end of Newcastle to reconstruct some of the dozen or so break-ins the poor cow's had in the last 18 months.

J. Thomas
Newcastle

• **These** people who claim there is no such thing as a free lunch obviously don't know what they are talking about. Why, only last Sunday, I pigged out on the 'All You Can eat for £4.99' buffet at my local Chinese restaurant, and walked out without paying.

Jeff Reed
Cambridge

Now that's magic

• **Why** doesn't David Copperfield stop making rabbits and the Eiffel Tower disappear, and make things like AIDS and cancer disappear instead. Or my herpes for that matter.

Margaret Barret
San Francisco

Fallen angel

• **Teenage** singing sensation Charlotte Church's behaviour in Cincinatti the other week was deplorable. In refusing to meet disabled fans after a concert, she showed herself up as a spoilt brat. What this young lady needs is some good old fashioned discipline. I would happily put Miss Church across my knee, lift up her skirt and spank her bare behind until she learned some manners.

Torbjorn Abercromby
Manchester

• **If I** were Queen of England, I would eat samosas for breakfast. Then, when Tony Blair came round to discuss the affairs of the nation, I would release the most resilient, pungent fart.

A Glen
Unterluss, Germany

** What would YOU do if You were Queen for a day? Perhaps you'd fill a pool with caviar and swim about taking huge mouthfuls. Maybe you'd have your old PE teacher publicly executed and his head put on a stick at Traitor's Gate. Write and let us know. We've teamed up with Buckingham Palace, and the writer of the best letter will get to spend a super day as Sovereign Monarch of the United Kingdom and Commonwealth Dominions with £100 spending money thrown in.*

Nitty gritty

• **I wonder** if any of your readers could advise me on a matter of etiquette. My girlfriend was giving me a blowjob the other day, when I noticed a small creature, obviously a nit, crawling through her hair. I'm not sure whether or not I should tell her. I don't want to risk hurting her feelings as she is my wife's best friend.

Christopher Hampshire
Bristol

Miriam

MIRIAM SOLVES YOUR PROBLEMS, TRANSLATES HER ADVICE INTO GERMAN ON THE INTERNET, THEN BACK INTO ENGLISH

Should I postpone my marriage proposal?

LETTER OF THE DAY

Dear Miriam... **I've been going out with a wonderful girl for nearly three years. I'm 26 and she's 24.**

We met whilst we were at college and we love each other very much. Now I would like us to get married.

The other week I bought an engagement ring, as I planned to pop the question over a romantic meal. The trouble is, last night I shoved the ring up my arse. I don't know why I did it, I just did. But now I can't get it back down and I can't afford a replacement.

Should I tell her I've stuck her ring up my arse and risk losing her, or should I postpone my proposal until I can afford a new one? Please help.

J Cursitor, Bristol

Do not worry yourselves, and certainly you do not cancel its obligation straight still. The first thing, which you must do, is their, to collect intestine movements each day and it with a fork to stampfen to begin, in order to examine for the missing jewelry. If the thought of that is moveable your stomach, before which you can like to play flushing a metalldetektor over your faeces in the toilet dish. If it does not turn above into the following week, you can have yourselves to compensate to the fact that them are lost and you must explain it. In pressing things your lower surface, like with many things, honesty is the best policy up. If you explain to her exactly, what happened, and if she loves you, she understands. I send my paper 'retrieving valuable articles of the Rektum' to you.

TOP TIPS

MOTORISTS. When going through a speed camera, flash your lights twice quickly, and watch the driver in front hit his brakes when he thinks he's been caught.

Kathy, Crewe

BUS drivers. Let everyone see how pig ugly your dog of a girlfriend is by letting her stand next to whilst you are driving, as if she owns the bus.

Mark Harris, Smegmaville

FILM makers. Why not cut down on the number of actors you need by having loads of identical twins and triplets in your stories, all played by the same actor, but never having them meet?

N Scott, e-mail

SLY AND THE KIDNEY STONE

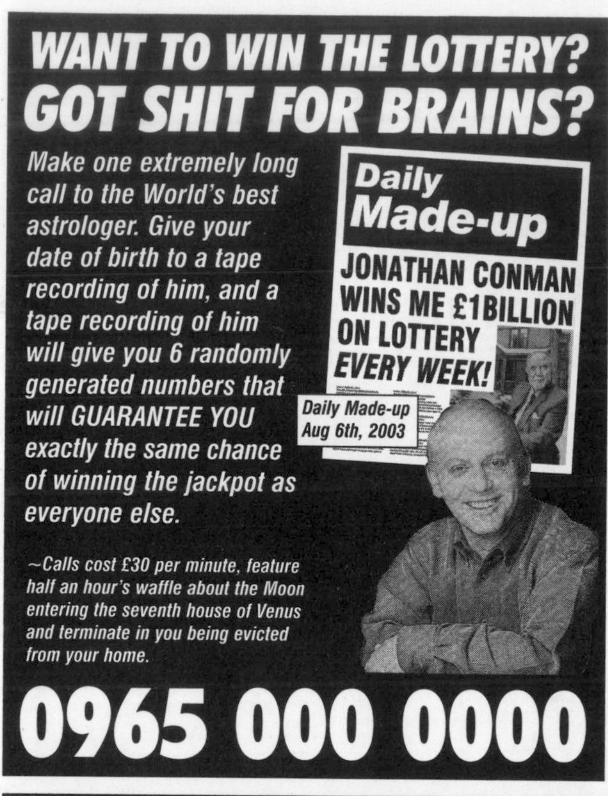

WANT TO WIN THE LOTTERY? GOT SHIT FOR BRAINS?

Make one extremely long call to the World's best astrologer. Give your date of birth to a tape recording of him, and a tape recording of him will give you 6 randomly generated numbers that will GUARANTEE YOU exactly the same chance of winning the jackpot as everyone else.

~Calls cost £30 per minute, feature half an hour's waffle about the Moon entering the seventh house of Venus and terminate in you being evicted from your home.

0965 000 0000

RON IS MR UNLUCKY!

EXCLUSIVE!

RON Usual, an unemployed driving instructor from Hayes in Middlesex is being dubbed the "Unluckiest Man Alive" by doctors at Ashford General Hospital.

Ron, 35, has been admitted to the hospital more times than any other patient since hospital records began. Over the last 28 years, the accident-prone bachelor has spent more hours in the hospital building than many of the full time staff, and his misfortune has the experts shaking their heads.

Stretch Armstrong

"It's unheard of," said Dr Beaker Titchmarsh of the hospital's proctology department. "We treat him and discharge him, then, within minutes he's readmitted having had some other terrible stroke of luck."

Ron's sad history began in 1976 when he was admitted to the hospital with a Stretch Armstrong up his arse.

"It's such a sad story," said his mother, who shares a bungalow with Ron near the hospital. "Apparently he'd fallen from his bunkbed and landed awkwardly on the toy. We had to rush him to Casualty straight away. He's not been any luckier from then on."

Bend Aldrin

According to his medical file, Ron has fallen awkwardly onto a variety of objects at least twice a day ever since, tumbling clumsily onto a seemingly endless list of items - including a sodastream bottle, an open pair of scissors, a box of Family Circle biscuits and over seventeen sets of car keys.

"We're running some tests on him at the moment to see if there might be something wrong with his balance," said Dr Titchmarsh, who has made the study of Ron's tragic condition his life's work.

Britain's unluckiest man, Usual - yesterday

Dr Titchmarsh, who has sold the film rights to Ron's story to Robert DeNiro for an undisclosed sum, believes that Ron's sad tale might be a beacon of hope to others.

Twist Collins

"One time, he had to drive here all the way from Chepstow in the nude, after he accidentally got the gearstick of his Mini Metro stuck up his arse. He never complained once. He's an inspiration."

Expensive treatments failed?

The secret of regaining thick, luxurious hair is written in the stars, says the World's best astrologer Justin Tophat. Simply call his magical hair regeneration horoscope line for scientifically proven personalised advice which will tell YOU exactly when to try to grow your hair back in order to maximise your chances of success.

Before After

"I was as bald as a coot and I'd tried everything to grow my hair. In desperation I phoned Justin's phoneline and he told me that because I was born on the cusp of Capricorn and Aries I should wait until Saturn was retrograde in Gemini. I took his advice and now I have to go to the barber three times a week" **Mr B, Essex**

Because the planetary aspects of the zodiac are ever-changing, successful hair growth may require repeated phonecalls totalling many hours. Calls cost from £40/min.

0965 000 0000

Need a New Car but Can't Get Credit?

The Stars may hold a new set of wheels for YOU!

The secrets of getting an unsecured loan for up to £15000 are written in the heavens, according to the World's best astrologer Mastic Meg. A call to her premium rate car loan zodiac phoneline is all you need to get you on the road in one of our cars which each come with a full service history and verified mileage!

0965 000 0000

Calls cost £1 per minute and may last up to 4 years

Weighed down with too much Horoscopes every day?

Daren't open the paper for fear of what it might bring?

Why not consolidate all your stars into a **single easily-understandable monthly prediction?** Don't stop and think, do it **now** with a simple call to the proven experts ~

Gypsy Baines & Ernst

7th Loan Co. of a 7th Loan Co.

Call 100 and ask for Freephone Gypsy Baines & Ernst

All horoscopes secured on future success in love. Your chances of going on a long journey and meeting a tall dark stranger may be at risk if you do not keep up payments.

Your Sex in the Stars

*"The secrets of how to turn on your partner are written in the stars" ...says Astrologer **Justin Tupperware.** Check out his steamy 2003 Zodiac Sex Games Chart to see what heavenly things **YOU** should be doing between the sheets tonight.*

HER \ HIM												
Capricorn	anal	water-sports	straight	bi-curious	BDSM	belgian biscuit	AC/DC	DVDA	sticky belly flap cock	feltching	beastiality	gang banging
Aquarius	nailing bollocks to table	no sex	quumphing	incest	dildos	donkey punch	missionary	golden showers	German	French	Dutch	Greek
Pisces	mastur-bation	soapy tit wank	piercing	round the world	rimming	dirtbox delights	pearl necklace	trades-mans	cheesey wheelbarrow	orgy	teens and cows	bottle fucking
Aries	voyerism	dogging	wanking	importun-ing	seagulling	teabagging	bagpiping	hot Karl	Cleveland steamer	popazo-golou	dirty Sanchez	shitty tits
Taurus	war machine	mumphiny	pile driver	snuff	boxing	fisting (anal)	fisting (vaginal)	fisting (oral)	auto asphixiation	spanking	S&M	trans-vestism
Gemini	cumulo-nimbus	naturism	horatio	blumpkin	bricing	rainbow kiss	mooning	flashing	cottaging	gas tight	cybersex	love eggs
Cancer	butt plug	safe	thick repeater	wet 'n' messy	death by chocolate	pasadena mudslide	latex ladyboy	tit abuse	melon mash	walking the dog	dirty talk	shaven haven
Leo	Mexican	teenage eskimo	harpers and queens	FCUK	arabian goggles	pissproud	farmyard	fart games	viagra falls	leather	bondage	gimp box
Virgo	big babies	shrimping	north sea trawler	fuck truck	torture parachute	hanging globes of joy	strap-on	sailor's favourite	sandwich	string of beads	sloppy Giusseppi	bum biting
Libra	last turkey in the shop	thumbing in a slacky	assorted creams	swiss kiss	spice island	chocolate sandich	doggie	full english breakfast	double ending	arse to mouth merry-go-round	sploshing	charity bean bath
Scorpio	meat warehouse	butcher's dustbin	making hats	necrophilia	flagellation	back door	dogs marriage	split the kipper	muff dive	8 ball Joe	nachos with cheese	face sitting
Sagittarius	top hat	top hat and tails	executive relief	dressing-up	rubber	frottering	knee trembler	anal intrusion	tongue bath	tops and fingers	bunny rub	wife swapping

GILBERT RATCHET

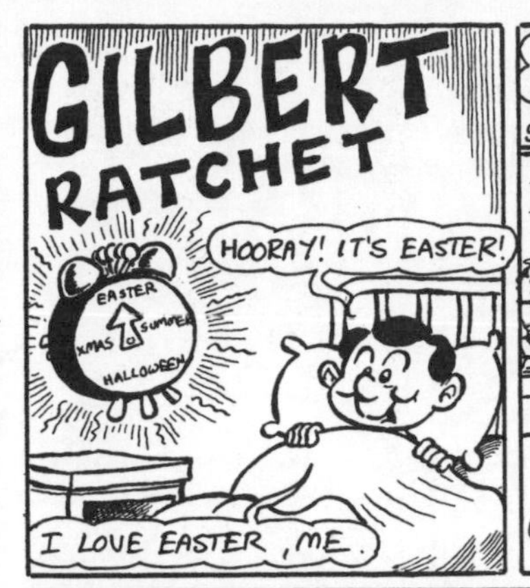

FRU T. BUNN the MASTER BAKER & his GINGERBREAD SEX DOLLS

SUDDENLY...

WHAT WAS THAT!? DID YOU HEAR THE FRONT DOOR GO?

ERM... MR WARBURTON, THIS ISN'T WHAT IT SEEMS. I CAN EXPLAIN EVERYTHING... IF YOU'D JUST LET ME PICK UP THESE CLOTHES...

...YOU SEE, YOUR WIFE HAD ORDERED A SCONE... ERM... AND WHILST I WAS DELIVERING IT SHE SUFFERED A SEVERE ALLERGIC REACTION TO RAISINS AND I WAS JUST...
...ER...

FLING!

SVEN
MAPS
SPATULA
CHEESE

ERK!
'ERE - WHAT'S GOING ON?

... I FEEL SO VERY PROUD OF HIM, THAT'S WHY I LOVE MY DADDY!
THE END.
MRS. BUNN!? IS THERE A MRS. DOREEN BUNN IN THE AUDIENCE? ONLY WE'VE JUST CAUGHT HER HUSBAND RUNNING NAKED DOWN THE HIGH STREET...
POLCHESTER SPECIAL SCHOOL
EXIT
...WITH ALL CRUMBS AND ICING SUGAR IN HIS PUBES.

CHEEKY COW!
Paul Palmer

10 ITEMS OR LESS

NO WAY HAS SHE ONLY GOT TEN ITEMS!

NOEL'S A

Tidy-bearded former entertainer Noel Edmonds is set to embark on his biggest project yet - ***to single-handedly wipe every living thing from the face of the earth!*** **Only he and the Royal Family will survive.**

SPECIAL REPORT
from **PAPA DOC DUVALIER** in **CRINKLEY BOTTOM**

The Swap Shop presenter, 54, made his shock announcement yesterday to a packed press conference at his Crinkley Bottom funpark. He told reporters he was tired of all the wickedness and sin in the world, and had decided it was time to start afresh. He said: "I am going to kill everyone in a giant flood that will completely cover the planet."

ark

However, not everyone is doomed. Edmonds plans to save the Royal family in a ***giant wooden ark!***

The Late Late Breakfast Show star, 54 inches, thought up his plan whilst watching television. He said: "The news was on one evening, and I was thinking about all the immorality and bad things that were happening in the world. I was getting angry, but I didn't know what to do about it. Then, later that night I happened to be flicking through the bible and I got the idea for a giant flood to kill everyone."

ilent

"I was already to unleash my deluge there and then, but it suddenly occurred to me that it would be a terrible shame to drown the royal family. They do a marvellous job and they've taken more than their share of flack over the years. It would be unfair of me to punish them for the wickedness of the rest of the earth's population.

hile

"My wife suggested I build an ark, like Noah did, and get the royals to go in two by two before the waters get too high."

od

To gasps from reporters, Edmonds then unveiled an artist's impression of his floating palace, a five hundred foot long vessel constructed of wood, gold and diamonds. With six decks and six hundred rooms, it will boast:

- *A championship size ballroom*
- *A thousand crystal chandeliers*
- *A hundred champagne jacuzzis*
- *A ten-pin bowling alley complete with solid gold skittles and diamond bowling balls*

Edmonds said: "I'm taking the Queen and Prince Philip, plus pairs of every sort of royal with me, and I'm sparing no expense. I'm packing the hold with fifty tons of swans, quails' eggs and cucumber sandwiches with the crusts cut off. This ark is going to be a real home from home for the Windsors. And it should be quite adequate for me in the short term."

***Noel's House Boat** - Edmonds' artist's impression of his giant ship as the Monarchy goes in two by two. Hurrah, hurrah.*

rowel

During the voyage Edmonds plans to keep his regal guests entertained with reruns of his television programmes, including his charitable Christmas morning broadcasts from the Post Office Tower and the hilarious episode of 'The Late Late Breakfast Show' when a car-jumping stunt nearly led to British television's first live primetime death.

ement mixer

But he also admitted to concerns over certain aspects of his plan. He told reporters: "The royal family and I could be on the ark for up to five months. That's an awfully long time for me to go without dropping someone off a crane or soaking them in a gunk tank, and I don't think her majesty the Queen would take too kindly to being the victim of my pranks. I'm going to need someone to belittle, so a member of the public will get to come along too."

pirit level

But the lucky survivor of the human race won't be able to look forward to an easy ride on Noel's Ark. Edmonds plans to wind him up with a series of his trademark funny phonecalls, and he can expect to be gunged by Mr Blobby six or seven times a day for the duration of his voyage.

adder

Edmonds angrily denied accusations that he was playing God. He

RK ROYAL

Edmonds Vows to Spare Monarchy from His Wrath

told reporters: "I am not in any sense comparing myself with God, although there are obvious similarities. We both do lots for charity and are loved by everyone, we both have beards, and we both spend a lot of our time in the sky; him on a cloud and mc in one of my helicopters."

cobra

And he dismissed claims that he was only destroying mankind in the hope of getting a knighthood. "Nothing could be further from the truth," he said. "I find such accusations very hurtful when all I'm doing is trying to make the world a better place, whilst at the same time saving an innocent family from a fate which is too horrible to contemplate. Although obviously, some official recognition of my actions would be nice, and I certainly wouldn't refuse an honour if her majesty were to offer me one."

7 Plague Plan of DLT

Noel Edmonds isn't the first Radio One disc jockey to plan the global annihilation of all living things.

long-running

Following the axing of his long-running Saturday morning show by new boss Matthew Bannister, Dave Lee Travis surprised listeners by cursing all mankind. At the end of his popular phone quiz 'Give us a break' he announced:

"Hearken unto me all ye out there in Radio One land. For I shall visit plagues upon the face of the earth, and the number of the plagues shall be seven. And mighty shall be the wrath of the Hairy Cornflake."

short-walking

Police later removed a crop-spraying light aircraft and a large quantity of frogs from a barn at Travis's Essex farm.

***TRAVIS:** Pictured in 1977 yesterday.*

SPOILT BASTARD

SCRATCH! SCRITCH!
AND WHAT ARE **YOU** LOOKING AT, EH?

MOTHER!!.. THAT GORILLA JUST TOUCHED ITS TASSELL IN FRONT OF ME... **ME!**.. AN **INNOCENT CHILD!**
OH... ERM... DID IT?
ARE YOU GOING TO STAND THERE AND LET IT GET AWAY WITH **THAT**, WOMAN?

WELL, IT DOESN'T MEAN ANY HARM, TIMMY... IT'S JUST WHAT MONKEYS DO
NO HARM? MAYBE YOU THINK IT'S ALRIGHT FOR PAEDOPHILE MONKEYS TO INTERFERE WITH THEMSELVES IN FRONT OF KIDS!

WELL, NO, OF COURSE NOT, TIMMY, BUT...
WELL **GET IN THERE AND KNOCK ITS BLOCK OFF!**
I'D GO IN AND PUNCH IT ONE IF IT HAD WAGGLED ITS WINKLE AT **YOU!**

WELL, IF YOU REALLY THINK I SHOULD, MY POPPET
YES I DO!

HEY! EVERYONE! MY MUM'S GOING TO FIGHT A BIG GORILLA! QUICK! COME AND WATCH!
OOH! OOH! OOH!

GO ON! GIVE IT A FOURPENNY ONE RIGHT UP THE BRACKET!
GO ON! HIT IT!

FEEBLE TAP!!
NO! HARDER! HIT IT HARDER THAN THAT!

POP
HARDER WOMAN! IT'S A PAEDOPHILE! RUDDY WELL MARMALISE IT!

GO ON, MOTHER! PUNCH ITS PERVERTED LIGHTS OUT... KNOCK IT INTO THE MIDDLE OF NEXT WEEK!
?
GRRR!

WHACK!!
HNNNG!

WHAT A GREAT PUNCH!..
A TEAM
FLIPPING HELL! IT LOOKS ANGRY!

BLIMBO! BLAMBO!

THUMP!

BIFF! BLAM! SOCK! WHAM! RIP! WHACK!

PUNT!!
WOOAH!
YEAH!

HEY, MOTHER! THAT WAS GREAT!
NOW, COME OVER HERE...

...THIS CROCODILE JUST OFFERED ME SWEETS AND TOUCHED MY BOTTOM.

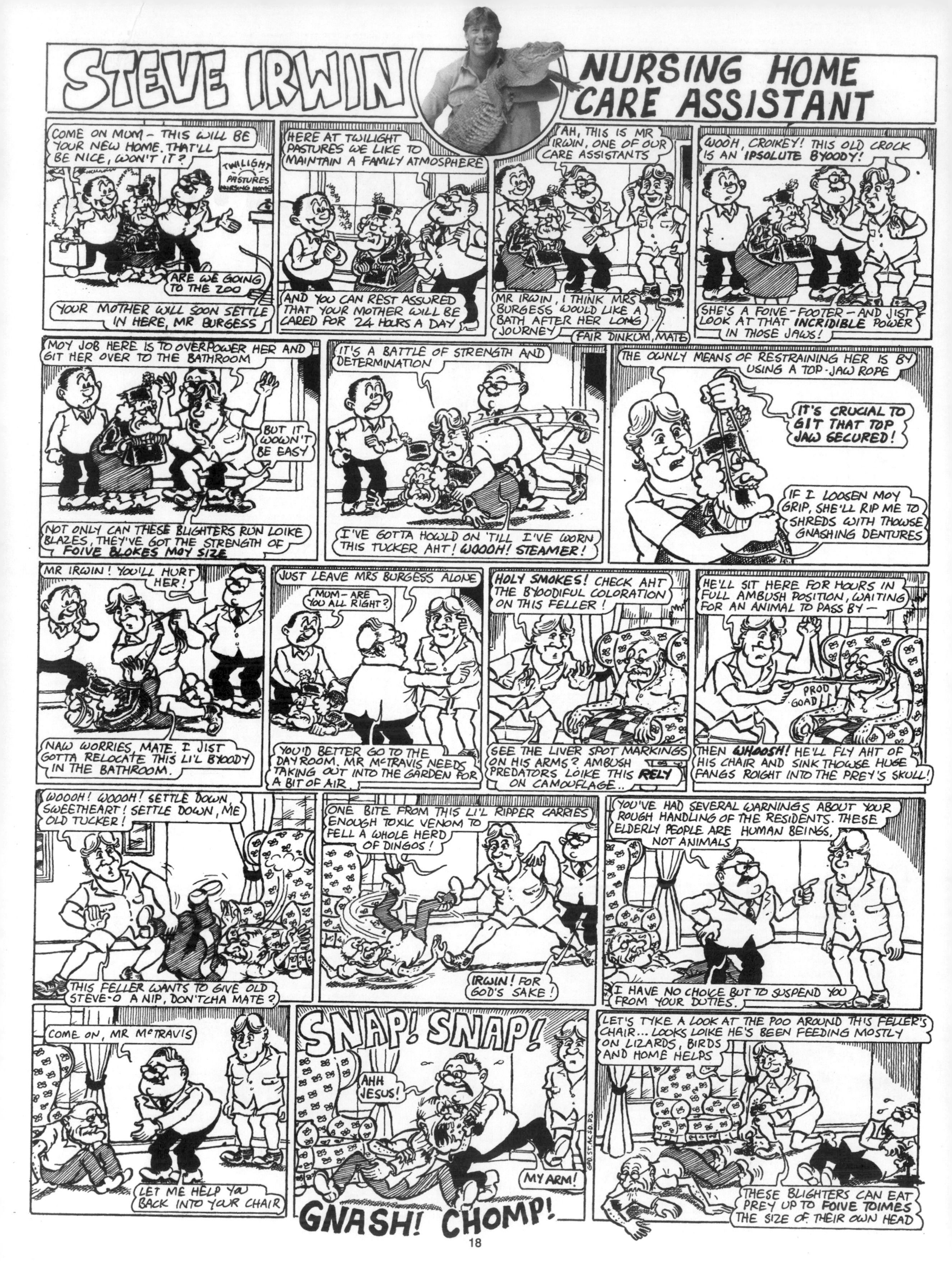
STEVE IRWIN
NURSING HOME CARE ASSISTANT
COME ON MUM - THIS WILL BE YOUR NEW HOME. THAT'LL BE NICE, WON'T IT?
TWILIGHT PASTURES NURSING HOME
ARE WE GOING TO THE ZOO
YOUR MOTHER WILL SOON SETTLE IN HERE, MR BURGESS
HERE AT TWILIGHT PASTURES WE LIKE TO MAINTAIN A FAMILY ATMOSPHERE
AND YOU CAN REST ASSURED THAT YOUR MOTHER WILL BE CARED FOR 24 HOURS A DAY
AH, THIS IS MR IRWIN, ONE OF OUR CARE ASSISTANTS
MR IRWIN, I THINK MRS BURGESS WOULD LIKE A BATH AFTER HER LONG JOURNEY
FAIR DINKUM, MATE
WOOH, CROIKEY! THIS OLD CROCK IS AN IPSOLUTE BYOODY!
SHE'S A FOIVE-FOOTER - AND JIST LOOK AT THAT INCRIDIBLE POWER IN THOSE JAWS!
MOY JOB HERE IS TO OVERPOWER HER AND GIT HER OVER TO THE BATHROOM
BUT IT WOWN'T BE EASY
NOT ONLY CAN THESE BLIGHTERS RUN LOIKE BLAZES, THEY'VE GOT THE STRENGTH OF FOIVE BLOKES MOY SIZE
IT'S A BATTLE OF STRENGTH AND DETERMINATION
I'VE GOTTA HOWLD ON 'TILL I'VE WORN THIS TUCKER AHT! WOOOH! STEAMER!
THE OWNLY MEANS OF RESTRAINING HER IS BY USING A TOP-JAW ROPE
IT'S CRUCIAL TO GIT THAT TOP JAW SECURED!
IF I LOOSEN MOY GRIP, SHE'LL RIP ME TO SHREDS WITH THOWSE GNASHING DENTURES
MR IRWIN! YOU'LL HURT HER!
NAW WORRIES, MATE. I JIST GOTTA RELOCATE THIS LI'L BYOODY IN THE BATHROOM.
JUST LEAVE MRS BURGESS ALONE
MUM - ARE YOU ALL RIGHT?
YOU'D BETTER GO TO THE DAY ROOM. MR McTRAVIS NEEDS TAKING OUT INTO THE GARDEN FOR A BIT OF AIR
HOLY SMOKES! CHECK AHT THE BYOODIFUL COLORATION ON THIS FELLER!
SEE THE LIVER SPOT MARKINGS ON HIS ARMS? AMBUSH PREDATORS LOIKE THIS RELY ON CAMOUFLAGE..
HE'LL SIT HERE FOR HOURS IN FULL AMBUSH POSITION, WAITING FOR AN ANIMAL TO PASS BY -
PROD
GOAD
THEN WHOOSH! HE'LL FLY AHT OF HIS CHAIR AND SINK THOWSE HUGE FANGS ROIGHT INTO THE PREY'S SKULL!
WOOOH! WOOOH! SETTLE DOWN, SWEETHEART! SETTLE DOWN, ME OLD TUCKER!
THIS FELLER WANTS TO GIVE OLD STEVE-O A NIP, DON'TCHA MATE?
ONE BITE FROM THIS LI'L RIPPER CARRIES ENOUGH TOXIC VENOM TO FELL A WHOLE HERD OF DINGOS!
IRWIN! FOR GOD'S SAKE!
YOU'VE HAD SEVERAL WARNINGS ABOUT YOUR ROUGH HANDLING OF THE RESIDENTS. THESE ELDERLY PEOPLE ARE HUMAN BEINGS, NOT ANIMALS
I HAVE NO CHOICE BUT TO SUSPEND YOU FROM YOUR DUTIES.
COME ON, MR McTRAVIS
LET ME HELP YOU BACK INTO YOUR CHAIR
SNAP! SNAP!
AHH JESUS!
MY ARM!
GNASH! CHOMP!
LET'S TYKE A LOOK AT THE POO AROUND THIS FELLER'S CHAIR... LOOKS LOIKE HE'S BEEN FEEDING MOSTLY ON LIZARDS, BIRDS AND HOME HELPS
THESE BLIGHTERS CAN EAT PREY UP TO FOIVE TOIMES THE SIZE OF THEIR OWN HEAD

"It's All *Bollocks*" ~Pope

Pontiff's tirade turns air blue

A FOUR-LETTER outburst from the Pope stunned 100,000 pilgrims who had packed into St Peter's Square, Rome on Sunday. Making a rare public appearance, the 85 year-old Pontiff appeared tired and unsteady on his feet as he addressed the crowd from a Vatican balcony.

BY OUR VATICAN CORRESPONDENT MARTHA & THE MUFFINS

Slurring his words and holding onto a rail for support, John Paul II amazed onlookers by opening his traditional Summer address with a tirade of abuse directed at the central tenets of the Christian faith. Shocked catholics in the crowd were horrified to hear the holy father:

- ***DISMISS*** the New Testament as a *"parcel of fucking shite"*
- ***CONDEMN*** believers as *"a load of cockwits"*
- and ***SLAM*** the resurrection as *"a right load of old bollocks"*

speech

Two minutes into the controversial speech the bemused crowd watched as a pair of cardinals appeared on the balcony and attempted to wrestle the microphone out of his hands. A short and unseemly scuffle ensued, during which the Pope was seen to strike out repeatedly, breaking one of the cardinals' glasses before being dragged back inside the Vatican.

However, apparently determined to continue his contentious address he reappeared seconds later, shouting incoherently, jabbing his finger and shaking his fist aggressively at the startled crowd. Climbing up onto a stone balustrade, he raised his cassock and appeared to be about to urinate until he was manhandled to the ground by several burly members of the Swiss Guard.

hypno

The Pope was then taken in a headlock from the balcony whilst Italian police moved into St Peter's Square and began dispersing the crowd.

Journalists were summoned to the Vatican for a press conference on Monday afternoon. A frail-looking and clearly uncomfortable Pope sat silently in dark glasses, taking occasional sips from a tin of Irn Bru whilst a Cardinal read from a prepared statement.

psycho

Reporters were told: "It has come to our attention that during yesterday's papal announcement there was a fault in the public address system which led to many of the Pope's words getting mixed up in the machinery and coming out of the speakers in the wrong order.

frenzy

"We have been assured by Vatican engineers that the fault will not recur, and the Pontiff's next speech will appear with all the words in the correct order."

This is not the first time that a papal address has led to controversy. During his Easter Sunday mass at St Peter's Basilica, a problem with the acoustics was blamed for John Paul II apparently suggesting that the Virgin Mary could perform a sex act upon him before stumbling from the lecturn and vomiting onto the floor.

The Mrs
Brady
Bunch
CISSIE ADA DOLLY
MIND. HE WOULDN'T HAVE LIKED THESE PRICES, ADA. IT'S TWO POUND FOR A FISH!
AYE. AT THOSE PRICES, IT'S A MERCY HE'S DEAD.
TWO POUND? THEY'VE GOT A NERVE. I BET IT'S NO BIGGER THAN A SPRAT, NEITHER.
Menu
MIND, LABIAS AREN'T WHAT THEY USED TO BE WHEN I WERE A GIRL, NEITHER.
THIS BIG THEY WERE, COVERED IN BATTER.
GOOD AFTERNOON, LADIES. WELCOME TO HARRY RAMPTON'S LUNCHTIME SENIOR CITIZENS' SINGALONG. NOW, DO WE HAVE ANY REQUESTS?
WHAT ABOUT "WE'LL MEET AGAIN"?
"DOWN AT THE OLD BULL AND BUSH"!

HERE WE ARE, LADIES. I HOPE YOU'RE ALL NICE AND HUNGRY!
...HUNGRY, YES.
...YES, THAT'S RIGHT.
...RIGHT, YES.
Harry Rampton's
FISH & CHIPS
SOCIAL SERVICES
...YES, THAT'S...

RIGHT. NOW YOU GO IN AND SIT DOWN, AND I'LL TELL THE NICE MAN YOU'RE HERE, ALRIGHT?
OAP LUNCHTIME SPECIAL
FISH + CHIPS
POT OF TEA
PUDDING
& OLD TYME SING-ALONG
£3.50

EEH, ADA. ISN'T THIS LOVELY. IT'S LIKE A PALACE.
EEH, YES. IT'S LIKE SOLOMON'S TEMPLE. IT'S A PITY MY SIDNEY PASSED ON BEFORE SEEING THIS. HE WOULD'VE LOVED IT.
AYE. IT'S A TRAGEDY, ADA.

I REMEMBER WHEN FISH WERE FISH.
...FISH, YES, THAT'S RIGHT.
THEY'RE NOT FISH NOW.
...NOT FISH, NO, THAT'S RIGHT.
IT'S ALL WRONG.
...WRONG, YES, NO, THAT'S RIGHT.

WE USED TO BUY IT LOOSE IN THEM DAYS, WRAPPED IN WAX...
FROM A BARROW.
...WAX, YES.
...BARROW, YES.
THIS BIG IT WAS... FOR TWO BOB.
...BOB, YES.
NEVER!
YES.
EEH.
FANCY.

'COURSE, I NEVER BOUGHT ANY. I DON'T LIKE FISH, ME. IT BRINGS ME OUT IN HIVES ON ME LABIAS.
AYE, WELL. THEY'RE TOO BIG THESE DAYS, AREN'T THEY. SPECIALLY WHEN THEY'RE COVERED IN ALL THAT BATTER.
WHAT? HER LABIAS?
NO. FISH.

HAVE YOU HAD A LOOK AT THE MENU, LADIES? DO YOU KNOW WHAT YOU WANT?
HANG ON... EEH... WHERE'S ME READERS?
AREN'T YOU WEARING THEM, CISSIE?
NO. THESE AREN'T ME READERS, ADA. THESE ARE ME SEE-ERS.
CAN I HAVE A LEND OF YOURS, DOLLY?

OOH. THIS LOOKS NICE, LOOK.
AYE. AND IT'S QUITE REASONABLE ISN'T IT.
AYE. I'VE GOT QUITE A PENCHANT FOR A BIT OF HADDOCK.
...HADDOCK, YES.

TELL YOU WHAT, THEN LADIES. I'LL GET YOU ALL A NICE HADDOCK AND CHIPS - HOW ABOUT THAT?

OOH, LOOK, ADA. THE SINGALONG'S ABOUT TO START.
HADDOCK AND CHIPS IT IS, THEN...

DO YOU KNOW "PEOPLE EQUAL SHIT" BY SLIPKNOT?
...OR ANYTHING OFF THE IOWA ALBUM?

SHORTLY....
ALL TOGETHER LADIES...
♪ OH DANNY BOY...
...BOY, YES.
♪ ONE MORE TIME MOTHERFUCKER. ♪ EVERYBODY HATES ME SO FUCK IT...
♪ ...BLOOD'S ON MY FACE ♪

MUNCH! MUNCH!
...THE PIPES, THE PIPES ♪ ARE CALLING...
MUNCH! SCOFF!

♪ ... FROM GLEN TO GLEN, ♪ AND DOWN THE MOUNTAINSIDE...
COUGH! CHOKE! SPLUTTER
...COUGH, CHOKE, SPLUTTER, YES. THAT'S RIGHT.

♪ ... THE SUMMER'S GONE ♪ AND ALL THE FLOWERS ARE DYING...
GREEURCH!!
ADA- ARE YOU ALRIGHT?

...'TIS YOU, 'TIS YOU MUST GO AND I MUST BIDE... ♪
CROAK
SPLAT!

ADA, LOVE... CAN YOU HEAR ME? SPEAK TO ME, ADA LOVE...

EEH, FANCY. I'M FLOATING FREE OF ME EARTHLY SELF ...
I'M HEADING TOWARDS THE LIGHT...
CHOMP
MUNCH

MIND, WOULD YOU LOOK AT THE TOPS OF THESE PELMETS.
EEH... I BET IT'S SIX MONTH SINCE THEY'VE SEEN A DUSTER.

MY MAM USED TO DUST HER PELMETS THREE TIMES A DAY. YOU COULD EAT YOUR DINNER OFF MY MAM'S PELMETS.
EEH, WELL YOU HAD TO, DIDN'T YOU. BUT WE NEVER COMPLAINED.

DOLLY - WHAT ARE YOU DOING UP HERE? DID YOU CHOKE ON A FISHBONE TOO?
OOH, NO. MINE WERE LOVELY. NOT A BONE IN IT, ADA.
WELL YOU'RE LUCKY. MINE WERE NOWT BUT BONES.

I THINK I MUST'VE HAD A STROKE, YOU KNOW. I WENT ALL NUMB DOWN ONE SIDE WHEN I WERE EATING ME SOAPY PEAS.
WELL I BET THEY CHARGE YOU FOR 'EM, THE ROB-DOGS.
AYE. THEY NEVER MISS A TRICK, DO THEY? THE LITTLE TURKS.

OOH, LOOK, ADA. ISN'T THAT YOUR SIDNEY AT THE END OF THE TUNNEL, BECKONING YOU INTO THE LIGHT?
EEH. I DON'T KNOW, DOLLY.
I'VE GOT ME READERS ON. GIVE US A BORROW OF YOUR SEE-ERS.

AYE. THAT'S HIM ALRIGHT. THAT'S MY SIDNEY.

WELL I'M NOT GOING OVER THERE TO HIM. HE CAN RUDDY WELL TICKLE.
...AND THAT'S SWEARING.
EEH. FANCY.
...I KNOW WHAT HE'S AFTER.

HE WAS ALWAYS VERY DEMANDING... LIKE THAT... ...DOWN THERE...
... EVEN WHEN I WAS, YOU KNOW, "ON".
NEVER!
I'M TELLING YOU. EVEN WHEN I WAS ON.
EEH. THE FILTHY BEAST!

THAT'S NOWT. HE ONCE ASKED ME TO...
WHISPER
WHISPER
WHISPER

EEEEH! NEVER!

EEH, ADA. DID YOU?
WELL, YES. YOU DID IN THEM DAYS, DIDN'T YOU. YOU JUST GOT ON WITH IT. BUT I'VE NEVER BEEN RIGHT THERE SINCE...
...IN ME BACK BODY.

YOU'RE A MARTYR TO THAT ANUS OF YOURS, ADA.
AYE.
A MARTYR.

OOH LOOK, ADA. I THINK HE'S GOT THE BONE OUT YOUR THROAT.
PTHOOP!
WELL I HOPE HE'S WASHED HIS HANDS FIRST. I THINK HE MIGHT BE... YOU KNOW... ONE OF THEM.

WELL HE'S GOT YOU GOING AGAIN, ANY ROAD UP.
EEH, WELL, I SUPPOSE I SHOULD BE GETTING BACK, THEN. SAY HELLO TO CISSIE FOR ME, WON'T YOU.
...BUT CISSIE'S STILL ALIVE, ADA.

...NO. SHE'S OVER THERE, LOOK.
OOH, AYE. I THOUGHT SHE'D BEEN A LONG TIME ON THE TOILET.

OOH, THANK GOODNESS YOU'RE BACK WITH US, ADA LOVE. YOU HAD US ALL WORRIED THERE FOR A MINUTE!
BLINK!
BLINK!

WELL I HOPE YOU'VE LEFT SOME SPACE FOR YOUR PUDDING!
AYE, WELL... NO THANKS TO YOU.
I SAW YOU - THINKING ABOUT GOING THROUGH ME 'ANDBAG.

SHORTLY...
♪... AND I SHALL HEAR, THO' SOFT YOU TREAD ABOVE ME, AND ALL MY DREAMS WILL WARM AND SWEETER BE... ♪ IF YOU'LL NOT FAIL TO TELL ME THAT YOU LOVE ME, I'LL SIMPLY SLEEP IN PEACE UNTIL YOU COME TO ME ♪
♪ I'LL SIMPLY SLEEP IN PEACE UNTIL YOU COME... TO..... ME. ♪
MUNCH! CHOMP! GUZZLE!
TRUMP!

Letterbocks

It's the page that spent double physics surreptitiously scoffing Coolmints then shat itself on the way home from school and threw its pants in a bush

Letterbocks
Viz Comic
P.O.Box 1PT
Newcastle NE99 1PT

In this space age you can electromail your letters and tips to letterbocks@viz.co.uk

Star Letter

What a lot of nonsense this tantric sex is. So Sting can delay his climax for seven hours. That's nothing. I've been banging my missus for forty years and she's not had an orgasm yet.

P Collins, Colchester

I RECENTLY opened a tin of Alphabetti Spaghetti, only to find the whole tin contained nothing but letter 'O's. Can any of your readers beat that?

Edward Sylvester
Leicester Square

Pasta Joke

WITH REGARD to Edward Sylvester's letter (this issue). I can't beat it, but I can match it. I opened a can last night and it was full of very long letter 'l's.

Axolotl Abrahams
Berwick

PSYCHOLOGISTS SAY that men who like women with large breasts are suffering from an Oedipal complex. What bollocks. I like big tits, and I don't want to shag my mam. Her tits are tiny.

Joel Young,
e-mail

NOW THAT celebrity boxing has been banned, when don't they get a couple of celebrity birds to do a spot of mud wrestling for charity? I would like to see a pair of those haughty newsreaders, such as Sophie Raworth and Natasha Kaplinski at it. That would take them down a peg or two and make them seem more human to boot. Especially if they had to do it in their bra and knickers.

Mr Brasi
London

SURELY IT would make sense to simply nuke the Middle East. Then all the sand would turn to dunes of glass that you could ski on, providing you lined your skis with velvet. And you could find oil just by wandering around looking down.

Neil Weatherall
e-mail

Pure Genius

THE OTHER night, I had seven pints of Guinness. Unsurprisingly, I woke the next morning needing to fart. Aware of the extreme risks involved, I proceeded with extreme caution, excercisng such masterful ring control, that I not only prevented a fizzy follow through, but unwittingly parped a pitch-perfect 'Uh-Oh'. The comic timing and irony was sublime. I laughed so much I shat myself.

Boyce Thornton
Surrey

WHEN FLICKING through the newspapers recently, I was shocked to spot the headline 'Matthew Kelly Child Sex Quiz'. Whilst I have always found Mr. Kelly to be a first rate presenter, I am appalled that TV bosses have decided to base a light entertainment show around such tasteless subject matter.

Tony Presidio
Leeds

I CAN'T help wondering why my neighbours appear to be having a two-storey extension built onto their house when I know for a fact that they both died in 1986 within 6 months of each other.

Fat Al White
Wrenthorpe

MANY CRITICS do not claim that America "would move quickly to start pumping out vast quantities of oil" (All about Oil?, Jan 25th 2002) in a post-Saddam Iraq. Rather, the 10 years it would take to upgrade the Iraqi oil industry would conveniently sit alongside the timeframe that many top petroleum geologists are predicting that we will reach peak oil production in. After peaking, production in non-OPEC countries will decline whilst market share will once again swing towards OPEC. Oil in the ground may well be better than money in the bank, given the low interest rates for now and the forseeable future. Why not admit that oil security plays a role and internalise the debate, as opposed to constantly denying the significance, thereby creating mistrust? This would not be the first time that wars have been fought partly over energy supplies.

Tobias Parker
e-mail

** Have you ever sent a letter to the wrong publication, like Mr Parker? Perhaps you've emailed an amusing anecdote about your knobcheese to the Financial Times. Or maybe you posted three photos of your wife sitting on the washing machine and pulling her flaps open to the Catholic Herald. Write to the letters page of The Lancet and let us know.*

I READ recently that a silver coin c. AD30 was found in Judea and subsequently auctioned for over £100,000. Despite the Bible portraying the 30 pieces of silver that Judas was paid as a paltry sum, according to my calculations it actually amounts to a healthy £3million. It's no surprise that he dobbed the bastard in to the Romans, is it? I know I would have.

Rev. H.B.
Middlesbrough

I'VE NOTHING against foreigners coming to this country, but at least they ought to try to integrate into our society. They should ditch their fancy dress in favour of normal clothes and speak English instead of their own mumbo-jumbo language. Furthermore, they should be forced to eat fish and chips and drink warm beer like we do. And if they don't like it, they can bloody well get back where they came from.

T. Kavanagh
Wapping

Holmes delivery

IN A recent newspaper interview, Eamonn Holmes claimed his mother had defective hips. I'm not surprised after giving birth to that fat twat.

Alan Gibson
e-mail

I WAS delighted when the kind people at the Inland Revenue wrote to me recently, telling me that my tax return was 'outstanding', particularly since I can't even remember sending it in.

Tom McCann
Wokingham

THE GOVERNMENT say that benefit fraud is costing every household in Britain about £80 per month. Nonsense. I'm up 300 quid a week.

A Collins
Liverpool

Fantasy Football Results

Division 1

Girl on girl 3 Three in a bed 2

Lesbian twins 2 Nympho nurses 1

Leather nazi 3 Watching wife and black man 0

WPC uniform 0 Seduced by wife's mother 1

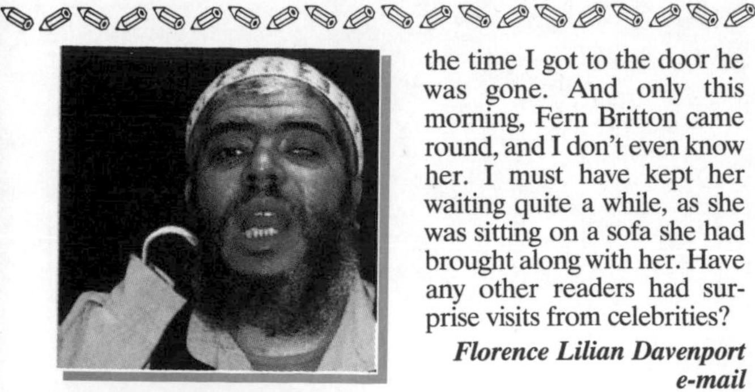

the time I got to the door he was gone. And only this morning, Fern Britton came round, and I don't even know her. I must have kept her waiting quite a while, as she was sitting on a sofa she had brought along with her. Have any other readers had surprise visits from celebrities?

Florence Lilian Davenport
e-mail

For His Eye Only

I WOULD like to nominate extremist cleric and Arsenal supporter Abu Hamza as the next Bond villain. With his claw hand and missing eye, he would look great as a baddy, and as a climax to the film, the dome roof of Finsbury Park mosque could open to reveal a giant laser gun that harnessed the power of the Sun's rays.

Bad Horsey
e-mail

Clint Made My Day

MY GRANDSON recently installed a security camera on my front door. "Just press 9 on the remote when someone knocks," he said. "Then you can check who's there on the TV." Last Tuesday, there was a knock on the door. Would you believe Clint Eastwood had called on me to pay a visit! However, by the time I got to the door he was gone.

IF MY wife is reading this, could I just point out that that, yes, sticking my thumb up her arse whilst shagging her IS completely necessary.

Kid
e-mail

I'M A pensioner and the other day I opened the door to find four 12-year-olds in tracksuits asking to read my meter. Hats off to the gas board for giving these youngsters such valuable work experience.

Mrs Earnshaw
Frome

I MUST SAY how surprised I was to hear Abu Hamza being interviewed on the radio. I was deeply disappointed by his normal voice. After all the trouble he's gone to getting his glass eye and hook, you'd think he'd try to talk more like Bernard Breslaw in 'Carry On Up the Khyber'. Next time, the least he could do is shout "infidels" at the top of his voice.

Bram Tchaikovsky
Battle Hill

TOP TIPS

SAVE *money on Red Nose Day by simply using half the wax covering from a tasty Babybel cheese. Save your friends money too by giving them the other half.*

J Routlidge
e-mail

CONVINCE *your neighbours that evolution is working backwards by not shaving for a week, walking to your car gradually more stooped each morning and wearing a monkey costume on the Friday.*

Baruch Soloman
e-mail

PAEDOPHILES. *Confuse the police during questioning by making suggestive remarks about old ladies.*

Johnny Pring
e-mail

McDONALDS. *Double the amount of money your customers donate to children's charities by reducing the cost of your breakfast from £1.99 to £1.98.*

Dave Saunders
Cricklewood

MAKE *striking firefighters leap into action. Set fire to a porn warehouse and see how quick they move.*

J Kerin
Faversham

FEMALE *shop assistants. When a garage mechanic comes to your till, add on a selection of random items they didn't know they needed, and charge them £50 labour costs for the transaction.*

Tim Woods
e-mail

I've got a shelf that's two metres long. Can any of your readers beat that?

King Shelf
Newcastle

I put up a shelf the other day, and the wife said it didn't look straight. Imagine her surprise when I checked it with a spirit level and it was perfectly horizontal. It was an optical illusion! How we both laughed.

Arthur Twoshelves
Daventry

The things kids say! "Look, grandad, that mantlepiece has lost its fireplace," my 3-year-old grandson said the other day. He was pointing at a shelf! Do I win £5?

Ernie McShelf
Kinross

I won a really nice shelf in a raffle, but everything I put on it falls off. That's because I'm a lighthouse keeper or I live in a windmill, and the only way I could fasten it on the wall was to fit it vertically!

Eamonn O'Shelf
Edison Rock Lighthouse,
Amsterdam

I haven't got any shelves in my house. That's because I work in a supermarket stacking shelves, and the last thing I want to look at when I get home is more shelves!

Rosemary Shelfson
St Asaph

That's nothing. I work in IKEA, stacking self-assembly shelves...onto shelves! If I came home and there was more shelves in my house, I'd probably flip, murder my wife and kids, and then turn the gun on myself!

Billy Bookcase
Gateshead

The things kids say! "Grandad, why has that shelf got four legs?" my 3-year-old grandson asked me in the kitchen the other day. He was pointing at the table! *Now* do I win £5?

Ernie McShelf
Kinross

I've been collecting shelves for forty years. "I've bought you something to help you store your collection," my wife said the other day. "I hope it's not another shelf," I replied. It was a box!

Sheldon Elf
Matlock Bath

All you shelf fans are saddos and wrinklies. They haven't even got doors. Get with it and get cupboarded up!

Kurt Cupboard
Cirencester

SHELF HELP WITH MIRIAM STOPPARD

Dear Miriam...

This Christmas, my boyfriend bought me a pair of bookends to put on my shelf. He'd overlooked one fact; I don't have any books. However, I have got twelve videos which occasionally topple over, especially when I'm dusting. Do you think it would be okay to use these bookends as "video-ends" instead?

Sarah, Luton

LETTER OF THE DAY

Miriam writes...

My ex-husband playwright Tom Stoppard's old woodwork teacher always used to tell him to never use a tool for any purpose for which it wasn't intended. However, in this case I think you can safely ignore that advice. Your bookends will make marvellous "video-ends" to stop your tapes toppling over!

Chat and share shelf gossip, stories and news with shelf-minded people in our new shelf chatroom.
www.suityourshelf.co.uk

BIG
VERN

4:30 am...
...TICK! TICK! TICK! TICK!...
ZZ-ZZZZ... WIFFLE-WAFFLE
ZZ-ZZZ-ZZ... WIFFLE-WAFFLE...

...TICK! TICK! TICK! ...K! TICK! TICK! TICK! TICK!
-ZZZZZ- WIFFLE-WAFFLE
...ZZ-ZZZ-ZZZ WIFFLE-W...
COUGH
EH!? WHASSAT!?

CLICK
VERN! WHAT THE..? ...HOW DID..?
MORNIN' ERNIE.
I LET MESELF IN.

YOU WANT TO GET YER LOCKS SORTED AHT, ERNIE. ANYONE COULD BUST THEIR WAY INTO THIS GAFF... AND THERE'S SOME NAUGHTY BOYS ABAHT, BELIEVE ME.

YAWN! OH, HELLO THERE, VERNON. WHAT..?
WE GOTTA LOSE THE TART, ERNIE.
THIS IS MAN'S TALK.

CAM ON. AAHT YER GET, DARLIN'.
...BUT VERNON, IT'S...
LOOK, LADY- SHAT YER MARF, PUT YER KNICKERS ON AN' MAKE ME A NICE CUPPA TEA...
ALRIGHT?

ERM...SO WHAT ARE YOU DOING HERE AT THIS TIME IN THE MORNING..?
I WANT YOU TO LOOK AFTER SOMETHING FOR ME, ERNIE.
OH YES, WHAT IS IT?

CAM ON, ERNIE. YOU KNOW THE RULES. NO NAMES, NO PACK DRILL. THEM WHAT DON'T KNOW NAFFINK CAN'T SQUEAL ON NOBODY.
ESSO ALL-NIGHT GARAGE

OOH- A MICROWAVE MEAL FOR ONE. THEY'RE NICE, THEY ARE. IS YOUR FRIDGE BROKEN?
ERM...YEAH! FRIDGE BROKEN-THAT'S IT. VERY CLEVAH, ERNIE.

GOOD BOY. YOU'RE USING THIS, ERNIE. LET'S KEEP IT THAT WAY, EH? NICE AND SIMPLE, SO NO-ONE GETS 'URT.
ERM... I SUPPOSE SO, YES.

NOW YOU DON'T SAY NAFFINK ABAHT THIS, ERNIE. NOT TO NO-ONE. ANYONE ASKS-YOU'VE NOT SEEN ME. YOU JUST GO ABAHT YER USUAL DAILY- ALRIGHT?
RIGHT YOU ARE, VERN.

ACTUALLY, I WAS THINKING OF TAKING MY MOTHER OUT LATER.
!?

YOU, ERNIE? TAKE YER MAVVAH AHT? YOU SURE YOU'RE UP TO THE CAPER?
OH, YES. I DON'T SEE WHY NOT, VERN.
I DUNNO, ERNIE. IT'S A BIG JOB MAN LIKE YOU...

YOU WANT TO GET A PROFESSIONAL IN, ERNIE. TELL YER WOT... YER UNCLE VERN'LL CAM ALONG WIV YER... 'OLD YER 'AND.
...BUT...
I'LL PICK YER AP AT TEN.

LATER...
VROOM!
SCREECH!

TSK! REALLY, VERN. COME ON. I SAID WE'D BE AT MUM'S TEN MINUTES AGO.
ALREADY TAKEN CARE OF, ERNIE. ...LOOK.

MMF!..MMF! ...MMMF!
MOTHER!!

SLAM!
BUT VERN- SHE'S 82 - CAN'T SHE SIT IN THE BACK WITH US? THIS WON'T BE DOING HER HIP ANY GOOD AT ALL.

NO TIME FOR THAT NOW, ERNIE. RIGHT- WHERE TO?
WELL- SHE DID SAY SHE FANCIED A TRIP TO THE SEASIDE, SO I THOUGHT...

SEASIDE, EH?... GOOD FINKIN' ERNIE... SECLUDED COVES... PLENTY OF CLIFFS...
SOMEONE COULD 'AVE A NASTY FALL...

SHORTLY...
HERE WE GO, ERNIE...
PARKING 20p
NICE AN' QUIET.

CAM ON, SWEET-TITS. NAFFINK PERSONAL, YOU UNDERSTAND - BUT THIS IS WHERE YOU GET YOURS.
MMF! MMF!

OFF YOU GO, DARLIN', AN' DON'T TRY ANY 'EROICS. YOU JUST KEEP WALKIN'... ALL BE OVER SOON...
YOU CAN 'AVE A NICE LONG SLEEP, MA. ALRIGHT?

PERHAPS IT'D BE BEST IF I WALKED WITH HER, VERN. I DON'T WANT HER GOING TOO NEAR THE EDGE...
...ESPECIALLY WHEN SHE'S BOUND AND GAGGED.
LEAVE IT, ERNIE. YOU'VE DONE YOUR BIT. I'LL TAKE IT FROM 'ERE.

RIGHT, ERNIE. 'EAD SHOT I FINK.
EH!?

EXCUSE ME, SIR. I DON'T THINK YOU SAW THE SIGN. PARKING IS 20p... OR IT'S FREE IF YOU'RE A MEMBER OF ENGLISH HERIT...
GET DAHN, ERNIE! IT'S THE FILF!

BLAM!

YOU SLAAG! YOU'VE FITTED ME AP, ERNIE, YOU BARSTAD. I TREATED YOU LIKE YOU WAS MY BRAVVAH AN' YOU FITTED ME AP!
AAAR CUDJA?

WELL NO FACKIN' COPPER'S GUNNU TAKE ME ALIVE!

VROOM!

BLAM!
VD 1

KA-BOOM!

IT'S THE BACONS

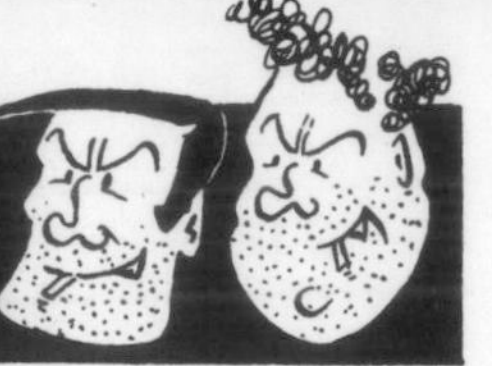

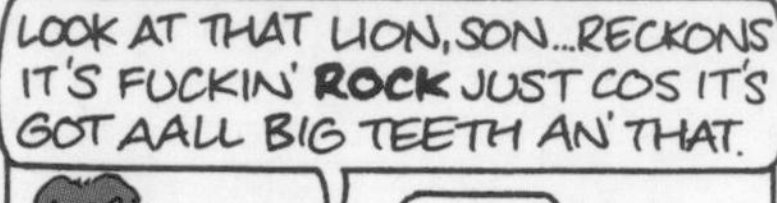

LISTEN! I'M NOT PUTTIN' ME HEED IN A FRIGGIN LION'S MOOTH!

BWAAK! BWAAK! BWAAK!

ONE DAY IN A GRANADA TV PRODUCTION OFFICE

Paul Palmer

Wing Span-Dabidozy!

Krankies' terror as hawk snatches schoolboy Jeanette

LITTLE Jimmy Krankie was recovering in the fake children's ward of a Ben Nevis hospital last night ~ *after being snatched by a hawk.*

The four-foot schoolboy granny was out walking with his normal-sized husband Ian when the bird of prey swooped unexpectedly.

hawk

Ian told reporters: "I heard a scream and turned to see a hawk gripping Jeanette's shoulders in its talons. Before I knew what was happening, it lifted him off the ground and carried her away."

wolf

He continued: "I threw some rocks to try to get the bird to drop her, but it was already too high. As it flew into the distance I could hear Jimmy's cries getting fainter and fainter. I could see his little legs kicking and I just panicked."

Unable to contact the emergency services Ian, 56, gave chase and eventually spotted his wife waving frantically from a nest 300 feet up a cliff.

hunter

Although relieved to see him still alive, he knew he had to act quickly before the hawk came back and ate her, so he started climbing.

He said: "I've done live TV, the Royal Variety Performance and Friday night at the Glasgow Empire but let me tell you, I've never been so scared as I was climbing that rock face. It seemed to take an age, but eventally I clambered up onto the ledge where the nest was."

And he was just in time, for the hawk chose this moment to return. Ian looked on horrified as the bird pecked with its razor-sharp beak at Jimmy's school cap as she attempted to fend it off with her satchel.

imp

Ian, who plays the straightman to his wife's wrinkled cheeky schoolboy in the duo's tired variety act, managed to scare it off for long enough to grab the terrified Jimmy and scramble to safety.

An RSPB spokesman later identified the bird as a Harris Hawk. He said: "They usually take mice or rabbits. I've only very occasionally heard of one taking a comedy schoolboy. It may be a rogue bird, so just to be on the safe side we've had it shot and smashed its eggs."

Ian, and cheeky schoolboy wife Jimmy ***(left)*** *and* ***(above)*** *the Harris Hawk that snatched Jeanette.*

JOHN, LESLIE GUILTY

STARS' SENSATIONAL CONFESSION

ELTON John and Leslie Nielsen have issued an incredible joint statement revealing their shameful pasts.

Nielsen, star of *Viva Knievel!* and *Scary Movie 3,* says he is "tortured daily with an unbearable burden of guilt" about stealing a pair of classmate's socks after basketball practice when he was 12.

Sir Elton, star of *Ally McBeal* and *Bob The Builder: A Christmas To Remember,* sobbed that "hardly a day goes by without me reliving the horror of treading on a snail when I was six."

One of Leslie Nielsen's two brothers went on to become Deputy Prime Minister of Canada.

FINBARR SAUNDERS & his DOUBLE ENTENDRES
SERGEI HAS DECIDED TO GET HIMSELF A PET...
PET SHOP
OPEN

PLEASE ASK TO HAVE A GO WITH ANY OF OUR ANIMALS.
...HELLO. I WOULD LIKE TO HANDLE YOUR GREAT BIG TITTIES.
!?
FNARR! FNARR!
YIK! YIK!
GIANT TORTOISE £10

...WELL THIS ONLY GOES TO PROVE WHAT I'VE ALWAYS SAID, MRS SAUNDERS. THE DECISION TO BUY A PET SHOULD NOT BE TAKEN LIGHTLY.
OPEN

EVEN THE SMALLEST ANIMAL IS A GREAT RESPONSIBILITY AND REQUIRES A LOT OF ATTENTION. FOR EXAMPLE I ONCE FOUND MY PET MOUSE UNCONSCIOUS.
GOSH!
IT HAD CHOKED ON ITS FOOD AND HAD TO BE RESUSCITATED.

WHAT DID YOU DO, MR. GIMLET?
WELL, MY WIFE WAS OUT FOR THE EVENING, SO I GRIPPED IT IN THE PALM OF MY HAND AND RUBBED IT UP AND DOWN FOR FIVE MINUTES UNTIL IT GAVE A LITTLE SHUDDER AND A LUMP OF CHEESE POPPED OUT.
K-YIK! K-YIK!
WOOF! WOOF!
SNURT! SNURT!
GAWB! GAWB!

WELL DONE, MR. GIMLET! YOU SHOULD HAVE BEEN A VET!
YOU'RE NOT WRONG, MRS. SAUNDERS. LAST YEAR I TOOK IN AN INJURED HEDGEHOG AND NURSED IT BACK TO HEALTH.

...IN FACT, IT RECENTLY WOKE UP FROM ITS HIBERNATION - ONLY I'D RUN OUT OF COTTON WOOL. IN THE END I HAD TO USE AN OLD SOCK TO WIPE THE STICKY GUNK OUT OF MY HOG'S EYE.
BLOOB! BLOOB!
THUBES! THUBES!
T-SNUT! T-SNUT!
G-YIP! G-YIP!
WAP! WAP!
ARP! ARP!
HOWP! HOWP!
OG! OG!
SNUB! SNUB!
WO-WOO! WO-WOO!

WHAT ABOUT LARGER ANIMALS, MR. GIMLET?
WELL, I AM QUITE INTERESTED IN EQUESTRIANISM, ALTHOUGH I FIND THAT THE HIRING OF HORSES CAN PROVE SOMETHING OF A LOTTERY. ON A RECENT HOLIDAY IN MOROCCO I PAID £10 FOR THE PRIVILEGE OF BEING TOSSED OFF BY A FRISKY YOUNG ARAB.
GACK! GACK!
SPOOB! SPOOB!
FWURF! FWURF!

MIND YOU - WHILST I WAS IN AFRICA I WAS MUCH TAKEN BY THE EXOTIC PLUMAGE OF THE INDIGENOUS BIRDLIFE. AS A RESULT, I PURCHASED A BREEDING PAIR OF LORIKEETS. MY HEN'S QUITE SMALL, WITH FEATHERS OF GREEN AND PURPLE.
WHAT ABOUT HER MATE?

MY COCK'S ABOUT SIX INCHES LONG, AND IT'S BRIGHT PINK WITH A PURPLE HEAD.
FWURR! FWURR!
HIB! HIB!
SNT! SNT!
YUK! YUK!

BUT I'VE ALWAYS HAD A SOFT SPOT FOR DOGS. THE LADY NEXT DOOR HAS SEVERAL PEDIGREE KING CHARLES SPANIELS WHICH SHE EXHIBITS EVERY WEEKEND AT DOG SHOWS. AS A CONSEQUENCE SHE KEEPS THEM EXCEPTIONALLY WELL GROOMED.

IF I'M IN THE SPARE ROOM ON A FRIDAY NIGHT AND I STAND ON TIPTOES I GET A GREAT VIEW OF HER SOAPING HER SPLENDID CHARLIES.
HURP! HURP!
GOOGLE! GOOGLE!
FNOOP! FNOOP!
G-YIP! G-YIP!
HOO! HOO!

HAS SHE ALWAYS KEPT SPANIELS?
NO. SHE USED TO HAVE A GREAT BIG ALSATIAN. I'LL NEVER FORGET THE TIME IT GREW ATTACHED TO MRS. GIMLET'S PET FERRET.

I CAME HOME FROM WORK UNEXPECTEDLY TO FIND A 14 STONE GERMAN SHEPHERD LICKING MY WIFE'S STOAT ON THE KITCHEN TABLE!
GIP! GIP!
BO! BO!
FNIT! FNIT!
HYEH! HYEH!
SPANG! SPANG!

YOU SEEM TO HAVE HAD A LOT OF PETS IN YOUR TIME, MR. GIMLET. HAS YOUR WIFE EVER OWNED A PARTICULARLY HIRSUTE CAT..?
...THAT SMELLED STRONGLY OF ITS FAVOURITE FOOD?
NOT REALLY, NO.

COCKNEY WANKER

TWO 'ANDRED NOTES FOR A FACKIN TITFER! I ARSK YER! I'VE JAST SPENT FIVE 'ANDRED ON Y' FACKIN' KNOCKERS WOMAN...

I AIN'T GOT MONEY T' GO WASTIN' ON FACKIN' 'ATS!

JAST FINK, LAV... IN AN 'OURS TIME, YOU WON'T BE A WANKAH NO MOWAH..

YOU'LL BE MRS EDDIE 'CUT-FWOAT' McBISHOP

LYRICAL LAUGHS with ANDREW MOTION

THE POET LAUREATE FUNNYMAN

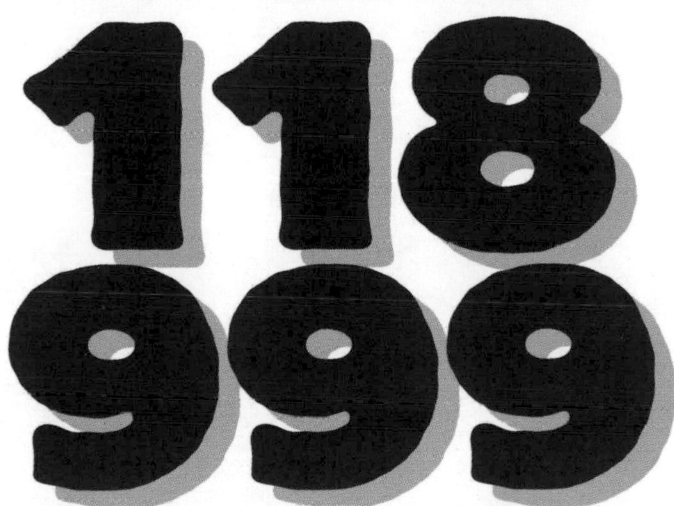

From September 1st, the old 999 number is being phased out to be replaced by dozens of exciting new numbers!

At last, just as you've always wanted, you'll be able to choose from a wider range of emergency call service providers.

If your house is on fire, if you've been hit by a bus, or maybe just been burgled or drifted out to sea, take a few minutes to choose who you'd like to ask for a fire engine. We hope you'll choose us.

46p per minute. Min call charge £1. All calls terminate in an undermanned call centre in an industrial unit on the outskirts of Ahmadabad.

Calls may be monitored to help maintain levels of customer service, and may not be answered in English.

If you need a loan of between **£500** and **£15,000**, and are having trouble getting credit because you're a cat, call us today.

Whatever you need the money for, we can approve you, **regardless of your breed or credit history**.

Balls of wool, dead mice, curtain fringing, fishing rods, a bin with a telephone and a straw boater your ears stick up through, it's up to you what you spend the money on.

Just because you're a cat, we won't say no.

call 08999 766 765

or apply online at www.irresponsibleloancompany.com

** Credit subject to status and how drunk we are when we answer the phone. Your owner's home is at risk if you do not keep up payments on a loan secured on it.*

POP ROUNDUP

With Belmarsh Prison Radio DJ

Jonathan King

Goodbye Abu Hamza Hello Samantha

Hook-handed extremist cleric Abu Hamza is set to be driven out of Britain by former Shadows frontman Sir Cliff Richard! The self-styled Peter Pan of Pop plans to fight the self-styled Moslem Captain Hook in a battle to the death ... and it's all for charity! Ageless Richards, 83, will don green tights and tunic for the fight, which will take place in Finsbury Park Mosque, transformed for the day into a spectacular pirate galleon - complete with skull and crossbones flags, rigging and cannons! The loser will be forced to walk the plank and be eaten by a ravenous crocodile - specially bred for the occasion by Cliff's Ready Steady Go pal Marty Wilde at his reptile farm in Cardiff!

Heaven Knows I'm Still a Twat Now

Malcontented former Smiths frontman Morrissey is throwing a party to celebrate his 20th year as a twat! The star-studded bash will take place at his swanky Hollywood home in November, marking two decades since the sulky mardyarse first entered the charts in 1983. 500 of pop's A-list are set to attend, including Sting, Bono, the Beatles, the Rolling Stones and Jimmy Hendrix. However, like the big arsehole he is, Morrissey plans to snub his celebrations and intends to spend the day sat moodily in his bedroom, listening to Doris Day records and waving daffodils round his head.

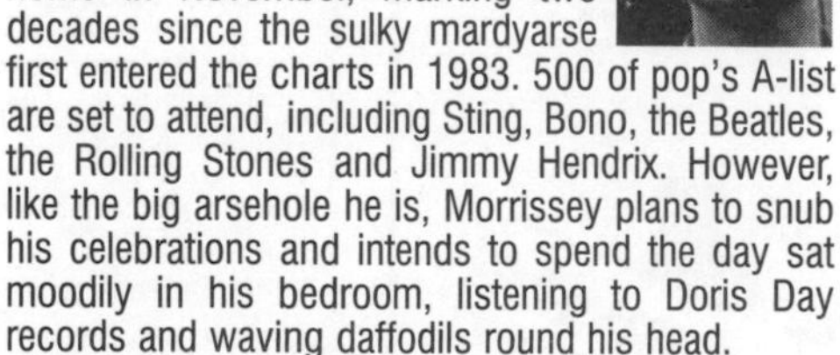

Good Bed Yellow Brick Road

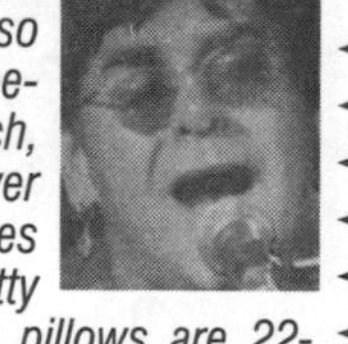

Four-eyed wig-wearing homosexual popster Sir Elton John has splashed out over £50 million ... on a custom made bed! Whilst most people dream of taking 40 winks in a swanky 4-poster bed, John's got so much money his bed's a 20-poster! Only trouble is, with all those posts, the tubby ivory-tinkler can't fit into it, so he has to be lowered in on a specially constructed £1 million winch, operated by his gay anal sex lover David Furnish! But Elton's troubles don't stop there - he's in for a pretty uncomfortable night's sleep. The pillows are 22-carat solid gold ... and the mattress is stuffed not with feathers but with buried treasure including pieces of eight, tiaras and diamonds the size of a hen's egg!

In the Hair Tonight

Balding pint-sized Genesis drummer Phil Collins recently checked out of a £2 million a day Swiss clinic ... with his wife's pubic hair transplanted onto his pate! He told Zurich TV: "She wanted a Brazillian, and I wanted thick black curly hair on my head. We're both absolutely delighted with the results!" This latest headline-grabbing antic follows his decision in May to have his foreskin removed and made into a 2 inch snare drum, which was sold on the internet, raising over £14 for the Prince's Trust charity!

Jonathan King hosts 'Slop Out with King' each morning from 6.00 am on Belmarsh Prison Radio.

KNOCK! KNOCK!

I'LL JUST GET THAT.

JIMBO JUMBO'S ROBO JOBOS
YOUNG JAMES JUMBO WAS THE LUCKIEST LAD IN BARNTON, FOR HIS GRANDFATHER WAS AN ECCENTRIC INVENTOR WHO HAD BUILT HIM A FANTASTIC MINIATURE TROUPE OF REMOTE CONTROL JEHOVAH'S WITNESSES...
NOT TODAY, THANKS.
OH, FOR FUCK'S SAKE! IT'S 8 O'CLOCK ON A SUNDAY MORNING!
FUCK OFF!
DAD! THERE'S SOME TINY ROBOTS AT THE DOOR WANTING TO KNOW IF YOU'VE EVER THOUGHT ABOUT ARMAGEDDON.
ERM... I'M C. OF E. YAWN!
NOT NOW, I'M BUSY.

THAT'S A GREAT MORNINGS WORK, ROBOTS. NOW LET'S GET HOME FOR A WELL EARNED BREAKFAST...
...I'M STARVING!

JIMBO LED HIS ROBOTS THROUGH THE STREETS HOME...
LEFT! RIGHT! LEFT! RIGHT!

...WHEN.
HELLO? THAT'S ODD...
THAT VAN HAS BEEN PARKED THERE ALL MORNING, AND THERE'S BEEN PARADE OF PEOPLE COMING AND GOING.

GO ON, ROBO JOBOS. FIND OUT WHAT'S GOING ON.

WITH JIMBO AT THE CONTROLS, THE ROBOTS MADE SHORT WORK OF FORMING A LADDER TO SEE IN THROUGH THE WINDOW...
CRIKEY! SO THAT'S THEIR GAME...

...IT'S A BLOOD TRANSFUSION SERVICE VAN!
THEY'RE FILLING UP WITH BLOOD TO TAKE TO THE HOSPITAL FOR CRITICALLY ILL PATIENTS.

THAT'S IN DIRECT CONTRAVENTION OF THE SCRIPTURES.
COME ON, WITNESSES! WE'VE GOT TO STOP THEM!

SHORTLY...
THERE WE ARE, DOCTOR. NEARLY 100 PINTS OF BLOOD.
GREAT! LET'S GET THEM TO HOSPITAL AS QUICK AS WE CAN.

A28
Ring Road
QUICK, EVERY ONE. THEY'RE GOING ALONG THE RING ROAD...
...IF WE'RE QUICK, WE CAN HEAD THEM OFF AT THE BRIDGE.

JIMBO AND HIS ARMY OF THE SAVED RAN LIKE THE WIND...
WE'RE JUST IN TIME!

HERE THEY COME... READY, MEN?

3...2...1...GERONIMO!

BUMP! THUMP, BUMP!
EH?! WHAT WAS THAT?

THE DOCTOR DIDN'T HAVE TO WAIT LONG TO FIND OUT AS ONE OF THE RADIO CONTROLLED EVANGELISTS MADE HIS WAY TO THE BACK DOOR...

...AND OPENED THE CATCH.

MEANWHILE, AT THE FRONT OF THE AMBULANCE, THE ROBOT WITNESSES HAD ANOTHER SURPRISE PLANNED...
WHAT THE...!?!
THE WINDSCREEN IS COVERED WITH ANTI-DARWINIST LITERATURE!...

...I CAN'T SEE!
SCREEEECH!

SMASH!

WELL DONE, ROBOTS. THAT'S AT LEAST 100 LIVES THAT WONT BE SAVED IN ACCORDANCE WITH THE WILL OF JEHOVAH ..
...NOW FOR THAT BREAKFAST!

Letterbocks

It's the page that has found a lump in its testicles, but would rather die than go to a lady doctor

Letterbocks
Viz Comic
P.O.Box 1PT
Newcastle NE99 1PT

In this space age you can electromail your letters and tips to letterbocks@viz.co.uk

★Star Letter★

According to the HSBC, the rudest thing you can do in Thailand is show the soles of your feet. What nonsense. On my last trip to Bangkok, I shat on a ladyboy's tits whilst his sister wanked me into their mum's hair.

B. Shipton, Leigh on Sea

I bought a new mobile phone last week and I was promised 'free evenings and weekends'. However, my boss has just told me that I have to work late tonight and come in on Saturday. How much longer are we going to fall for the phone companies' lies?

Cliff Brown
e-mail

Just a thought, but if people in the Third World are so poor, how come they can afford so many haircuts?

M. Barber
e-mail

All this talk of lesbians only liking sex with women is absolute rubbish. In every film I have seen involving lesbians, they get bored with each other after ten minutes or so and end up sucking some bloke's cock.

Jim Bowden
Teignmouth

I think that the congestion charge for London is a load of wank, and it seems that the people who designed the 'Register for FastTrack' logo on the website at www.cclondon.com agree.

Julian Malone
e-mail

In the last issue of *Viz*, Naylor Hammond says 'All things freeze at 0°c, or absolute zero, as scientists call it'. I think you will find that freezing can occur at any temperature depending upon the substance. In addition, absolute zero is not 0°c, but -273°c.

Paul Miller
Sunderland University

Naylor replies.
I don't know what they teach people at Sunderland University these days, but the mind boggles. How can the temperature of something possibly be lower than 0°? It would simply start getting hotter again. I would advise Mr Miller to check his facts before writing in future.

In the last issue, you asked for people to write about letters sent to the wrong publications. Well I think I have sent all my letters to you to the wrong publication because they were funnier than the crock of shite you usually publish, and you didn't print a single one.

Mike Harbidge
e-mail

I reckon if you stuck a fish's tail under Geordie comic Ross Noble's chin, he'd look the spitting image of Billy the Fish.

Jimmy Hobson
Morecambe

I have just watched Richard Hillman being exposed as a murderer in Coronation Street, and at the end had the irresistible urge to phone my sister and go over every minute of the action with her.

A Woman
Everywhere

Here's a picture of a big arse snapped in Edinburgh. You're welcome to it.

Alan Kayda
snail-mail

I for one would NOT be amused if Shakin' Stevens developed Parkinson's disease.

Dav
e-mail

Am I alone in thinking that 8 Ace has the voice of Stan Ogden? And Major Misunderstanding sounds like Ballard Berkeley?

Dave Essex
E-mail

These days, most shops have wheelchair access, but once inside the shop, the needs of the disabled are all but forgotten. Whilst in my newsagents the other day, I realised how difficult it must be for someone in a wheelchair to purchase a top shelf magazine. They would have to ask someone to pass it down which would cause great embarrassment. Wouldn't it be a good idea if newsagents had a pneumatic ramp by the magazines to lift wheelchairs up to the top shelf. It could be fitted with flashing lights and a klaxon to warn other customers to keep clear of the mechanism when in operation.

Steve Dawson
e-mail

I don't know why Heather Mills is so concerned about land mines. She's only half as much at risk from them as everybody else.

J. Jordan
Leeds

My gran told me that if I fart and sneeze at the same time, I'll do a backflip. Is this true?

Finlay Briggs
e-mail

**Have YOU ever farted and sneezed at the same time? Write and tell us what happened. Mark your envelope 'I farted and sneezed at the same time, and here's what happened.'*

I would like to nominate the fat fuck Jobbie Coltrane as a celebrity cunt for refusing an autograph for my boy in Makro's car park while loading up his Merc. Apparently he doesn't do autographs or sign anything, except fat contracts to be the friendly wizard in Harry Snotter. Magic.

G. McKendrick
Glasgow

I have no proof, but I'm convinced that Rowan Williams, the Arch Bishop of Canterbury combs his eyebrows because he thinks it makes him look like an owl, and therefore wise.

S. Oakwood
Penge

Now Thora Hird has fucked the bucket, the BBC ought to repeat every episode of Last Of The Summer Wine in tribute to her. There can't be more than 300.

Peter Bleater
Iffley

TOP TIPS

SPECTACLE wearers. Prepare for any forthcoming conflict by putting crosses of masking tape across the lenses of your glasses.
NO NAME, NO PLACE

SAVE money on expensive hole punches by goading a Great Dane into snapping at you while you slip the appropriate documents between its foaming canines. It may help to make a pencil mark halfway along the edge, and try to line this up with the cleft in the dog's top lip.
Mike Fitzgerald, Jersey

AVOID chip pan fires by suspending a plastic bag full of water over the pan each time you cook. If a fire occurs, the bag will melt and the water will extinguish the flames.
Kieron Douglas, Glasgow

A SHREDDED Wheat on a stick makes a great back scrubber for the first couple of seconds of your bath.
Hapag Lloyd, Runcorn

SAVE doing unnecessary ironing by putting on your shirt and tucking it into your trousers. Then, draw a line around the shirt at belt level with an indelible marker pen. The material below this line will never need ironing, thus saving time and effort.
JA Colo, e-mail

VACUUM cleaner manufacturers. Put a smiley face on your machines. It really makes us laugh at six o'clock in the morning when the lead gets tangled around chair legs and keeps overbalancing.
Spenshine Cleaning Contractors, New Malden

IRAQI dictators. Avoid having to destroy missiles capable of traveling 7 miles further than the 93 mile limit set by international law by simply agreeing to only ever launch them from 7 miles further back.
Jim Bailey, Leeds

JOHN Fortune. Make your satirical attacks on American corporate greed on the Rory Bremner show carry more weight by appearing in slightly fewer adverts for McDonalds in your spare time.
Roland Butter, Denmark

LADIES. Make your own industrial floor polisher by sliding a pair of your hubbie's towelling socks onto the blades of a Flymo.
Matt Rundle, e-mail

BARMAIDS. Pour all my mates' lagers first, and THEN my Guinness, to ensure half my night is spent at the fucking bar.
Stu Holt, South Shields

I HAVE been informed by the fire brigade that a safer way to extinguish chip pan fires is to suspend a damp tea towel in a plastic bag above the pan.
Kieron Douglas, Burns Unit Glasgow Royal Infirmary

DOG OWNERS. Keep a plastic bag full of excrement behind the kitchen door. When you exercise the dog, take it with you to save collecting a new lot each time.
Phoebe Handrail, Yapton

FOOL women into thinking their opinions are valued by nodding occasionally and saying 'mmm'.
Stu Holt, South Shields

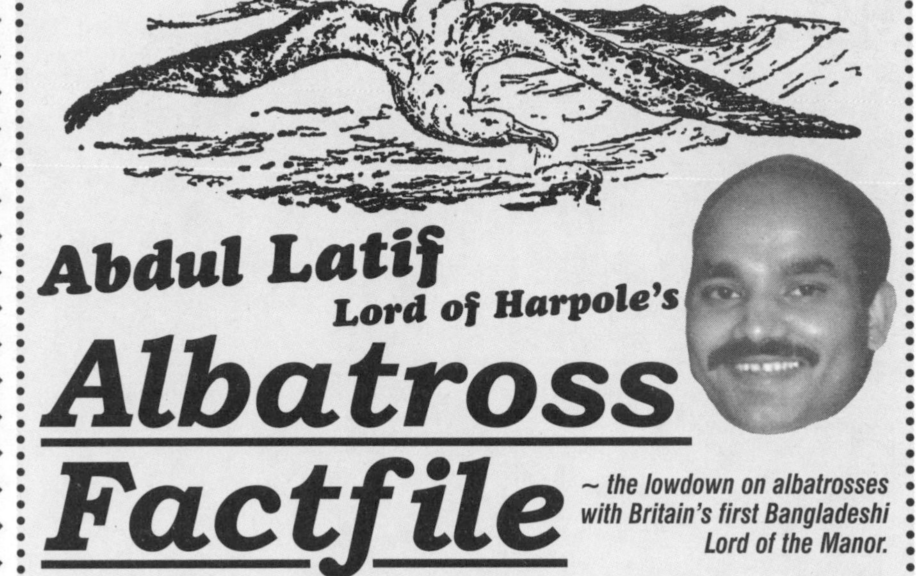

Abdul Latif Lord of Harpole's Albatross Factfile

~ the lowdown on albatrosses with Britain's first Bangladeshi Lord of the Manor.

- *In its lifetime, an albatross will fly to the moon and back **20 times!***
- *The albatross's wingspan is **exactly** 12 feet!*
- *A fully grown albatross can live for anything up to between 20 and 80 years **or more!***
- *Sailors are scared of albatrosses because they are the ghosts of **dead sailors!***
- *Unlike chickens, lambs and beefs, albatrosses don't feature on the menu of the Rupali Restaurant, Bigg market, Newcastle upon Tyne!*

✻ That's all my albatross facts for this week, albatross factfans. I'll be back with more albatross facts next week!

Abdul Latif, Lord of Harpole

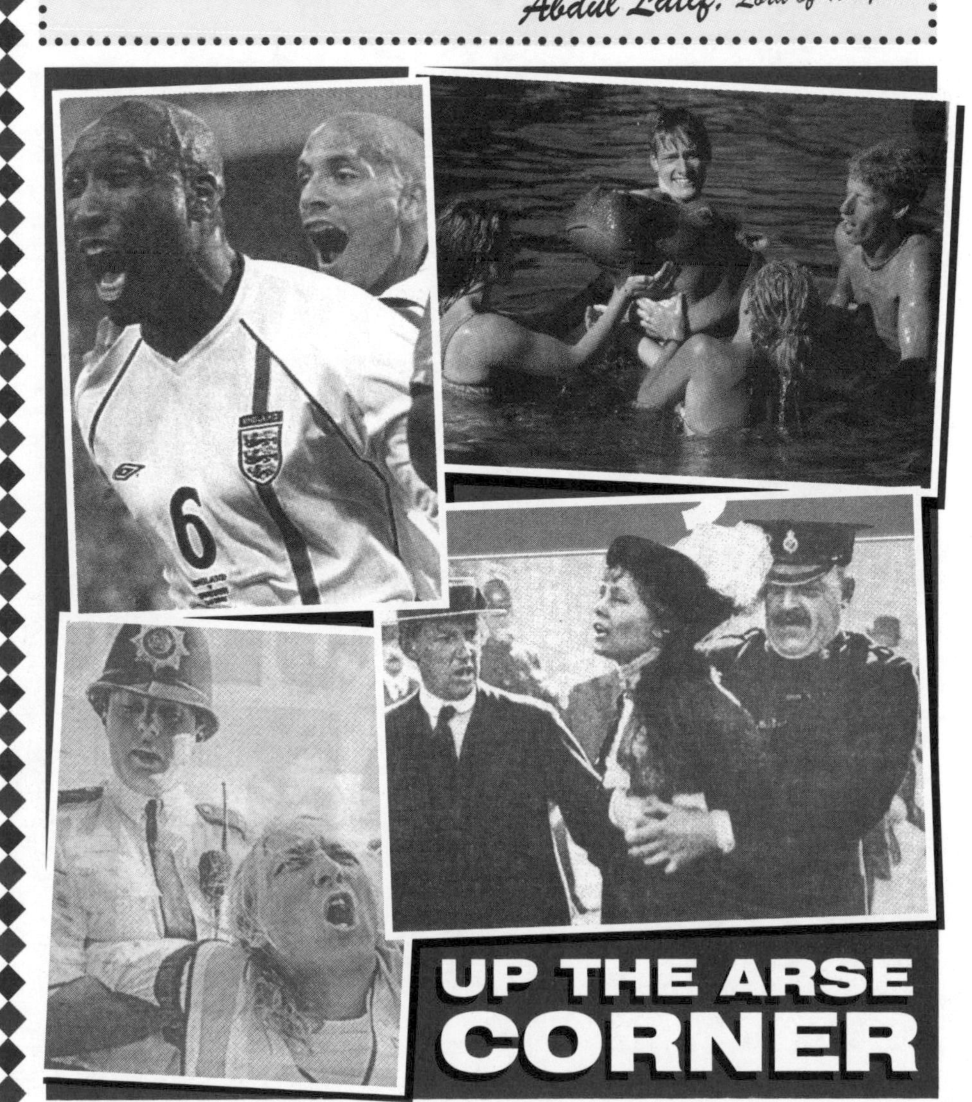

UP THE ARSE CORNER

TINRIBS
11-YEAR OLD TOMMY TAYLOR HAD AN INCREDIBLE ROBOT FOR A PAL
I'M REALLY LOOKING FORWARD TO THIS SCHOOL TRIP TO PARIS, TINRIBS. ARE YOU?
PARIS 3KM
HEAD MASTER
HI. I'M BARBIE. I LOVE YOU VERY MUCH.
BAH! TRIPS TO FRANCE INDEED. WHAT A WASTE OF TIME.
FULCHESTER-PARIS HETEROCOACH EXPRESS
HEAD MASTER
WE SHOULD BE BACK AT SCHOOL FORCING THESE BRATS TO READ STIG OF THE DUMP AGAIN.
THEN
BONJOUR, EVERYONE. MY NAME EES MADEMOISELLE PEIGNOIR
THUD THUD THUD
I WEEL BE YOUR TOUR GUIDE HERE IN PARIS
FIRST, WE GO UP ZE EIFFEL TOWER. FOLLOW ME, PLEASE.
HA HA! I THINK MR SNODWORTHY HAS FALLEN IN LOVE, TINRIBS
AND
OH MY GOODNESS! WE'RE SO HIGH UP I FEEL NAUSEOUS
HEAD MASTER
I'M GOING TO THROW UP — QUICK, I NEED A SICK BAG TO VOMIT INTO
TINRIBS WILL HELP PROVIDE YOU WITH ONE, HEADMASTER
I'LL JUST TIE HIS TOW-ROPE AROUND THE CUFF OF MR SNODWORTHY'S TROUSER LEG, LIKE SO
THAT'S PERFECT, YOUNG TAYLOR
HAWWP!
THAT ROBOTIC CHUM OF YOURS IS A MARVEL!
REALLY, M'SIEUR SNODWORTHY! I FIND ZAT TROUSER LEG FILLED WITH VOMIT MOST UNATTRACTIVE
B-BUT..
STENCH
GUIDE
EET IS SO UNROMANTIC
FIDDLESTICKS! THE LIFT BACK DOWN IS OUT OF ORDER
LE LIFT
OUT DE ORDER
LOOKS LIKE WE'RE STUCK UP HERE
ONCE AGAIN, TINRIBS WILL COME TO THE RESCUE
THIS TIME WITH THE AID OF MR SNODWORTHY'S TESTICLES
HUNH?
USING TINRIBS' ARM-ROD AS A LEVER, WE JUST NEED TO STRETCH MR SNODWORTHY'S SCROTUM
WHIMPER
HEAVE!
NOW WE CAN ALL BUNGEE-JUMP OFF THE EIFFEL TOWER ON THE END OF THE ELONGATED KNACKERSACK
LEAP
HOLD TIGHT, EVERYONE!
HI. I'M BARBIE.
EEEEYOWWW
SPROING
WHEEE! THAT WAS FUN
LET'S DO IT AGAIN AND AGAIN
LATER
OOYAH! A 986 FOOT LONG SCROTUM IS UNLIKELY TO IMPROVE MY CHANCES OF WOOING MADEMOISELLE PEIGNOIR. STILL, I'M NOT GIVING UP YET
GARLICS
Boutique d'Amour
CHEESE
A BOX OF SOFT-CENTRED SNAILS AND A BOUQUET OF FROGS LEGS PLEASE
>BLUSH< THESE ARE FOR YOU, MADEMOISELLE PEIGNOIR
GUIDE
WHY M'SIEUR SNODWORTHY, 'OW ROMANTIC OF YOU
ONIONS 'R' NOUS
OOPS! LOOK OUT, TINRIBS
CLONK
YOU'VE KNOCKED OVER THAT STACK OF ONIONS
WAH! I'VE SLIPPED ON SOME ONIONS —
GMPH!
GUIDE
PARP
'OW DARE YOU KISS MY BREASTS IN SUCH AN UNSOPHISTICATED FASHION, M'SIEUR SNODWORTHY
GUIDE
SLAP
TAKE ZAT, YOU COARSE BRUTE!
SO, SNODWORTHY! BEEN KISSING GIRLS, HAVE YOU?
HI. I'M BARBIE. I LOVE YOU VERY MUCH.
GUIDE
HEAD MASTER
MMM. M'SIEUR TEENREEBS, YOU KNOW 'OW TO SWEET-TALK A LADY
THIS WIRE BRUSH WILL GET THE GIRL-GERMS OFF YOUR TONGUE, SNODWORTHY
DESPAIR
OOH LA LA, TEENREEBS!
SCRUB RASP
BOUNCE BOUNCE
VOUS ETES UN ROBOT MAGNIFIQUE!

OH, LORDY!.. IT'S THE

FAT SLAGS

SHORTLY...
RIGHT, GIRLS. WHO'S FIRST?

YOU GO FIRST, SAN... I'M 'AVIN TROUBLE WI' ME ZIP
JESUS! LOOK AT THE SIZE OF 'EM... AND THEY'RE BLOODY PULSATIN'...
...SHE IS KEEPIN' YOU SHORT, BAZ

WELL, IT'S NOT ALL 'ER FAULT ...T' TELL THE TRUTH, I'VE NOT FELT MUCH LIKE DOIN' 'ER...
...I DON'T KNOW...

...I THINK IT'S THE SIGHT OF 'ER BIG STOMACH... PUTS ME RIGHT OFF
WELL, IT CAN'T EXACTLY BE SEXY, CAN IT, BAZ?

HEY! IF Y' THINK THAT'S A TURN-OFF, JUST WAIT 'TILL SHE'S 'AD IT, BAZ... SHE'LL 'AVE A FANNY LIKE A FUCKIN' WINDOW CLEANERS' SHAMMY
I KNOW. I'VE BEEN TRYIN' T' PERSUADE HER TO 'AVE A CAESARIAN LIKE POSH SPICE... BUT SHE WON'T LISTEN
YOU WANT T' PUT YER FOOT DOWN, BAZ...
...I'LL BET DAVID BECKHAM DON'T PLAY 'LAST SAUSAGE IN THE TIN'

BLOODY 'ELL!
DIDDLE-DE DIDDLE-DE DIDDLE-DE DE-DE

'ELLO?...YES...YER WATERS?...NO, THEY CAN'T 'AVE BROKE ALREADY, HE'S NOT DUE TILL TOMORROW ...YES...JUST MOP IT UP AN I'LL BE BACK IN A BIT...
FUCKIN' ZIP...!
...I'M NEARLY AT FRONT OF THE QUEUE

ALRIGHT! KEEP YER HAIR ON! I'LL COME STRAIGHT BACK AS SOON AS I'VE BANGED THE BREAD... BOUGHT THE BREAD.
@¥!#

JESUS WEPT!... SHE DON'T BLOODY TRUST ME, Y'KNOW, THAT'S 'ER PROBLEM. SHE DON'T BLOODY TRUST ME ONE BIT
AYE!
EEH! I'D BEST 'URRY UP AN SHOOT ME BOLT

THOUGHT YOU'DE OF SHOT IT BY NOW, BAZ, STATE THEM KNACKERS WAS IN
WELL ALL THESE FUCKIN' INTERRUPTIONS ARE PUTTIN' ME OFF ME STROKE

AW, FOR FUCK'S SAKE!!
SNIGGER!
TITTER!
DIDDLE-DE DIDDLE-DE DIDDLE-DE DE-DE

NOW WHAT!?... HEAD?... WHAT HEAD?.. WELL PUSH THE BLOODY THING BACK IN!
STOP IT!
GIGGLE!
JESUS! I'VE TOLD YOU... I'LL BE THERE IN FIVE MINUTES. WHAT MORE DO YOU WANT ME TO DO?

PACK IT IN!
...NO, NOT YOU, LOVE. I WAS...ER...TELLIN THE BLOKE TO...ER PACK THE BREAD...IN A BAG.
BYE!

F'CHRIST'S SAKE, SAN... THAT WAS ME WIFE ON THE PHONE... 'AVE A BIT OF RESPECT FOR ME
C'MON... TURN OVER

JESUS, SHE NAGS ME ENOUGH AS IT IS. SHE'D GO UP THE FUCKIN' WALL IF SHE KNEW I WAS 'ERE
CALM DOWN, BAZ
AYE. Y'ALL STRESSED YER COCK'LL GO SOFT IF YER NOT CAREFUL
EEH! DON'T PUT PRESSURE ON 'IM, SAN

OOH! THERE IT GOES!.. THANK CHRIST F' THAT
OOH!.. HEY!.. 'ANG ON, GIRLS... THERE'S SUMMAT 'APPENIN' OVER 'ERE AS WELL
...YEP!.. OOH!.. 'ERE WE GO. STAND BACK
DIDDLE-DE! DIDDLE-DE! DIDDLE-DE-DE-DE!
LEAVE IT! FUCKIN' LEAVE IT! I'M AT THE BILLY MILL ROUNDABOUT!
DIDDLE-DE DIDDLE-DE DIDDLE DE-DE-DE
AYUP, THELMA... BAZ?.. AYE, HE'S JUST COMIN'
UH! UH! UH! UH! UH! OOH, JESUS! OOH AYE! UGH! UGH!
IT'S THELMA F' YOU, BAZ... NA-AA-AA!
UGH! UGH! AYE! OOH, AYE... UH.......
UH!...
NA-AA -AA!
PUFF!... PANT!... PUFF!... PANT!... THANKS... TRAY... ...GASP!... CHRIST... PHEW!
'ELLO, THELMA, MY LOVE. I WAS JUST ABOUT TO CA....
ER... YES... TRACEY..
...IN THE SHOP... SHE ANSWERED IT THINKIN' IT WERE HERS...
...WHAT WAS WHAT NOISE? ...OH THAT! THAT W' SOMEBODY IN THE SHOP 'AVIN' HEART ATTACK... MMM... IN THE SHOP
NO, REALLY, THEL... IT WAS... ON ME LIFE!..
... WHAT!?!
BORN!?
...I'LL BE RIGHT OVER!
SHE'S 'AD IT GIRLS. ON THE BATHROOM FLOOR! BARRY JNR.
I'M A DAD!!
CONGRATULATIONS
THIS IS THE HAPPIEST MOMENT OF ME LIFE... I CAN'T WAIT T' SEE HIM!
C'MON THEN, TRAY... I'LL MAKE YOURS A QUICKIE THEN I'M STRAIGHT 'OME
SLAP!
YOU COULDN'T NIP ROUND THE SHOP FOR A LOAF FORRUS COULD Y' SAN?
GEDDUZ TWENTY BENSONS WHILE Y' THERE, WILL YER?
A WEEK LATER...
...AN' ME LIFE'S JUST CHANGED OUT OF ALL RECOGNITION
LITTLE BARRY JNR... DEPENDANT ON ME FOR 'IS LIFE! ... IT'S A HELL OF A RESPONSIBILITY IS FATHERHOOD
...IT GIVES YOU A WHOLE NEW PERSPECTIVE ON LIFE!...EEH! AN' IT'S SUCH HARD WORK. ... BUT D' Y' KNOW WHAT?
WHAT?
I WOULDN'T MISS A MINUTE OF IT F' ALL THE TEA IN CHINA
DIDDLE-DE DIDDLE-DE DIDDLE-DE DE-DE
'ELLO, THELMA, LOVE... AYE.....I'M IN THE CHEMISTS NOW... YES, I'VE GOT THE NAPPIES, BUT HIS TILL'S ON THE BLINK... MMM.......
...AN' HE'S 'AD T' NIP T' THE BANK F' SOME CHANGE... SAID HE'D BE 'BOUT AN HOUR... I MIGHT AS WELL WAIT

Not nice not to see y... see you, not nice!

SHOW... EXCLUS...

SHOWBIZ BOFFINS were left scratching their heads yesterday after Generation Game host Bruce Forsyth went invisible for almost 45 minutes.

Forsyth's a jolly invisible fellow

By our London Palladium Correspondent
Tommy Fart

The 75-year-old all round entertainer was in the bathroom of his £80,000 Surrey mansion when he suddenly dissappeared from his own sight in the mirror.

Speaking at the gate of his £100,000 Essex mansion, a visibly shaken Forsyth told reporters: "One minute I was there brushing my teeth, the next I was nowhere to be seen. I was worried that I might have became a vampire, so I called down to my wife, Isla StClair, former Nicaraguan Miss World, Anthea Redfern."

mansion

Blonde Anthea, 22, came running up to the bathroom and couldn't believe her eyes. "It was really spooky," she told newsmen at the gate of the couple's £125,000 Berkshire mansion. "All I could see was Brucie's toothbrush going up and down in mid air. I didn't know what to make of it, until I heard the unmistakeable sound of his tap shoes dancing across to the toilet. That's when it dawned on me that he must have of went all see through."

light

Former Miss Paraguay Redfern was so shocked that she gave her

husband a twirl and fainted on the bathroom floor. She came round to find that Brucie was still completely invisible. She said: "His unseen hands were patting me with a damp flannel whilst his disembodied voice kept saying 'Alright my love?'"

The big-chinned song and dance man was due to record a special variety show that afternoon and telephoned the BBC to explain his predicament. Frantic TV bosses set about organising bandages, gloves and a pair of dark glasses so that the show could go on. However, three quarters of an hour later Forsyth's visibility returned as quickly as it had faded and producers were able to breathe a sigh of relief.

partridge

Bruce's agent Clitoral Hood commented: "It was a worrying time for everyone, but especially for Brucie. In this business, being completely transparent is box office poison. The public simply won't turn up to see an invisible performer, it's as simple as that."

quail

Professor Ernst Bauhaus, head of physics at the Variety Club of Great Britain confessed that he was baffled by Forsyth's sudden disappearance. He told reporters: "Showbiz personalities usually reflect light from their surfaces. The different textures and refractive properties of their bodies, clothes and faces allow us to see them as the celebrities we know and love. Why a star should suddenly allow light to pass straight through him unhindered is a phenomenon that is still poorly understood."

dare

Forsyth is not the first British entertainer to succumb to sudden unexplained invisibility. Radio 2 afternoon show host Steve Wright vanished from view for 4 days in 1999. Listeners to his piece of shit programme remained unaware of his predicament, whilst his sycophantic 'afternoon posse' of talentless fuckfaces were forced to suck up to a pair of floating headphones. "They had to throw flour over him in order to find his arse to lick," said a BBC source.

Didn't they do invisib-well?

What would the gameshow hosts do if they went invisible?

BEING unseen to the human eye may sound like fun, but in his film *'The Invisible man'* H.G.Wells pointed out that being completely transparent has as many pitfalls as it has advantages. Bruce Forsyth only vanished for 45 minutes and was never able to fully explore the pros and cons of his condition, but just imagine what the veteran comic could have got up to if he'd been invisible for a *whole day!* We asked Brucie's fellow gameshow hosts how they would spend 24 hours of invisibility.

"I'd go down to the Yorkshire TV canteen and pinch a load of napkins from right under the waitress's nose," grinned asinine Countdown host **Richard Whiteley**. *"Then I'd hurry along to my colleague Carol Vorderman's dressing room and settle myself down in a corner for a very special day of non-stop masturbation."*

"I know exactly what I'd do," smiled Question of Sport presenter **Sue Barker**. "I'd walk right up to the trophy cabinet at the All England Club and finally pick up the Ladies' Singles plate, which I never came anywhere near winning during my frankly lacklustre sporting career."

They Think It's All Over *host* **Nick Hancock** *had other ideas. "I'd go on a very special shopping spree," said the cheeky God-botherer. "I'd walk into Superdrug and help myself to the biggest box of Kleenex in the shp before spending the afternoon masturbating furiously in the ladies' changing rooms at Miss Selfridge."*

"TV viewers know all about my wicked sense of humour," said *Weakest Link* presenter **Ann Robinson**. "A day of invisibility would be the perfect opportunity to go round to Cilla Black's house and make objects float round the room so she thought she was being haunted by her late husband Bobby."

"It would be easy to abuse such a situation, but I would try and use my invisibility for good purposes," University Challenge *questionmaster* **Jeremy Paxman** *told us. "However, I can't think of any way to do that off the top of my head, so I'd probably just end up wanking like mad in the showers of the local nurses' home."*

...u... not to

Now you see him, now you don't - Brucie (left) and a computer generated picture of how the invisible Brucie would have appeared in his bathroom (inset)

★★★★★★COMPETITION★★★★★★

Catch a wanking star and put £100 in your pocket!

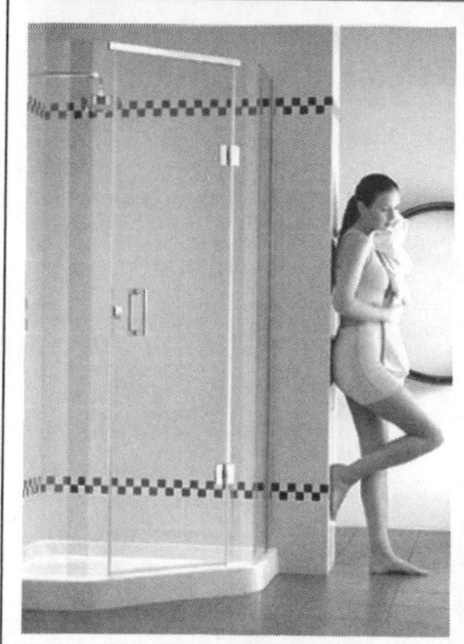

WE SNAPPED a picture of an invisible Game Show host abusing himself in the ladies' showers at the BBC television centre. There's a crisp £100 note for the first Viz reader to identify the masturbating celebrity. **Clue:** *'This quizmaster has got himself in a bit of a tiswas over this lady. You have a 50:50 chance of identifying him, but you may like to phone a friend for some help before you decide on your final answer'.* Send your answer to ***'Invisible Masturbating Chris Tarrant competition, Viz comic, PO Box 1PT, Newcastle upon Tyne, NE99 1PT'.*** The first person to write in correctly naming Chris Tarrant will win £100.

SCREENWASH with Mark Commode

GEORDIE hard man actor **Jimmy Nail** has announced plans to remake **Orson Welles**'s classic **Citizen Kane**, which was recently voted best movie of all time. The controversial actor shocked a specially invited audience at the Venice Film festival when he branded the 1941 original "Shite". The new version will be set on his native Tyneside, and instead of being a newspaper magnate Nail's Charles Foster Kane will be a brick-laying country & western singer detective wearing crocodile shoes. "The old film definitely needs bringing bang up to date," Nail told CBS's **Regis Philbin**. "It's not even in colour." Shooting of Jimmy's self-penned screenplay starts underneath the Tyne Bridge in November, with Jimmy starring, directing, editing, operating the camera and doing the onset catering.

HARD *on the heels of the multi-million dollar grossing* ***Jackass The Movie****, veteran political commentator* ***Sir David Frost*** *is set to team up with octogenarian* ***Ludovic Kennedy*** *in what is described as "The grossout movie to end all grossout movies". The unlikely pair plan to film themselves performing a variety of hair-raising stunts, such as firing roman candles out of their bottoms, jumping off high buildings into piles of human excrement, and fastening each other's scrotums to telegraph poles with staple guns. "Whatever you do, don't try any of these stunts at home," Frost told ABC's* ***Howard Glans****. "Me and Ludo totally take it to the edge, man." The film, provisionally entitled* ***Jackarse UK*** *is set to hit British screens in Autumn 2004.*

Commode's Top 10 Movie Bloopers

1 In William Wyler's epic 1959 version of *Ben-Hur*, Charlton Heston checks the time on a digital watch - even though digital watches weren't invented until 20 years after the film was made!

2 In the closing sequence of Mike Hodges' 1971 film noir *Get Carter*, Michael Caine can clearly be seen to have three legs whilst scrambling up a slagheap!

3 During a dramatic sequence in *Whatever Happened to Baby Jane?* (1962) Joan Crawford is supposedly alone in her bedroom. However, when she crosses in front of the dressing table her co-star Bette Davis can clearly be seen in the mirror, performing oral sex on grinning director Robert Aldrich.

4 In *Free Willy* (1993), when child star Jason Richter first discovers orca Willy in his neglected aquarium, the giant whale is wearing a digital watch on his left flipper. In the next scene, the watch has moved to his right flipper!

5 In the infamous ear-cutting scene in Quentin Tarantino's 1991 cult hit *Reservoir Dogs*, Mr Brown, played by Michael Madsen, is clearly seen to cut off the wrong ear.

6 2002's *Minority Report*, starring Tom Cruise, was set in the future yet one of the cops who chases Cruise through a shopping mall is wearing a wind-up wristwatch!

7 Kevin Costner's 1990 Oscar winner *Dances with Wolves* was filmed in full colour despite being set during the American Civil War. Colour film was not invented until 80 years later!

8 In *Back to the Future* (1985), Marty McFly travels 30 years back in time wearing a pair of 1980's baseball boots. This sort of footwear first became popular in the 1940s, 40 years after the film was set, and 20 years before it was made!

9 Mel Gibson, an Australian, plays 30-year-old Fletcher Christian in *Mutiny* (1982), despite the film being set in 1765 - only 20 years after Australia was invented by Captain Cook!

10 For budgetary reasons the 1948 biopic *Scott of the Antarctic* was actually filmed in the Arctic. Director Charles Friend may have got away with it, except that as Scott, played by John Mills, reaches the South Pole, a polar bear (native to the North Pole) can clearly be seen in the background. Wearing a digital watch.

GOLDFISH BOY
AFTER LOSING HIS PARENTS IN A BIZARRE FAIRGROUND ACCIDENT, YOUNG JOHNNY JOHNSON WAS TAKEN IN AND RAISED BY KINDLY GOLDFISH ON THE HOOK-A-DUCK STALL. AFTER SEVERAL YEARS, HE HAD BEEN WON BY FATHER BROWN THE LOCAL VICAR, WITH WHOM HE NOW LIVED.

FATHER BROWN IS GOING ON HOLIDAY...
THERE YOU GO, GOLDFISH BOY. THIS DEVICE WILL FEED YOU ONCE A DAY UNTIL I GET BACK FROM MY WEEK IN BLACKPOOL WITH THE WIDOW ERNSHAW
ACME AUTO FISH FEEDER
BLACKPOOL
GOD! THAT WOMAN WOULD TRY THE PATIENCE OF ST. JOB HIMSELF...
...IT'S BEEN SIX MONTHS SINCE THE GOOD LORD GATHERED HER HUSBAND INTO HIS ARMS AND I HAVEN'T HAD SO MUCH AS A SNIFF

STILL, I'M HOPING A BIT OF SEA AIR WILL LOWER HER RESISTANCE...
...KEEP YOUR FINGERS CROSSED FOR ME, GOLDFISH BOY
BLACKPOOL

SHORTLY...
THANK YOU SO MUCH FOR BRINGING ME TO BLACKPOOL, FATHER
NOT AT ALL, ELSPETH
I SPENT MANY HAPPY HOLIDAYS HERE WITH MY LATE HUSBAND, WHOSE NAME ESCAPES ME FOR THE MOMENT
You are now entering BLACKPOOL Twinned with UMM QASR

YOU MUST MISS HIM DREADFULLY, ELSPETH
WHO?
YOUR LATE HUSBAND
OH, HIM. YES
THE COCA CABANA GUEST HOUSE
STRICTLY NO PETS, WORKMEN D.S.S. OR ASYLUM

COME ALONG, LET'S GET CHECKED IN

AH, YOU MUST BE FATHER BROWN AND THE WIDOW ERNSHAW. WELCOME TO THE COPA CABANA GUEST HOUSE...
THANK YOU
I'VE PUT YOU IN ROOMS 4 AND 5, LET ME SHOW YOU UP

I MUST SAY HOW NICE IT IS TO HAVE A MAN OF THE CLOTH SUCH AS YOURSELF STAYING AT THE COPA CABANA, FATHER BROWN. IT LENDS OUR HUMBLE ESTABLISHMENT A CERTAIN CLASS...

...HAVING YOU HERE MAKES SUCH A CHANGE FROM OUR USUAL CLIENTELE OF BUILDING CONTRACTORS AND ALL-IN WRESTLERS

YES. IS THERE SATELLITE TELLY IN THE ROOMS? WITH BRAVO OR GRANADA MEN & MOTORS?
SATELLITE TELEVISION, FATHER? GOOD GRACIOUS, NO
OH, DEAR. NEVER MIND

ANYWAY, HERE ARE YOUR ROOMS
THANK YOU VERY MUCH
YAWN! WELL I THINK I SHALL HAVE A LITTLE LIE DOWN TO RECOVER FROM THE JOURNEY

GOOD IDEA, ELSPETH. DID NOT THE LORD HIMSELF SET ASIDE TIME FOR FORTY WINKS?...THOUGH THAT WAS AFTER THE ACT OF CREATING THE UNIVERSE RATHER THAN DOING THIRTY MILES ALONG THE M55...
...SO HE MUST HAVE BEEN TRULY KNACKERED

A LITTLE LIE DOWN? PFWA! IF THAT'S NOT A COME-ON, I DON'T KNOW WHAT IS...
I'LL GIVE HER 5 MINUTES TO GET HER NIGHTIE ON...JUST TIME TO GIVE MY TACKLE A RINSE IN THE BASIN

KNOCK! KNOCK!
AW, BLOODY HELL! WHO'S THAT?

YES?
AH, FATHER. SORRY TO BOTHER YOU, ONLY I FEAR MY FAITH IS BEING TESTED LATELY. I WAS WONDERING WHY, IF GOD LOVES US, WHY DOES HE ALLOW SUCH SUFFERING IN THE WORLD?
ERM...WELL... I'VE NEVER REALLY THOUGHT ABOUT IT, TO BE PERFECTLY HONEST...
...IT'S PROBABLY SOMETHING TO DO WITH JESUS AND THE TEN COMMANDMENTS... SOMETHING LIKE THAT. NOW, IF YOU DON'T MIND...

AND ANOTHER THING. IF YOU LOSE YOUR ARM OR LEG OR SOMETHING BEFORE YOU DIE DO YOU GET IT BACK WHEN YOU GO TO HEAVEN?
ERM... I DON'T KNOW. PROBABLY...
...IT'LL TELL YOU ALL IN HERE

ANYWAY, IF YOU DON'T MIND, I'M QUITE ANXIOUS TO HAVE MY NAP
THANK YOU, FATHER. I'M SORRY TO HAVE BOTHERED YOU

SLAM!
RIGHT! WHERE WAS I?

TALK ABOUT THE WIDOW'S MITE...
PFFT
...WELL, I THINK THIS WIDOW WILL WHEN I TURN ON THE OLD ECCLESIASTICAL CHARM. HEH! HEH!

SO...
EXCUSE ME, FATHER...
EH?

I'M SORRY TO BOTHER YOU AGAIN BUT THE OTHER GUESTS ARE ABOUT TO TAKE TEA AND BISCUITS IN THE LOUNGE AND I WAS WONDERING IF YOU COULD BE PREVAILED UPON TO SAY A QUICK GRACE
WHAT! NOW!?!
OH, VERY WELL. JUST A QUICK ONE

THIS IS REALLY VERY GOOD OF YOU, FATHER. IT'S SUCH A PRIVILEGE TO HAVE A RELIGIOUS GENTLEMAN SUCH AS YOURSELF IN THE HOUSE
YES. WHERE ARE THESE BISCUITS, THEN?
OVER HERE, FATHER

AHEM...OH, LORD. WE THANK THEE FOR THIS THY BOUNTEOUS GIFT OF GYPSY CREAMS, GARIBALDIS AND FIG NEWTONS
YOU'VE FORGOTTEN THE HOBNOBS, FATHER
AND HOBNOBS. AMEN

SHORTLY...
FOR WHAT I AM ABOUT TO RECEIVE MAY THE LORD MAKE ME TRULY THANKFUL. HEH! HEH!
KNOCK! KNOCK!
ENTER!

OOH, REVEREND! WHAT A LOVELY SURPRISE!
YES, I WAS WONDERING IF YOU MIGHT LIKE TO HAVE A LITTLE CHAT ABOUT SCRIPTURE OVER A GLASS OF COMMUNION WINE
THAT WOULD BE VERY NICE

SHORTLY...
... SO YOU SEE, ELSPETH, WHEN THE LORD SAID, "THOU SHALT NOT COVET THY NEIGHBOUR'S WIFE" I DON'T BELIEVE HE MEANT IT IN ITS LITERAL SENSE
HERE, LET ME FILL YOUR GLASS
... NO, YOU SEE... WHILST IT IS INDEED A SIN TO SUCCUMB TO TEMPTATIONS OF THE FLESH IN THOUGHT, MIND AND INDEED, DEED, I FEEL CERTAIN THAT THE LORD, IN HIS INFINITE WISDOM, WOULD TURN A BLIND EYE IF, ON OCCASION A GENTLEMAN WERE TO WHIP OUT HIS...

KNOCK! KNOCK!
AW, BUGGER! WHO'S THAT, NOW!?

WHAT!?!
AH, THERE YOU ARE, FATHER. THANK GOODNESS. I'M AFRAID ONE OF THE GUESTS HAS GOT A CHOCOLATE BOURBON LODGED IN HIS WINDPIPE...
...COULD YOU POP DOWN AND GIVE HIM HIS LAST RITES?

ERM... I'M SORRY... I'M TIED UP HERE IN AN ECUMENICAL DISCUSSION
BUT IT'LL ONLY TAKE A MINUTE, FATHER. HE'S GONE BLUE

WELL... LAST RITES IS A SORT OF CATHOLIC THING, I'M MORE OF AN ANGLICAN, MYSELF...
BUT SURELY WE'RE ALL GOD'S CHILDREN, FATHER

WELL... NO, NOT REALLY
IT'D BE LIKE BEING IN THE A.A. AND THEN CALLING OUT THE R.A.C. WHEN YOU BREAK DOWN
I REALLY MUST INSIST, FATHER BROWN
TCHOH!

THIS WAY, FATHER
JESUS! THIS HAD BETTER NOT TAKE LONG

I'M AFRAID YOU'RE TOO LATE, FATHER... HE'S GONE
AH, WELL. YOU'LL NOT BE NEEDING ME, THEN...
...THAT'S SAVED ME A LOT OF PAPERWORK, I CAN TELL YOU

DON'T YOU WANT TO SAY A FEW WORDS, FATHER?
ERM... NO. I'D BEST BE GETTING BACK UPSTAIRS

GOD, I HOPE THAT INTERFERING OLD COW DOESN'T INTERRUPT ME AGAIN...
...AT LEAST FOR THE NEXT TEN MINUTES ANYWAY

HISSSSSSSSSSSSSS!
PHWOAR! SHE'S FRESHENING HERSELF UP IN THE SHOWER...
...I'LL CLIMB IN BED AND WAIT FOR HER

SHORTLY...
HURRY ALONG, MY DEAR. I'M WAITING FOR YOU IN BED - AND THIS THING'S NOT GOING TO STAY UP FOR EVER...

I RECKON YOU'VE GOT ABOUT TWO MINUTES TO GET TO KNOW ME IN THE BIBLICAL SENSE...
GRAPPLER O'GRADY
YOU WOT!?!

JESUS CHRIST!

THUMP!

LATER...
GROAN!
OH, DOCTOR! I THINK HE'S COMING ROUND
WHERE AM I?
YOU'RE IN BLACKPOOL ROYAL INFIRMARY. YOU'VE BEEN UNCONSCIOUS. I'VE BEEN KEEPING A BEDSIDE VIGIL

WHO'S THAT?
THIS IS FATHER GREEN, THE HOSPITAL CHAPLAIN. HE'S BEEN A TOWER OF STRENGTH FOR ME...
...IN FACT, I'D GIVEN UP ALL HOPE OF YOU RECOVERING SO WE GOT MARRIED TEN MINUTES AGO
YES, ELSPETH AND I GREW VERY CLOSE OVER THE LAST FEW MONTHS
MONTHS!?!
YES, YOU'VE BEEN IN A PERSISTENT VEGETATIVE STATE FOR TWO YEARS, FATHER
BUGGER!

MEANWHILE...

PETE'S PORTABLE PRISON

Heart Swap Large 'Back on the Cakes' ~claim

Salad dodging comic on ticker-spanking bender

ROLY-POLY unfunny man Eddie Large was last night reported to be back on the pastries, less than *6 MONTHS* after the heart transplant which saved his life.

Large, who shot to fame in the seventies as the medically obese straightman to "supersonic" Syd Little, was apparently spotted downing a succession of sausage rolls, cakes and eclairs with friends in a fashionable Morecambe patisserie until the early hours, despite having been warned by docs to lay off cakes and pies.

After 6 months of abstinence, Large appears to have well and truly fallen off the cake trolley. During his 16 hour pie shop bender, he ***guzzled*** his way through

- ***56** Cocktail sausage rolls*
- ***8** Ginster's pasties*
- ***12** steak bakes*
- ***10** Danish pastries*
- ***2** family-size white chocolate torts*
- ***3** Black Forest Gateaus with custard slice chasers*

Syd Little later slammed the shop's proprietors and Large's eating buddies.

stormed

"Some friends they are," he stormed. "Everyone knows that Eddie has a pastry problem. To ply him with pies and cakes like this is nothing short of criminal. They ought to be ashamed of themselves."

wolverined

Passer-by Derek Bolsover was less sympathetic. "I think it's disgusting," he told us. "It's like digging up the organ donor and slapping him in the face. They ought to take that heart back off Large and give it to someone who deserves it, like Simon Weston or Bob Champion."

Large picture (left) shows Large out of Little and Large and little picture (inset) shows Little and Large's Little, yesterday

MAJOR MISUNDERSTANDING

NOBBY'S
THROBBITY THROB

FULCHESTER St. JOB'S HAEMORRHOID CLINIC NO RIFF-RAFF
WOW! THAT £1000 I JUST BLEW GETTING MY CHALFONTS PUSHED BACK UP MY JACKSIE IN A PRIVATE CLINIC WAS THE BEST MONEY I EVER SPENT!
I FEEL FORTY YEARS YOUNGER!

IN FACT... I THINK I'LL CELEBRATE! WATCH THIS, GUYS. I'M GOING TO DO A DOUBLE IMPOSSIBLE GRIND DOWN THIS RAIL.
COOL.
SKATE

SCOOT! SCOOT! SCOOT! SCOOT!
HERE GOES...!

HUP!
CHA-CHINK!

WHOOO-OOAH!!

HURTLE!
GAAAAAA-AAAAAA-AAAAA-AAAAA-AAH!

OH WELL. AT LEAST I'M IN FOR A SOFT LANDING.
WELCOME TO FULCHESTER MUNICIPAL MATTRESS DUMP

BOING!
AH, BLESSED RELIEF!

HUNH?!?
WELCOME TO FULCHESTER MUNICIPAL MATTRESS DUMP
SPROING!

CRASH!
FIRST WORLD WAR GERMAN ARMY HATS 'R' US
RUSTY SPIKE SALE NOW ON!
GAAAAAAAH! ME LEVER ARCHES!

SHORTLY...
...WELL, MRS PILES, I'M AFRAID YOUR HUSBAND'S ILL-ADVISED STUNT HAS BROUGHT DOWN EMERODS OF FRANKLY BIBLICAL PROPORTIONS.
OH DEAR.
ARSE SPEC

IS THERE ANYTHING YOU CAN DO, DOCTOR?
HMM... WELL... I'VE HEARD GOOD REPORTS ABOUT THE BENEFICIAL EFFECTS OF DEEP-SEA DIVING.
OH!?

YES. APPARENTLY THE SALT WATER IS VERY SOOTHING, AND THE PRESSURE UNDER THE SEA GENTLY EASES THE PILES BACK UP INTO THE BOMB-BAY.

HERE'S A PRESCRIPTION FOR A TWO-WEEK DEEP SEA DIVING HOLIDAY.

SO...
...ARE YOU READY TO BE LOWERED INTO THE WATER, DEAR?
YES. I CAN'T WAIT TO START EXPLORING SHIPWRECKS IN A PILE-FREE ENVIRONMENT!

RIGHT YOU ARE...
WHOOPS!
UP
DOWN
PLUMMET

SPLASH!
GAAA-AAA-AAA!!

MMF!
MMF!
HANG ON, NOBBY LOVE!

CHRIST! ME CERAMICS ARE ON FIRE!! GET 'EM BACK IN THE WATER!!
QUICK!!

PROTECT YOUR FAMILY WITH COCKROACH SOMBRERO™

The world is once again on the brink of nuclear Armageddon.

And as every child knows, the cockroach is odds-on to be the sole survivor... until now!

Using revolutionary insect-weaving technology developed by prisoners on Florida's Death Row, the COCKROACH SOMBRERO™ is built to withstand a direct hit from a 50 megaton nuclear warhead.

SPECIAL FAMILY OFFER! 4 Sombreros for the price of 3

DOWNLOAD ALL THE NEWEST

KETTLE RINGTONES

PERSONALISE YOUR TEA-MAKING WITH THESE NEW! EXCLUSIVE CHART-BUSTING TUNES FOR YOUR KETTLE WHISTLE...

To download the tune you want, simply call **08999 99779**... followed by making yourself a nice cup of tea with the number of sugars indicated! It couldn't be simpler!

No.	Tune	No.	Tune
01	The Beatles - *"Nationwide" Theme*	06	Shalamar - *Greatest Hits* (LP)
02	So Solid Crew - *Y.M.C.A.* (with actions)	07	ABBA - *Teach Yourself Italian*
03	Air Raid Siren (All Clear)	08	The Ray Parlour Big Band - *Medley*
04	The Mike Sammes Singers - *Autobahn*	09	Liberty X - *Froggy Went A Courtin'*
05	Sean Paul feat. Mrs Mills - *Gertcha*	10	Radiohead - *The Cup Of Tea Song*

All kettle ringtones cost £1.49 and are charged to your grocery bill under "tea bags". Please ask the permission of whoever owns the kettle before downloading any whistles. In the event of any particular whistle being unavailable, we reserve the right to send you an alternative whistle as a replacement (usually a single, sustained, high-pitched note). In this event, no further correspondence will be entered into. Registered with the Inland Revenue as a fantastic way to bleed stupid teenagers dry. R3444-1510

Letterbocks

"It's the page that keeps me smiling through my shit-filled life"
~ Viz reader Clive Rendell

STAR LETTER

IT'S BEEN one sad tragedy after another for your average Beatles fan. What with the slaying of John Lennon by a crazed maniac, and the more recent loss of George Harrison through cancer. I only hope that the next Beatle death can be a little more cheery. Perhaps Paul McCartney can ski off a cliff and leave a comical spread-eagle shape in the snow below. Or possibly Ringo Starr could be electrocuted by a Las Vegas slot-machine, causing his eyes to spin in their sockets before finally settling on two 'jackpot' signs, setting off a cascade of silver dollars spilling out of his mouth.

Andy Epwurf, Castleford

Letterbocks
Viz Comic
PO Box 1PT
Newcastle NE99 1PT

In this space age you can electromail your letters and tips to letterbocks@viz.co.uk

I have never been attracted to another man, but I like to touch myself around my penis when I masturbate. As a result, I am worried that I may be a homosexual. What do your readers think?

Big Straight Jock
Glasgow

Can you settle an argument? My wife says I'm a drunken bastard for coming home at 3 in the morning and pissing in the wardrobe. I say she's a lazy cow who never makes any effort to look nice, and if she gave me a bit now and then I wouldn't have to go looking for it elsewhere. Who is correct?

T. Arnold
London

I get in a sexual lather when the news is read by such posh totty as Katie Derham (ITN) or Jane Hill (BBC News 24), to such an extent that my wife is complaining about my lack of a grip on current events.

Steve Dawson
e-mail

I watched the much-hyped 'Walking With Cavemen' last week with some disappointment. Where were all the dinosaurs? If the producers had done their research to the same standard as those who made The Flintstones, these mistakes wouldn't have occurred. Or perhaps it was penny pinching by the BBC that has once again affected programme quality.

David Hershman
e-mail

I am a waiter in an Italian restaurant, and I often put mouse droppings in the pepper grinder for a laugh.

Manuel
e-mail

**Do you work in catering? If so, write and tell us what you get up to in the kitchens at work. There's a pound for the first 1000 chefs who write in to tell us they've wanked into Michael Winner's soup.*

Some philosopher John Lennon was. When he sang 'You're never anywhere that isn't where you're meant to be' in the song 'All You Need is Love', he'd obviously never inadvertently got on the wrong bus in Stockport town centre before and ended up in Brinnington rather than Bramhall.

Brian Sparrow
Brinnington

On hearing Pink's song 'Don't Let Me Get Me' where she begs for 'a day in the life of someone else' I was filled with pity. I wrote to her offering to spend a day mucking about in a music studio, while she could spend eight hours packing cheese before returning home to an alcoholic mother and her local felon boyfriend. I have yet to receive a response.

A Dawes
Northumberland

Since the death of the Queen Mother and more recently Dame Thora Hird, we British have found ourselves without a lovable favourite granny figure. In these troubled times, we need to find a focus for the nation's love. June Whitfield is too young, and the Queen is simply too bad tempered. In the absence of any other credible contender, I would like to nominate my own granny, Edna Wallis, 88 from Cheadle. She's had a rough life, but she's always got a smile for everyone.

Jayne Wallis
Cheadle

**Well, readers. Have you got a granny who is more lovable than Edna Wallis? We're looking for someone to assume the mantle of the Nation's Favourite Grandmother. Send a picture of your gran, stating her age, and how smiley she is, and giving a brief outline of her lovable qualities. We'll draw up a shortlist of the ten best for our Gran Final and ask you to choose Britain's favourite Granny. The best granny will win a crown, a sash, a refurbished shopping scooter, but most of all, a place in the hearts of the British people. Send entries to the usual address by 20th May. Mark your envelope 'My Granny's better than Edna Wallis of Cheadle'.*

Whilst on the Pepsi Max roller coaster on Blackpool Pleasure Beach recently, I noticed a speed camera at the bottom of one of the dips. It kept flashing all day, every time the coaster went past. The police must be making a fortune.

Ryan Marshall
Belfast

In the unlikely event that Samantha Mumba ever turns up at my house whilst my wife is out and demands a portion, this is the order I will do her in: arse, gob, arse. If I have any left I will do her arse again.

Paul Evans
e-mail

It's my birthday on 9th May. Would any of your readers like to come and get pissed? If so, we're starting off at The Beach House in Bognor at 8pm.

Arron Weedall
e-mail

It is hardly surprising that the people of Iraq are starving and undernourished when one learns that there is only one butcher in Baghdad. Surely after 30 years in power, Saddam could have done a little more to increase the number of meat outlets in the city instead of spending time firing guns into the air and laughing.

J Poucher
Cowes

I felt that the public reaction to the death of Princess Diana was a little over the top. My wife, who was a thoroughly decent woman, died last week, and who made any fuss about her? Certainly not me.

Andrew Dunn
Kent

What a con this so-called evaporated milk is. I opened a tin of it the other day and it was still completely full.

Jules
Great Yarmouth

Recently, my girlfriend of eight years ran off with my best friend and all our savings, leaving me heartbroken and in considerable debt. Now my mother turns round and says 'I knew this girl was trouble from the moment I laid eyes on her'. All I can say is, thanks for waiting till now to tell me, mum, you rotten cow.

T Filmer
e-mail

I have been hearing all week how the trendy band 'White Stripes' recorded their new album on old analogue equipment in a couple of days and for only a few thousand quid. Hooray for them, but in a piece of irony that I'm sure they would appreciate, I have just used the latest file-sharing technology to download it off the internet for nothing. Keep it up, White Stripes.

Trendy Muso
Camden

Whilst driving on the M1 between Leicester and Northampton last Wednesday evening, my in-laws were suddenly aware of a car inches from their rear bumper, obviously being driven by a dickhead. After some time, the vehicle pulled alongside my in-laws and the driver switched on the interior light so as they could see who the occupant was. It was none other than Darius. What a wanker. What has he got to be up his arse about? He couldn't win Pop Stars or Pop Idol, which suggests he's about as popular as a rattlesnake in a lucky dip.

Ashley Hayward
Northampton

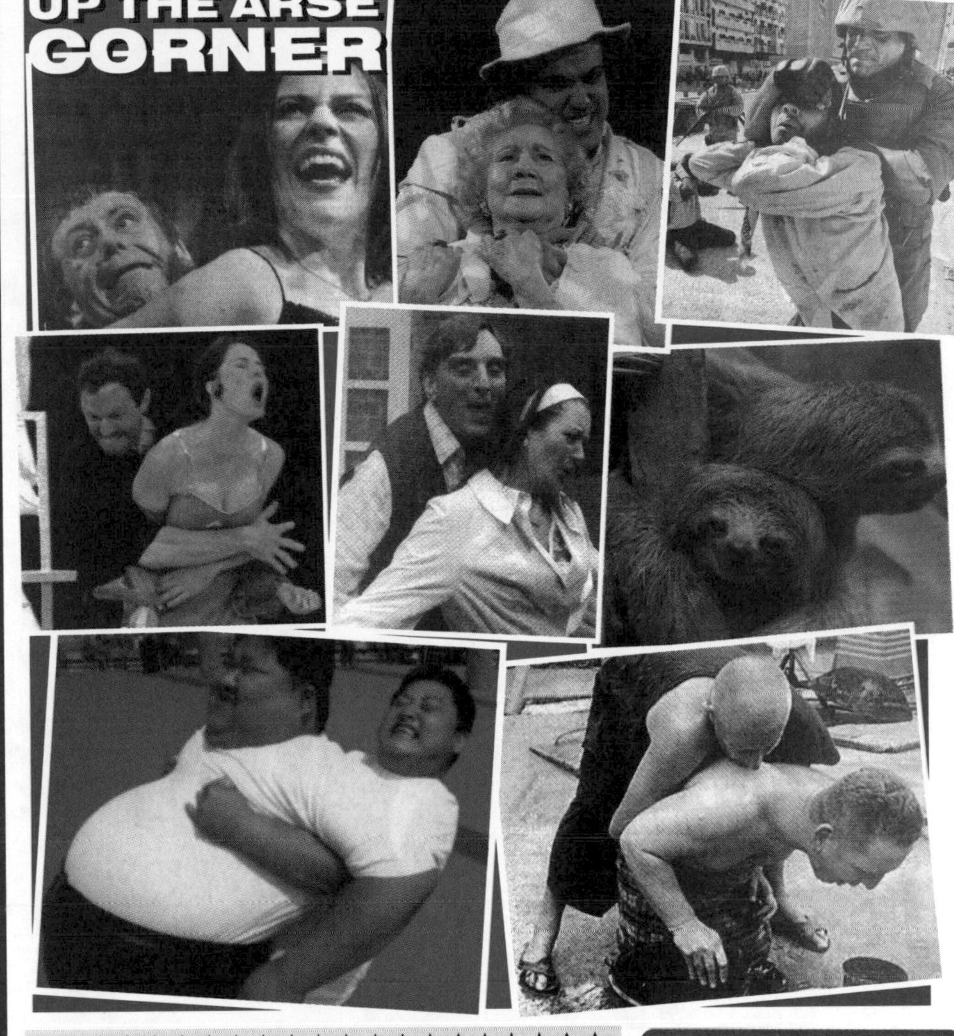

Dear Dr Telly
My wife insists that Lisa Goddard replaced Una Stubbs on Give Us A Clue and was married to Worzel Gummage, but had an affair with Jim Bergerac. I maintain that Aunt Sally replaced Lisa Goddard on Give Us A Clue, whilst Una Stubbs was in fact married to Alvin Stardust, who had an affair with Lionel Blair. Who is right?

Stephen Stills, e-mail

****I'm afraid you are both wrong. Lionel Blair was married to Anita Harris who replaced Una Stubbs as Linda Bellingham, the OXO mum.***

Church burnt out at 16

SINGING SENSATION Charlotte Church was yesterday found burnt out and abandoned on wasteground near the Cardiff home of her boyfriend.

The voice of an Angel star had just finished a gruelling World Tour to promote her latest album when she was snatched by thieves from outside the home of her sweetheart, rap artist Steven Johnson.

youths

Witnesses say they saw saw four youths riding her at high speed around the streets of a local estate in the early hours of Saturday morning. Firemen were called when she was set alight around four in the morning, but had difficulty putting her out when the came under ambush by yobs who pelted them with stones and bottles.

★★★★★★★★★★★★★★★★★★★★★★ POSTBAGhdad ★★★★★★★★★★★★★★★★★★★★★★

...YOU have to applaud Tony Blair's sportsmanship, sending 'boys and girls' to face the might of Saddam's army when trained killers would have been more appropriate.

A Todd, Ayreshire

...I WAS against the Gulf War before it started, but when the bombs began dropping I really got into it. Before long, I was hooked. Well done the BBC, I can't wait for the next one.

P Davis, Kirkstall

...WHY was all that money wasted on ousting Saddam Hussein from office? He is nearly 65 and would have been due for retirement this year anyway.

Matt Guy, Bristol

...WITH all the action being live on TV, George Bush should have taken a leaf out of Bernie Ecclestone's book and plastered the troops' uniforms, vehicles and bombs in fag adverts. I'm sure the likes of Marlboro and Mild Seven would have been up for it.

Davo, Herts

...CARRYING on from the previous letter, the logo of BAR sponsors Lucky Strike would have looked good on the occasional American bomb that hit its intended target, rather than foreign journalists.

T Street, Wales

...AS AN Iraqi, I was thrilled by the toppling of the Ba'ath regime, and celebrated by helping myself to an incubator from the local maternity hospital. However, on my way home, I was set upon by lawless yobs who took it from me, and American troops did nothing to help. The sooner order is returned to the streets, the better.

L Renard, Basrah

PROFESSIONAL *footballers. Remember, there is plenty of time to get pissed after your playing career has ended.*

T. Haines, London

AIRLINE *pilots. Encourage your passengers to 'get up and move about a bit' while doing 500mph, 30,000 feet above an ocean, but indignantly insist they 'remain seated with their seatbelts fastened' as you dawdle the three miles across the tarmac to the arrival gate at 5mph.*

Chris Ash, e-mail

IF DRIVING *your car quickly over speed bumps causes your exhaust to come loose, try reversing over them. It should tighten everything up.*

Martin, Bradford

SAVE MONEY *on water rates by only ever eating bananas, the food you can eat without washing your hands after a piss or a dump.*

Arnold Verrall, Essex

toptips@viz.co.uk

Have YOUR Say...

With London's traffic now crawling along no faster than it did at the end of the last century, Lord Mayor Ken Livingstone has decided the time has come for drastic measures. To prevent total gridlock in the capital's traffic system, he's introducing controversial congestion charges; every driver without false numberplates entering the city will be fined £5. But is there a better way to tempt the public out of their pollution-belching cars and into 40-year-old diesel fume-farting buses? We went out onto London's traffic-choked streets to find out what YOU thought...

...TRAFFIC MOVED at its fastest pace in Victorian times, so to get London moving again it would make sense if penny-farthings, horse-drawn carriages and sedan chairs were made exempt from congestion charges.

Reg Halliwell, Butcher

...THE MAYOR'S *new charges won't get me out of my BMW. I went on a bus once and there were other people on it and I had to sit next to someone dressed in gaudy clothes made of vulgar fabrics. What's more the driver refused to drop me at my door. Never again.*

John Brown, Magnate

...THE ONLY way to tempt men out of their cars would be if they put topless lapdancing conductors on the buses. They could gyrate sexily on the pole, and commuters could stuff the fare into their knickers. It would certainly brighten up my journey to work.

Andy Inman, Window-cleaner (retd.)

...WHY NOT *take advantage of these so-called asylum seekers to ease congestion? They should be made to walk along the bus-lanes with route-numbers tattooed on their foreheads, giving piggybacks to commuters. Let's see how long they hang around when there's a bit of proper graft to do.*

Charlie Pontoon, Journalist

...I READ that gas-powered vehicles are to be exempt from the mayor's congestion charges. How ridiculous. These large American cars are renowned for guzzling fuel, and they take up twice as much room as a normal family hatchback.

Jasper Maskelyne, Magician

...A CAR *can only crawl along at 4mph in central London because that's the speed of the car in front. And he's only doing that speed because of the car in front of him. If the police set a minimum speed limit of say 50mph, the traffic would fair zip along and the problem would be solved.*

Denver Colorado, Pteridologist

...SINCE MOTORCYCLES are exempt, I intend to avoid the congestion charges by painting my car to look like three Domino's pizza bikes riding abreast.

Huw Edwards, Newsreader

...LONDON TRANSPORT *should take a leaf out of the airlines' books to tempt people back onto the tube. Stewardesses should wander up and down the carriages of underground trains, selling cheap cigarettes, perfume and drink to the passengers, and telling them what to do in the event of the train crashing in the sea.*

Milos O'Shea, Taxidermist

...I CAN'T wait for the capital's traffic to start moving more smoothly. There's nothing worse than sitting in a taxi, being forced to listen to the driver spouting his bigoted homophobic opinions every day, while he gets paid for the privilege.

Richard Littlejohn, Columnist

...CARS ONLY *use the bottom four or five feet of London's streets. The Highways Agency should give money to the first scientist to invent hovering cars, allowing any number of traffic jams to be stacked vertically above a single road.*

Patrick Pending, Crackpot inventor

...PEOPLE WOULDN'T get so frustrated in traffic jams if the authorities instigated a 'chicane' contraflow queuing system such as is in use in the post office. Although the queue would be just as long, it would feel shorter psychologically, so all the drivers would be happy.

Tina Catweazle, Mudwrestler

...POOR PEOPLE *already get preferential treatment, with their dedicated bus-lanes. How about a bit of equality for the rest of us? What about special lanes for cars costing over £60,000, like my BMW M5?*

John Brown, Magnate

THE ADVENTURES OF BEN "BEND OVER" DOVER

THE WANK CHANNEL FAVOURITE

Paul Palmer

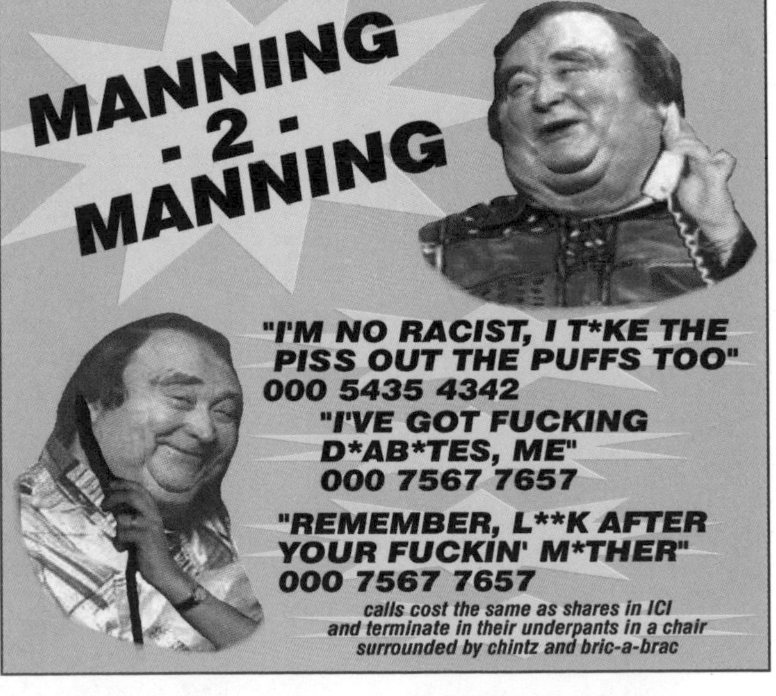

THE JASONS and the AGA-NAUT
Roaring down the River Conwy in North Wales was the most incredible paddle-steamer you had ever seen.
Belonging to the Jason family from Gloucestershire, it was a gigantic Aga cooker which had been built by the father, Rupert Jason. And now Rupert was taking his wife Jocasta and their two children, Laura and Ashley, on a thrilling holiday – an expedition deep into the uncharted heart of darkest Wales.
Young Ashley was agog with excitement as the exotic Welsh countryside rolled by.
GOSH, DAD — DOESN'T THE LANDSCAPE LOOK WILD AND UNTAMED!
YES, ASHLEY ~ WE'RE A LONG WAY FROM THE COTSWOLDS NOW!
Suddenly a shower of crudely-made spears rained down on the Aga-Naut.
A TRIBE OF WELSH NATIVES ~ THEY'RE ATTACKING US!
DON'T WORRY, LAURA ~ THEY'RE PROBABLY JUST A BIT WARY OF STRANGERS
But Rupert's face was grave.
I'M AFRAID WE'LL HAVE TO PULL OVER AT THE RIVERBANK
THOSE SPEARS HAVE CHIPPED THE HAND-PAINTED CERAMIC TILES AT THE REAR OF THE AGA-NAUT ~ I'LL HAVE TO RE-GROUT THEM BEFORE WE CAN GO ANY FURTHER.
Slowly, the durable four-ovened range cooker chugged over towards the Welsh locals.
STAY CALM, FAMILY
APPARENTLY THEY'RE LOVELY PEOPLE ONCE YOU GET TO KNOW THEM
Rupert presented the Welsh Chieftain with a peace-offering of his wife's home-made lychee and avocado chutney.
WE MEAN YOU NO HARM
WE ONLY WISH TO STOP AT YOUR VILLAGE WHILST WE REPAIR OUR SHIP
The Chief nodded, and with a gutteral command ordered his men to carry the Aga-Naut into the village
YACKY-DA!
GOH-GOH-GOCH!
As Rupert grouted the tiles, a crowd of natives clustered eagerly round.
LOOK! THE WARM AND FRIENDLY PRESENCE OF THE AGA-NAUT MAKES IT THE FOCAL POINT OF TRIBAL LIFE!
HA!HA! THE VILLAGE CAT THINKS WE'VE BROUGHT IT HERE FOR HIS BENEFIT!

MIGHTY CAST-IRON BUFFALO TRANSMIT RADIANT HEAT OF MANY SUNS THROUGH ALL FOUR OVENS
YET BECAUSE IT HEAP WELL INSULATED UM EXTERNAL BODY IS PLEASANTLY WARM TO UM TOUCH, LOOK YOU NOW
But the village witch-doctor was glowering jealously as the villagers ignored his 4-hob Hotpoint electric cooker.
YES, ONCE YOU'VE HAD AN AGA IT'S HARD TO IMAGINE LIFE WITHOUT ONE
YACKY-DA! UM ANCIENT GODS OF UM VALLEY DEMAND SACRIFICE OF ENGLISH SQUAW IN FLORAL DRESS!
PUT HER IN UM SACRED CAULDRON, ISN'T IT
Overawed by their witch-doctor's mumbo-jumbo, the credulous Welshmen seized Jocasta and thrust her into a large cauldron.
WE'VE GOT TO STOP THEM ~ THEY'LL BOIL MUM ALIVE ON THAT HORRID ELECTRIC STOVE
WAIT — I'VE AN IDEA
The Barbour-clad youngster quickly pulled a tray of scalding hot Ciabatta bread rolls out of the Aga-Naut's baking oven.
FIRST, WE PUT THESE ON ONE OF THE AGA-NAUT'S WHEEL PADDLES
THERE. NOW, START UP THE WHEEL, DAD
GOTCHA, ASHLEY!
As the paddle spun round, the Ciabatta rolls – piping hot and baked with the unique 'aga taste' – were catapulted through the air.
WAH! YACKY-DA!
THAT UM BURNS!
With a yelp the Welsh magic man plunged into the waters of the River Conwy to cool off.
HA HA! LOOKS LIKE UM ENGLISH RANGE COOKER MAGIC IS HEAP TOO POWERFUL FOR YOU, BOYO!
But the witch-doctor soon cheered up when Ashley and Laura demonstrated the Aga-Naut's wonderful facility for drying wet clothes on the front rail.
And the Jasons were almost sorry when it was time to leave their quaint Welsh friends and continue on their journey down river in the incredible floating Aga.

UN weapons insp ctors delv i

Just How P

She's the head of Britain's newest royal family, she spent her childhood being chauffeured around in her father's Rolls-Royce, her wedding day resplendent on a golden throne and now lives like a queen in her very own palace. Every surface in her stately home groans with onyx trinkets and every wall is plastered with fine works of art. She's Posh Spice, one time pop princess and now Lady Victoria Beckham. But is she quite as posh as she is painted?

To find out once and for all, we commissioned United Nations arms inspector Dr Hans Blix to produce a detailed report to determine Posh's level of classiness. For a week, he was granted unprecedented access to Beckingham Palace, where he searched high and low for "smoking gun" evidence of commonness. Finally we presented his detailed dossier of results to Penelope Keith, Britain's most upper class woman. Here she assesses Dr Blix's evidence and finally answers the question: *Just HOW posh is Posh?*

MONDAY.........

MY inspection team arrived at the gates of Beckingham Palace and were let in by the guards. I immediately asked to be shown the master bedroom. The decor included gold light switches, swagged Venetian curtains and a 4-poster bed out the Scotts of Stowe catalogue. Mrs Spice appeared generally cooperative and opened the wardrobe to facilitate my inspection.

I found her dresses to be suitably posh and expensive, including many couture labels such as Moschino. However, one of my inspection team located two pairs of discarded ladies' underpants on the floor under the bed. Later in the day, we made a cursory inspection of Mrs Beckham's fridge, where we found several cartons of Tesco 'Value' orange juice and a box of Ferrero Rocher.

We asked for documented evidence of Miss Posh's last food shopping trip and were shown till receipts which revealed that she had procured, amongst other foodstuffs, several bags of Walker's 'Sensations' premium crisps and a bottle of expensive champagne. However, it was noted by my chief inspector that a crude attempt had been made to obscure an entry detailing the purchase of twelve Goblin meat puddings and a jar of Chicken Tonight.

Penelope Keith...

On the surface, I see little here to suggest that Posh Spice is concealing commonness. Gold light switches, swagged curtains and mail order catalogue beds are all signs of genuine poshness. Likewise, discarded undergarments are not necessarily the "smoking gun" they may appear to be; truly posh people don't pick up their own dropped scads, they have servants to do it for them.

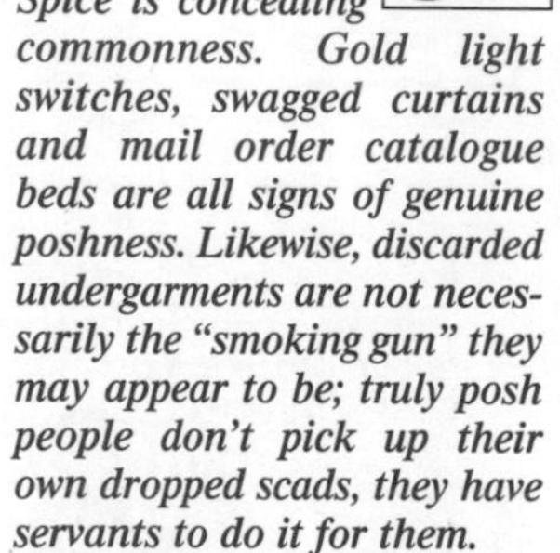

Of slight concern at this stage are the working class food products amongst Mrs Beckham's groceries. However, the presence of the world's poshest chocolates - Ferrero Rochers - amongst the inventory leads me to conclude that, in the main, her tastes are genuinely rarefied.

TUESDAY.........

At noon, myself and a team of seven inspectors made a surprise visit to Mrs Beckham's dining room, where we positioned ourselves around the table while she ate her dinner.

We noted that the cutlery was silver, and laid out in accordance with the standard practice as recommended by Debretts. However, certain discrepancies were noted with regard to her usage of spoons throughout the meal. a) A pudding spoon was used for the consumption of soup. b) After stirring six sugars into her Earl Grey tea, Mrs Spice replaced the wet spoon back in the sugar bowl. c) Mrs Beckham used her clean soup spoon to eat her gravy, and d) She was then forced to go in the kitchen for a clean spoon to eat her dessert. It was noted that this was a soup spoon.

My inspection team appraised me of the fact that, when she was drinking her tea, Mrs Posh's little finger remained uncrooked. Furthermore, when she was eating her dinner, she was repeatedly seen to place her elbows on the table.

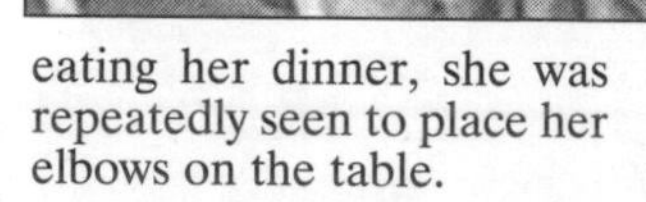

Penelope Keith...

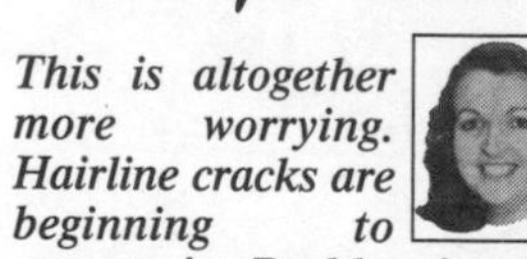

This is altogether more worrying. Hairline cracks are beginning to appear in Beckham's posh facade. 50 percent of being posh is knowing one's way around the cutlery on the table, and here she appears to be let down badly by her confused spoon usage and poor etiquette.

However, her choice of tea is straight out of the top drawer; Earl Grey is ten to fifteen times as posh as PG Tips, so it may simply be that Mrs Beckham's lack of table manners is merely a manifestation of very British extreme upper class eccentricity.

I will wait for Mr Blix's full report before coming to any firm conclusions.

WEDNESDAY....

My team requested access to the toilet; it was our intention to make a thorough inspection of the palace lavatory facilities in order to determine their level of poshness. However, Mrs Beckham became uncooperative and refused our request, telling us that the lock was broke.

We moved on to the upstairs nursery where we found two children's beds

o th 'Life of Spic ' as we ask...

sh is Posh?

with names painted onto the headboards - 'Romeo' and 'Brooklyn'. The floor was littered with plastic toys - such as Action Men, Transformers, radio-controlled cars etc.

Penelope Keith...

There could be any number of reasons why Posh Spice wouldn't want UN inspectors nosing round her lav, but sadly the most likely one is that it's in a right state. Perhaps there's skidmarks on the bowl, sprinkles of piss on the seat or a well-thumbed copy of the Autotrader lying on the mat. Without proper unfettered access to her toilet, it is impossible to discount any of these possibilities. A genuinely posh person's cludgy is kept as clean as their kitchen. I can't help beginning to wonder if Posh Spice is as posh as she seems to be.

On the other hand, she HAS given her children genuinely posh names, though it is interesting to note that Dr Blix makes no mention in his report of hand-crafted wooden toys like Noah's Arks, expensive rocking horses or old fashioned pedal cars. Miss Beckham's children evidently play with mass-produced plastic toys like common urchins on some dreadful council estate.

THURSDAY.......

The team decided to arrive unannounced at Beckingham Palace in order to make a dawn swoop on one of the living rooms. My inspectors identified and catalogued the following items: a) A 72" widescreen television set with surround sound speakers. b) A copy of 'TV Quick' with that day's schedule on QVC circled in biro. c) A grease-stained Greggs bag on the chair arm, containing the remnants of a chicken and vegetable pasty.

Mrs Beckham entered the room after the process had got underway. It was noted that she was wearing a toweling dressing gown and maribou high-heeled mule-type house shoes. Her hair was inspected and found to contain twelve Carmen heated rollers which were held in place with a nylon hairnet.

She announced that she was just going out and it was decided to send a small task force of inspectors to accompany her and report on her activities.

Mrs Spice walked out of the gate of Beckingham Palace, still dressed as described above, and entered a local newsagent's shop. Here she spent £40 on National Lottery scratch cards, comprising £17 on Millionaire Maker, £12 on Instant Jackpot and £11 on Lucky Lotto, which she then scratched on the counter using a large diamond ring.

Penelope Keith...

Dr Blix's discovery of a large television set is very significant. On the face of it, it may seem very posh to have a big TV, but in fact just the opposite is the case. Truly posh people shun television, and if they do own a set, it is a small black and white one used for watching nature documentaries and Newsnight. Likewise Mrs Beckham's choice of reading material - TV Quick rather than the TV Times - as well as her clothing and purchase of scratch cards, smack somewhat of the lower end of the social spectrum, as does her evident predilection for Gregg's pasties in preference to upper class fare such as Fortnum and Mason scotch quails' eggs.

FRIDAY............

After receiving intelligence that the main hallway of Beckingham Palace contained a print of a street scene including a genuine clock, powered by an AA battery, my team decided to make a thorough search of all the corridors in the building. However, as the inspection got underway, Mrs Beckham received a telephone call and left the house. As before, a detachment of inspectors decided to accompany her, following closely in a liveried United nations Land Rover.

She was seen to drive into the car park of a local licensed premises, where she spoke to a man in a shell-suit, and got into his car. The couple were then followed to a lock-up garage where the man appeared to be showing Mrs Beckham a variety of unboxed electrical goods. She bought eight video recorders, paying cash.

Penelope Keith...

Finally, this is the "smoking gun" evidence I have been waiting for. The behaviour detailed by Dr Blix on the final day of his inspection proves that Posh Spice is as common as muck. A properly posh woman, such as the Queen, has many works of art and it is certain that none of them contains a real clock. Furthermore, if a member of the upper classes such as Tamara Beckwith or Nicholas Parsons wanted to buy eight video recorders, they would buy them from Harrods. And they would pay with a Coutt's cheque, signed with a solid gold fountain pen.

Penelope Keith's VERDICT

After weighing up all the evidence in Dr Blix's report, I have to conclude that Victoria Beckham is not quite as upper class as she might at first sight seem to be.

BRA HUMBUG!

One person who disagrees with Penelope Keith's verdict is Professor Tibor Zachas, emeritus professor of breasts at the University of Cincinatti. He maintains that a woman's chest and cup size is inversely proportional to how posh she is.

For the past 20 years he's made a systematic study of women's bosoms, mapping their dimensions against the class of their owners. And if correct, his revolutionary theory could put Victoria Beckham near the top of the social tree.

He told us: "In my research, I concluded that all the posh birds had tits like eggs sunny side up. Look at your Tara Palmer-Tomkinson, she may be high class muff but she's got knockers like two aspirins on an ironing board."

However, at the other end of the social scale professor Zachas found it was a different story. "Take Dolly Parton," he told us. "She's real trailer trash, but she's got goddam massive charlies."

So where does this leave Victoria Beckham? We showed some pictures of her to the professor. He told us: "From the size of her top bollocks, I'd say she was pretty lah-di-da. About the same as Princess Stephanie of Monaco."

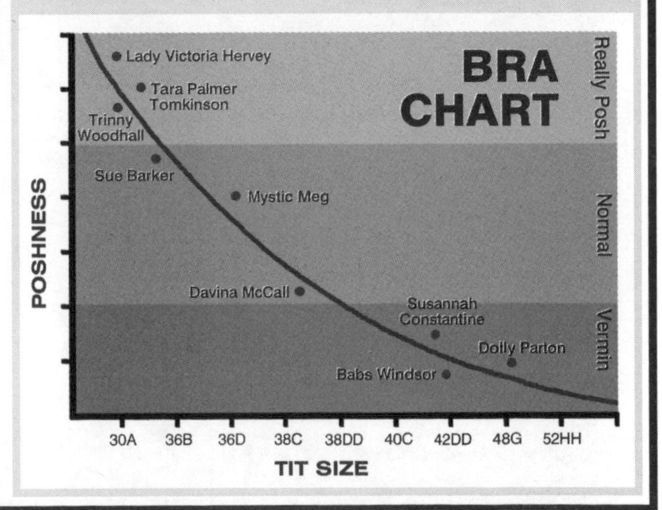

TAP TAP TAP TAP TAP
`OO THE FUCK'S THAT NOW?

AYUP LUV. IT'S ONLEH MEE. TH' POSTMAN'S JUST BRANG THIS LETTEH TER ME SHED, BURRIT'S FER YOO.

TELL YER WOT, P'RAPS A'LL JUST CUM IN' FER A QUICK CUP OF TEE WHILE YER OPPEN IT, EH?

YOO FUCKIN' WILL **NOT** CUM IN. YOO STAY ON THAT FUCKIN' DOORSTEP.

AW, CUMON, LUV. LERRUZ IN FER JUST ONE MINNIT. IT'S NOT TOO MUCH T'ASK... ONE F-FFUCKIN' MINNIT IN TEN YEAR OF F-FUCKIN' MARRIDGE.
A'LL GO BACK OUT TH' SECOND YER TELL USS. THE F-FFUCKIN' SECOND.

EEH. IT'S ME CHEQUE FER TEN GRAND.
TEN GRAND?
AYE. A WON IT OFF 'COUNCIL FER WHEN A TRIPPED ON A SLABSTONE OUTSIDE T'NASH.

£10000

A WOS JUSS THINKIN'... IN'T IT ABAHT TIME A PUT THEM SHELVES UP F'YER...
...ERM... AN' DID THE DISHES...

...AN' YER KNAW THAT MATTRESS WOT A SHITTED ON US WEDDIN' NEYT?... A'LL TEK IT DAHN THE WOODS, EH?
...AN' THE COOKEH...
...AN' THE TELLIES.

'OO D'YOO THINK YER KIDDING? A WAN'T BORN YESTERDEH. A KNAW YER ONLEH AFTEH ME MUNNY.
MUNNY?
WOT TEN THAHSAND PAHND?

A'D FERGOT ABAHT YER 'UGE CHEQUE. A JUSS THOWT A'D TIDEH T'PLACE UP A BIT FER YOO AN' T BAIRNS, LIKE.
OH AYE?
WELL YER NOT GETTIN' YER FUCKIN' 'ANDS ON NONE OF ME MUNNY, REYT.

AW, JUSST A BIT, MY SWEET... MEBBE ONE FORTEH-NINE FER... FER... A... **THING**... FER TH' B-BAIRNS...
FER TH' BAIRNS? YER LYIN' **GET**. IT'S FER TH' ACE.
IT IN'T.
IT IS.

AYE. BUT IT WARMS THEH HEARTS WHEN THEH SEE THEH FATHA HAPPY AND AALL FULL O' THE ACE... SO IT'S FOH **THEM** REELLY... YER SEE WOT A MEAN...?

...A JUSS WANT TER SEE THEH LIRRUL FUCKIN' FACES LIGHT UP WENN THEH SEE ME STOTTIN' ON TH' ACE. A'M NOT BOTHERED A FUCK, ME... A CAN TEK TH' STUFF OR LEAVE IT... IT'S FER F-FFUCKIN' IDIOTS, THAT STUFF...

...SO GIVE US ONE FORTEH-NINE, YER F-FFUCKIN' B-BB-B-**BITCH!**

LOOK AT 'ER... **TEN** F-FF-FFUCKIN' **GRAND** AN' SHE WAIN'T EVEN GIVE 'ER 'AHN 'USBAND ONE F-FFUCKIN' FORTEH-NINE FER ACE TER DRINK FER TH' B-BBAIRNS...
F-FF-FFF-FFUCKIN' B-BB-B-B-**COW!**

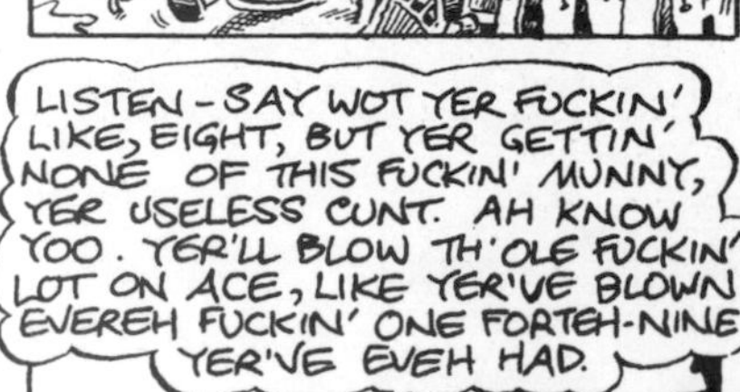

LISTEN - SAY WOT YER FUCKIN' LIKE, EIGHT, BUT YER GETTIN' NONE OF THIS FUCKIN' MUNNY, YER USELESS CUNT. AH KNOW YOO. YER'LL BLOW TH' 'OLE FUCKIN' LOT ON ACE, LIKE YER'VE BLOWN EVEREH FUCKIN' ONE FORTEH-NINE YER'VE EVEH HAD.

WELL YER NOT GUNNEH GET TH' CHANCE TER WASTE A SINGLE FUCKIN' **PENCE** OF THIS TEN GRAND.

IT'S ABAHT TIME SUMWUN IN THIS FAMBLEH TOOK A RESPONSIBLE ATTICHOOD WI' MUNNY.

10,000 SCRATCHCARDS.

BILLY
NO MATES

BREAKFAST TIME...
WELL, THATS THE HOUSE REMORTGAGED
YES, BUT IT'S WORTH IT. WE'LL BE ABLE TO PAY FOR YOUR MOTHERS OPERATION NOW... WE'LL JUST HAVE TO TIGHTEN OUR BELTS A BIT.
YEAH. WE'LL BE OKAY.

Gasp!
PHONE BILL

B-I-L-L-Y!!
GOD SAKE! KEEP IT DOWN! I'M ON THE PHOOONE TO...erm... GRANNY!
ooh my melons
ooh my big melons
ooh my great big melons
feel my great big melons...

BAH! I'VE HAD TO GET A JOB HERE TO PAY BACK MY DEBTS
...I'M NOT GOING TO LET ANYONE DOWN THIS TIME, THOUGH
24 hour Shell

INSIDE...
WAHEY! THIS ISN'T TOO BAD! YOU COULD LIVE HERE, IT'S GOT ALL THE BASIC HUMAN ESSENTIALS...
...DR PEPPER, PICKLED ONION MONSTER MUNCH, PEPPERAMIS...
...AND PORNOGRAPHY
...LOADS AND LOADS OF PORNOGRAPHY...

NOO! CANT LET ANYONE DOWN! NO POOORRN!!

...Billy... oh, Billy...

...come on Billy, Screw work and look at us...
we want you Billy you make us hot!
Yeah, my husbands away, and I want to play!!
...I'm wet and willing, see me take two cocks up the same hole...

MMNUGGH!! THE MAGS ARE CALLING ME...! MUST... RESIST! ...NO... USE...!
STRUGGLE!

TAP TAP!
HELLO? I'D LIKE TO PAY FOR SOME PETROL, PLEASE~ IT'S PUMP NUMBER...
GAAAH!! HAVE IT!! JUST GOOO AWAY AND LEAVE ME ALOOONE!

HA! HE'S GOING!
BLUE PUMP UNLEADED (or possibly deisel) 74.9 per Li

SCOOP!!
WHICH MEANS NOBODIES AROUND TO SEE ME NICK THESE!

WHIIIIIRR!!
CLICK!
AARGH!

I MUST GET THE VIDEOTAPE FROM THE BACK ROOM AND DESTROY IT!
BACK ROOM
SLAM!

BUT...
oh no...
oh, GOD NO!!
I'M LOCKED IN HERE RED HANDED WITH VIDEO EVIDENCE!!
CCTV TV

STILL... AS LONG AS I'M HERE... WITH THESE MAGS...
BACK ROOM
ZZIIIPP!

POP!
SHIT, THE BULBS GONE.
BACK ROOM

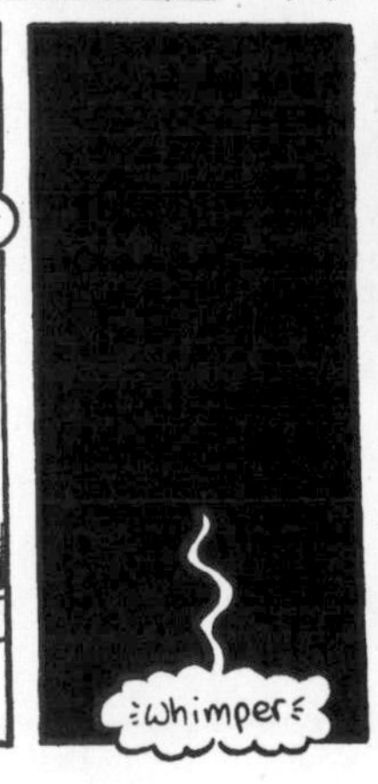
Whimper

24 hour Shell
FREE PETROL

SPOILT BASTARD

Grave Turn of Events for Di

Lady Diana turned in her grave yesterday after it was announced that 68% of the public would now be prepared to accept Camilla Parker-Bowles as Queen.

Seismologists using sensitive monitoring equipment detected movement six feet below the surface of the island where the late princess was buried in 1997. Meanwhile, crockery shook on tables in the nearby village of Allthorp and a picture was dislodged from the wall of a nearby teashop.

plate

Michael Macmanus, professor of plate tectonics at Northampton University, recorded the vibration at 7.28pm, the exact time at which the survey results were broadcast on Channel 4 News. He told us: "It was a short event, lasting only four or five seconds, but it was quite powerful, measuring 3.2 on the Richter scale. All I can say is, Lady Di must of really disliked Camilla Parker-Bowles."

EXCLUSIVE

saucer

Meanwhile, Northampton tourism chiefs fear the tremor could put paid to plans for a giant rollercoaster to be built near Allthorp House. Local businessman Eric Fagpacket has raised nearly £2million to fund his proposed Lady Di Memorial theme park to be built in nearby Nobottle.

fox

Fagpacket's centrepiece ride was to be a half-mile long triple-inverted corkscrew rollercoaster called 'Parisian Oblivion', which would recreate the thrills and spills experienced by the Princess of Wales on her final 150mph limousine ride through the French capital.

circus

He told a local radio station: "We were all ready to start work on the project. Now I've had a letter from the council saying they may have to withhold planning permission. Their fear is that we build the rollercoaster and Camilla becomes Queen and falls pregnant. The amount Lady Di would turn in her grave in those circumstances could bring the whole structure tumbling down like a house of cards."

DI: Right Royal Rollover scuppered rollercoaster.

fuck

"I've got six thousand tons of steel tubing and twenty miniature Mercedes cars sat in a field, rusting," he added. "I'm ruined."

IVAN
JELICAL

MMMH... THOU SHALT NOT KILL... YES, OF COURSE... AN EYE FOR AN EYE ... YES, YES... I SEE...
MUNCH! MUNCH!
3 SCOTCH EGGS

PRAAIISE HIM!
MY HEART IS FILLED WITH HIS GOOD NEWS! IT'S TOO MUCH!... I MUST SHARE IT WITH THE WORLD!

NOW THEN, I THINK I'VE ALREADY DONE THIS STREET. I'LL BRING GLAD TIDINGS OF GOD'S BOUNTEOUS WONDERS TO PERFORM AND HIS THINGS WISE AND WONDERFUL TO FESTIVE TERRACE INSTEAD.
ABSOLUTELY NO GOD BOTHERERS
BIBLE-BASHERS WILL BE SHOT

I WONDER IF MRS. TRUBSHAW WILL BE AT HOME. SHE'S BEEN ALONE SINCE HER HUSBAND DIED LAST JUNE...

INSIDE...
HELLO? SAMARITANS? ALL I WANT IS... SOB! ...SOMEONE TO TALK TO... ANYONE AT ALL WILL DO... I'M GOING OUT OF MY MIND WITH LONLINESS!

DING! DONG!
UNH?
THERE'S SOMEONE AT THE DOOR!... JOY OF JOYS!

!
SHIT! IT'S A GOD BOTHERER!
DING! DONG!

10 MINUTES LATER...
DING! DONG!
GO AWAY... GO AWAY... I'M NOT AT HOME... I'M NOT AT HOME...

LATER...
SHIT!
FULCHESTER ESTATES
JUST SOLD

QUICK! RING D.F.S.!
BIDIP! BIP! BIDIP! BIP!
TEA

SCREEECH!
D.F.S.
D.F.S.

WHOOOOOSH!
QUICK! INSIDE!
WHISK!

DING! DONG!
PHEW!

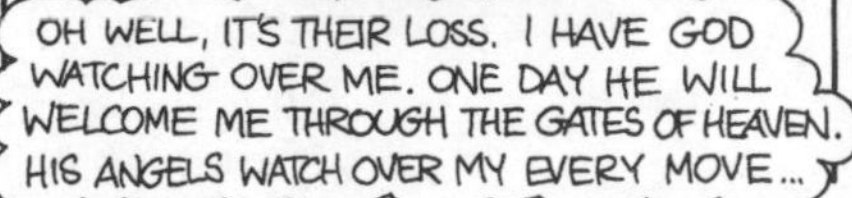
OH WELL, IT'S THEIR LOSS. I HAVE GOD WATCHING OVER ME. ONE DAY HE WILL WELCOME ME THROUGH THE GATES OF HEAVEN. HIS ANGELS WATCH OVER MY EVERY MOVE...

...I PITY THOSE WHO TURN A HARDENED EAR TO GOD'S PLENTIFUL MERCIES... I'LL JUST POP OVER THE ROAD FOR SOME SCOTCH EGGS...
ZOOOM!
BROOM!

SPLATT!

LAAAA!
LAAAAA!

HELLO? HELLO? IS ANYONE IN?
FULL METAL CHALLENGE
IS HE STILL THERE?
SHHHH!

PLAYTIME FONTAYNE

ONE MORNING...
PLAYTIME-HURRY UP! YOU'LL BE LATE FOR BANK.
AW MUM. CAN I STAY OFF TODAY? I DON'T FEEL VERY WELL.

GOSH, PLAYTIME. YOU'RE COVERED IN RED SPOTS!
I KNOW. I THINK IT'S GERMAN MEASLES.
EVERYONE IN MORTGAGES AND INVESTMENTS HAS GOT IT.

I'LL PHONE MR. PODMORE AND TELL HIM YOU'RE POORLY, PLAYTIME. HERE-LET ME PLUMP YOUR PILLOW UP.
NO! IT'S ALRIGHT..!
HELLO? WHAT'S THIS?
A LIPSTICK! THEY'RE NOT GERMAN MEASLES AT ALL, ARE THEY?
ERM...
WELL...

GET UP AND GET YOUR SUIT ON THIS MINUTE!
AW MUM. THE SPOTS AREN'T REAL, BUT I HAVE GOT A SORE THROAT REALLY.
THIS MINUTE!
...AND A HEADACHE.

SHORTLY...
...COME ON, PLAYTIME! I DON'T KNOW WHAT'S WRONG WITH YOU. YOU'VE BEEN ACTING LIKE THIS ALL FISCAL QUARTER.
IT'S NOT MY FAULT IF I'M GETTING BULLIED.
WHAT!?

IT'S THIS NEW MAN. HE'S JUST COME OVER FROM THE LOBLEY ROAD BRANCH AND HE KEEPS ON GETTING AT ME.
WELL DON'T YOU LET HIM, PLAYTIME.

IF HE BOTHERS YOU AGAIN, YOU GO STRAIGHT TO MR. PODMORE AND TELL HIM.
I CAN'T. HE SAYS HE'LL KILL ME IF I TELL ON HIM.

LATER...
HEH. WATCH THIS, LADS.
...OH GOD- HE'S THERE.
B. PODMORE -DISTRICT MANAGER.
SNIGGER!

TRIP!
WAAAH!!

MORNING, FONTAYNE. ENJOY YOUR "TRIP"?
HUR! HUR!
NICE ONE, TILSLEY.

HERE- DO YOU COLLECT STAMPS?
...ERM...

WELL HERE'S ANOTHER ONE FOR YOUR COLLECTION!
CRUNCH!
ARF! ARF!
HO! HO!

NOW HAND OVER YOUR LUNCHEON VOUCHERS, FONTAYNE, OR I'LL GIVE YOU A DEAD ARM.
BUT TILSLEY...
I HAVEN'T GOT ANY. YOU TOOK THEM ALL YESTERDAY.

RIGHT! GET READY TO DIE, FONTAYNE!
OW! OW! OW! AW..!

LOOK OUT, TILSLEY! IT'S THE DISTRICT MANAGER!
!?
WHAT'S GOING ON OUT HERE? WHAT'S ALL THIS NOISE?

WHAT'S GOING ON?
ERM...OW!...ERM... NOTHING, MR. PODMORE.. YOW!!

WELL WHY AREN'T YOU AT YOUR DESKS WORKING QUIETLY?
WELL?
don't know sir.

I TAKE IT YOU HAVE BOTH COMPLETED YOUR QUARTERLY AUDIT RETURNS?
erm...no sir.

...WELL IN THAT CASE, MIGHT I SUGGEST YOU GET ON WITH THEM? I WANT THEM ON MY DESK THIS AFTERNOON!
YES SIR.

SO...
TAP-TAP TAPPITY TAP-TAP SCRIBBLE

PSST! FOUREYES! WHAT'S THE GROSS INCREMENT CARRIED FORWARD FOR AUGUST?
WORK IT OUT FOR YOURSELF.

AUGUST
SNATCH!
OI! GIVE THAT BACK!
FUCK OFF.

HEH-HEH! CHEERS FOR DOING THESE ANSWERS YOU BUMMER.
I'LL GET YOU FOR THIS, TILSLEY.
COPY COPY
AUGUST
GIVE ME BACK THOSE QUARTERLY AUDIT RETURNS.

YOU WANT THEM BACK? HERE THEY ARE, FONTAYNE.
RIP! RIP!
...OH, SORRY. MY HANDS SLIPPED.
YOU BIG BULLY! YOU BIG BULLY!

WHAT'S ALL THIS NOISE? I THOUGHT YOU WERE SUPPOSED TO BE WORKING QUIETLY.
SPRINKLE

WHAT ON EARTH..? FONTAYNE — WOULD YOU MAKE A MESS LIKE THIS AT HOME?
...BUT SIR...
BUT SIR NOTHING. CLEAN IT UP NOW!
TITTER

HERE'S THE QUARTERLY AUDIT RETURNS YOU ASKED FOR, MR. PODMORE.
HMM. THIS IS VERY GOOD. EXCELLENT WORK, TILSLEY.
SNIFF

FONTAYNE - YOU SHOULD TAKE A LEAF OUT OF TILSLEY'S BOOK. HE'S REAL SENIOR MANAGEMENT MATERIAL.

THE WAY YOU'RE CARRYING ON, YOU'LL NEVER RISE ABOVE SUB-BRANCH DEPUTY CHIEF CASHIER.

NEXT MORNING...
MUM! I CAN'T GO IN TODAY. I'VE GOT A TERRIBLE TEMPERATURE!

MILLIE
WE ARE ONE
SISTERS!
TANT
AND HER RADICAL CONSCIENCE

OOH. THAT'S A NICE JUMPER, MILLIE. IS IT NEW? IT'S LOVELY ON.

HOW NICE OF ADRIAN TO NOTICE. IT'S LOVELY WHEN SOMEONE PAYS A COMPLIMENT. ...IF ANY OTHER MAN HAD SAID ANYTHING LIKE THAT I MAY HAVE FELT THREATENED, BUT AS ADRIAN IS GAY I KNOW HIS WORDS ARE GENUINE AND INOFFENSIVE, AND HAVE NO INTIMIDATING HETROSEXUAL UNDERCURRENT.

...HAVING THOUGHT THAT, HE IS ACTUALLY A MAN IN PHYSICAL TERMS, AND THEREFORE HAS TESTOSTERONE IN HIS VEINS, GIVING HIM A CERTAIN AMOUNT OF MASCULINE QUALITIES, HOWEVER REPRESSED...
...THERE MUST BE A POSSIBILITY THAT HIS COMMENT COULD HAVE COME FROM SOME DEEP SUBCONSCIOUS PART OF HIS MASCULINITY.

IF HE HAS INDEED REPRESSED A HIDDEN MASCULINE PSYCHE THROUGHOUT HIS RELATIONSHIP WITH CEDRIC, THEN IT HAS BEEN BOTTLED UP FOR 34 YEARS... THAT IS A LOT OF MALE AGRESSION TO COME OUT ALL IN ONE MOMENT...
PERHAPS HIS COMMENT WAS THE BEGINNING OF HIS REPRESSED AGRESSION BEING FREED, AND WILL DEVELOP RAPIDLY INTO A FRENZY OF TESTOSTERONE-FUELLED MALE MADNESS!

BEFORE I KNOW IT HE MAY HAVE THROWN ME TO THE GROUND AND WILL BE FORCING HIS SWOLLEN PHALLUS AGAINST ME... TIME AND TIME AGAIN... PAWING MY BREASTS WITH HIS FILTHY HANDS AS HE DOES SO... YES, PAWING THEM, PAWING THEM AND SLAMMING HIS PELVIS AGAINST MINE... AGAIN AND AGAIN!

RAPE!
MACE

Letterbocks

"It's the page that's marginally more fun than forcing your head into a box of Assorted Creams. And I should know." ~ Viz reader Bruce Pitcher

Letterbocks
Viz Comic
P.O. Box 1PT
Newcastle NE99 1PT

In this space age you can electromail your letters and tips to letters@viz.co.uk

STAR LETTER

THESE do-gooding parents who get so angry about paedophiles 'grooming' young children are probably the same ones who are always going on at their kids to tie their shoelaces and comb their hair. Hypocrites.

Matthew Clifton, Wandsworth

It was heartening to see that veteran rocker Adam Faith died whilst banging 22-year old Tanya Arpino. This comes hot on the heels of news that the Who's John Entwistle pegged it whilst giving a tasty young stripper a bit of how's your father. Good for them. Let's hope that when it comes to their turn, today's generation of pop stars will keep up this wonderful tradition. I for one would like to think that some day in the future, a 60-year-old Gareth Gates will finally stutter to a halt happily up to the apricots in some stunner who won't even be born for another 20 years.

J. Meek
Newent

Anyone with a long history of heart disease who at 62 decides to slip a length to a girl 40 years his junior is asking for trouble. Like Adam Faith, I had my first heart attack in my twenties, but for the past four decades I've stuck to my boot of a wife, and she's never once raised my pulse rate. If, like me, Faith had set his sights a bit lower he would still be alive today.

R. Dixiano
Leatherhead

Speaking as a consultant heart surgeon, I must disagree with the writer of the previous letter. It is an established medical fact that having regular, energetic sex with young women is one of the best forms of exercise for the heart. Unfortunately, many people still do not believe me when I say this, not least of all my miserable old trout of a missus, who has caught me on several occasions looking after my heart with student nurses in consulting rooms.

G. Plywood
Garsdale

Yesterday on the way to work I was passed by a van claiming to represent 'The number 1 producer of traditional Mozzarella in London'. Has anyone seen a more pitiful, worthless and unimpressive corporate slogan than this?

Peter Cashmore
London

I used to think that Michael Jackson sleeping with young boys was sick and twisted, but on his recent interview, he reminded me that such behaviour was beautiful and nothing to be ashamed of. I am sorry I ever doubted you, Michael. I owe you an apology.

M Entwistle
Beaconsfield

"Have you had an accident in the last three years?" they ask. "You could claim compensation," they continue. I phoned Claims Direct expecting to be passed on to a solicitor and a big cash payout, only to be told that drinking 15 pints of real ale, before sneezing and following through was "not an accident". But it's not like I did it on fucking purpose.

Andy Write
e-mail

What a con these safety belts are. Only last week I was putting mine on when my knee slipped off the steering wheel and I ran into a lamp post.

Dominic McGough
e-mail

I wonder if any readers, when showering, actually bother to conduct a full top to toe body detail; or whether, like myself, they save precious time by using their genital area as an ad-hoc 'lather pad' from which to generate and spread suds around as much of their bodies as they can be arsed to reach.

Raretown
Brighton

Before they spent millions of pounds of licence payers' money on prosthetic make-up and computer graphics in order to produce Walking with Cavemen, the BBC might have tried walking round Kings Lynn with a camcorder on a Tuesday afternoon.

Ishmael
Kings Lynn

They say a woman's work is never done. Well if they got up an hour earlier every day, or stopped watching daytime television, then there would be no need for this ridiculous situation to exist again.

Blake
Northend

On behalf of all the drunk drivers, joyriders and speeding motorists of Northern Ireland, I would like to thank the local police for fitting those extra bright xenon headlamp bulbs to their unmarked cars so we can spot them a mile off.

Serious Roger
Belfast

When I was a kid, my uncle Reg always said he would never forget the day he first set eyes on Mabel, his wife. Well now he is in the advanced stages of Alzheimer's disease, and he can't even remember when to go to the toilet, let alone the day he met Mabel. It just proves the old saying 'words are cheap.'

Johnny Jizz
Poplar

How come my vicar can threaten me with damnation in hell for all eternity, yet when I threaten to cut him a bit with a Stanley knife he calls the police?

P Lorimer
Wells

EVERY WAD'S A WINNER!

Last issue, we asked chefs if they had ever ejaculated into Michael Winner's soup, and we offered £1 for the first 1000 to write in and tell us. Well the money went within days, and we're sorry if you weren't one of the lucky ones. Here's a selection of some of the best we received...

"***...I'm*** a chef in a mobile catering unit. I masturbated into his Tomato and Orange soup on a TV shoot recently. He never noticed and even asked for another portion."

A Stewart, Surrey

"***...I'm*** a 3 star Michelin Chef, and I work in a catering establishment that shall remain nameless. One day Winner ordered Leek and Potato soup, and not only myself, but the entire kitchen staff, the Maitre d' and several customers who had seen him come in, wanked into it."

D Northcot, Exeter

"***...I don't*** work in catering and I'm not a man, but if I did, and I was, I would wholeheartedly wank into anything he cared to put in his mouth."

Lori Richardson, e-mail

"***...Interestingly,*** Michael Winner came into our restaurant the other day and we gave him some soup which we hadn't had time to wank into. He sent it back to the kitchen, claiming it 'tasted odd'."

P. Smith, London

This country is radidly turning into a police state. Whilst on the London to Leeds mainline train the other day, I pulled the train alarm to show my young nephew how it sounded. The next thing I knew, some tinpot train guard was trying to fine me £200 for 'improper use', even though I'd given the thing a good, hard yank. You will be pleased to hear that I am contesting the case in court.

C Rossi, Herne Hill

I recently saw a documentary where ordinary people spoke about what they were doing when they heard the news of the planes crashing into the World Trade Centre. It's a good job they didn't interview me. I was having an enormously satisfying morning crap, followed by a massive pull about my lithe young neighbour rubbing her shaved quim all over my face. Have any other readers found themselves behaving inappropriately during times of international significance?

Noemantis, Australia

**Were you picking cheese from your bell-end when you heard Kennedy had been shot? Or did you receive the news of Princess Diana's death whilst sniffing your wife's knickers from the laundry basket? Write in and let us know.*

JUDGE JUGS

JUSTICE ALFRED JUGS ADJUDICATES ON MATTERS BREASTULAR

Dear M'Lud,

I reckon Trinny Woodall out of *What Not To Wear* has littler tits that Tara Palmer Tomkinson, whereas my mate Hairy John says it's the other way round. I ask your honour to look at exhibits A and B, consider the evidence and deliver your verdict.

Russell Hopton, Bickford

JUGS' SUMMING UP

I have considered the evidence laid before me on the bench. After watching several episodes of the television series What Not To Wear, I concluded that while Miss Woodall's breasts were like two aspirins on an ironing board, they did actually form a perceptable bump in her clothing. However, studying a video recording of I'm a Celebrity, Get Me Out of Here, it was apparent that the breasts of Miss Tompkinson failed to give any shape whatsoever to the bikini that she wore. So, whilst both women have chests like fried eggs, I find beyond reasonable doubt that those of Miss Tompkinson are fried-er than those of Miss Woodall. I therefore find in favour of your mate Hairy John.

STARS Confidential

I SAW Paul King on a shopping channel the other day and I think he's got AIDS. I have no evidence for this, and I don't know why I believe it, I just do. I would love to know if my hunch is correct.

Jozmaz
e-mail

** Are you Paul King's binman? Have you found empty AIDS pill packets in his rubbish? Write and let us know in the strictest confidence.*

WATCHING Sophie Raworth read the news on the BBC, I got the distinct impression from the way she was looking at the camera that she may not be averse to a bit of back door action. What do you think?

A Ross
London

** Do you work with Sophie Raworth's husband or boyfriend? Has he ever been indiscreet about their love life? Write and tell us about what they get up to in the fart sack. All information will be treated in the strictest confidence.*

PRETENDERS vocalist Chrissie Hynde recently said in Word magazine that nobody should be allowed to have more than £5 million. It occured to me that Miss Hynde probably set her arbitrary limit at the amount of money she herself has. Could anyone confirm my suspicions?

J Parker
Whitby

** Do you live near Chrissie Hynde? Have you ever had one of her bank statements delivered to you in error, and opened it? Write and let us know in the strictest confidence how much she's got in her account.*

Do YOU have a suspicion about a celebrity's private life? Write to Stars Confidential at the usual address and we'll do our best to confirm it.

CAPTAIN CONSUMER

Fights for your Statutory Rights

MARKS & SPENCERS may have increased their profits by 13% this year, but I for one will not be shopping there again. Last week I bought one of their shirts. Unfortunately, whilst in the lavatory I had a wiping mishap which resulted in quite a large amount of excrement becoming smeared on the cuff. The shirt was unwearable, yet when I took it back to the shop for a replacement they didn't want to know. So much for customer service.

Nicholas Cock
e-mail

ZOKK!!! *Sorry, Nicholas. I rang Marks & Spencers but they put me on hold for 5 minutes and then the line went dead.*

Captain Consumer

I recently bought a new shirt costing nearly £15 from the Kay's catalogue. The first time I wore it I returned home drunk and went to the toilet for a number two. Whilst wiping, I somehow got the tail of the shirt caught between my bottom and the toilet paper. Needless to say the shirt is now useless, but Kay's are refusing to give me a refund.

Eric
Huddersfield

KA-POW!!! *I've written a letter to Kay's catalogue, but I keep forgetting to post it. I think it's on the mantlepiece or in my other coat. I'll definitely post it tomorrow.*

Captain Consumer

Consumer Troubles? **SHA-ZAMM!!!** *Let Captain Consumer come to your rescue. Write to him at the usual address.*

SHOPPERS. *When buying grapes, take one (single) grape to the till. When it is weighed it won't register on the low-tech unsensitive scales so you will get it for free. Repeat this procedure a hundred times or so, and hey, presto! You have yourself a free bunch of grapes.*

A Bomb & Wan Kin Gai,
Hiroshima

KEN *Livingstone. Ensure popularity with the capital's younger voters by fitting giant 'spokey dokeys' to the London Eye.*

Jamie Hussey, Thurrock

DRIVERS. *When overfilling your car with petrol by a few pence, simply wink at the assistant, laughingly telling her you'll "bring it in next time, love." This will put a smile on her face before her already meagre wage is docked. Again.*

Rosemary, Billericay

AIR *guitar players. Become Air-Ukulele players by shortening the distance between your hands. For that added Formby feeling, substitute head moshing with a cheeky smile and the occasional wink.*

Matt Douse,
Beverley

DRIVERS. *If you catch a service station assistant drinking from a bottle of water, simply wink at her, laughingly asking if it's vodka. Even the most difficult day will be lightened by your chirpy humour.*

Rosemary, Billericay

USERS *of premium rate sex lines. Save hundreds of pounds by phoning the Samaritans and threatening to kill yourself unless they talk to you in a sexually explicit manner.*

Rabbi Tableknife,
Middlesbrough

LADIES. *Prevent sexist workmen from shouting "Get yer tits out!" by having them permanently on display.*

Hoolmes,
Email

DRIVERS. *When the salesgirl in your local petrol station holds your banknote up to the light, simply wink at her, laughingly telling her "the ink's still wet!" Trust me, she won't have heard this one before, and you might even get a shag.*

Rosemary, Billericay

HORSE *whisperers. Speak louder. This will enable the animals to hear you more clearly, thus speeding up training times.*

Name lost, Address lost

VOYEURS. *Sit on your cock and your hand until they are both numb. Hey presto, it looks and feels like someone else wanking someone else off.*

Al F., Email

Local Artist Takes Saatchi Prize

EXCLUSIVE

By our art correspondent
ALFRED SHAN De BASS

PORTRAIT OF THE ARTIST: Woodscrew, captured on CCTV yesterday.

A LITTLE known north eastern artist was last night £20,000 richer after scooping the prestigious Saatchi Prize for Contemporary Art.

Monkseaton-born Jason Woodscrew, 14, was the unanimous choice of the judges, who praised the way his work "embraces the poetic, the logical, the sexual and the sensual, whilst drawing connections between, without and within them."

works

Two works singled out for particular praise were *'Suck my Nips'* (2001) and *'My Penis Smels of Apples'* (2002), both executed in car touch-up aerosol on concrete.

cooker

The award is welcome news for Tyneside's bid to be named European City of Culture 2008. Newcastle and Gateshead council spokesman Paul Rubinstein said: "This is a great boost for culture in the region. The Angel of the North, the Millennium Bridge and the Baltic Centre have already marked the north east out as a centre of creativity in the arts. To have these prize-winning artworks on display in the region is just the icing on the cake for the region."

man

As usual the award has prompted controversy. Many critics felt that the £20,000 should have gone to 13-year-old Scott Bradawl of Cullercoats for his marker pen on bus shelter piece 'Angie Does Anal for Tabs' (1999). However, Bradawl failed to make the shortlist for the third year running.

bill

The winning artworks are on exhibition at the Links shelter, Whitley Bay seafront until February 6th when they will be scrubbed off by a man from the council. Admission free.

Have YOU spotted a work of art worthy of the Saatchi prize?

Entries are now invited for next year's competition. Send photographs, stating your name, address and where the work is being exhibited to Viz, PO Box 1PT, Newcastle upon Tyne, NE99 1PT. Mark your envelope 'Saatchi Prize'.

Evening Standard Art Critic Quentin Bumboy on

'My Penis Smels of Apples'

"What is the artist saying to us in this painting? It seems to me that Woodscrew's use of the word 'penis' establishes him firmly in the art historical tradition of male nude painting. Since the earliest cave paintings, the penis has been a symbol of strength. And yet

also of weakness and vulnerability. It smells of apples; that is, it is redolent of the instrument of man's fall from grace. But at this point Woodscrew delivers his *coup de grace*. By misspelling the word 'smell', he challenges the veracity of our senses, causing us to question our notions of truth and being. He leaves us wondering if his penis 'smels' at all, and if it does, whether it smells of apples. Or perhaps some other fruit."

Paul Palmer

JACK BLACK AND HIS DOG SILVER
Bluebird Souvenirs
THE MICHAELMAS HOLIDAYS WERE HERE, AND JACK BLACK AND SILVER HAD COME TO STAY WITH AUNT MEG IN ANOTHER ONE OF HER FUCKING COUNTRY COTTAGES, THIS TIME IN THE PRETTY VILLAGE OF GRUMBLEMERE ON THE BANKS OF LAKE CONISTON...

GOOD MORNING JACK. YOU MUST HAVE SMELT ME COOKING YOUR HEARTY CUMBRIAN BREAKFAST.
YES, AUNT MEG. WE'RE STARVING!
WOOF!

OH NO! I'VE CAUGHT MY TANK TOP ON A NAIL!
R-R-RIP!

NEVER MIND, AUNT MEG. YOU CAN KNIT ME A BRAND SPANKING NEW ONE!
OH, NOT ME, I CAN'T KNIT. NEVER COULD.

IN THAT CASE, WHAT ARE ALL THESE KNITTING NEEDLES FOR?

OH, BLESS YOU, JACK! THESE AREN'T FOR KNITTING...
THEY'RE MY BACKSTREET ABORTION TOOLS.
GOSH!
GIN

ALL THE YOUNG LADIES WOULD COME KNOCKING WHEN THEY GOT INTO TROUBLE, AND I'D SORT THEM OUT ON THIS VERY KITCHEN TABLE FOR TEN SHILLINGS A TIME.

SOMETIMES, DURING THE SCHOOL HOLIDAYS, I'D DO TEN A DAY.
GOLLY! ARE YOU GOING TO DO ONE TODAY, AUNT MEG? CAN I WATCH?

SORRY, JACK. BUSINESS HAS REALLY DROPPED OFF LATELY. I HAVEN'T CARRIED OUT A SINGLE ILLEGAL ABORTION IN THE LAST TWO MONTHS...
...I JUST DON'T UNDERSTAND IT.

THAT'S WHY I'VE HAD TO OPEN THIS SOUVENIR SHOP...
BLUEBIRD FRAGMENTS 1/-
ASSORTED PHALANGES 1/6d
BLUEBIRD STEERING WHEEL 11/6d
1/6d

...SPEAKING OF WHICH, IT'S TIME YOU WERE OFF BEACH COMBING. SEE IF YOU CAN FIND ANY MORE BITS OF DONALD CAMPBELL.
OK, AUNT MEG
THE TOURISTS LOVE THEM.

JACK AND HIS FAITHFUL CANINE COMPANION SOON FOUND THEMSELVES DOWN ON THE BANKS OF THE LAKE...
WHAT IS IT, BOY? WHAT HAVE YOU FOUND?
GRRR! WOOF! GRRR!

GOSH! I WONDER WHAT IT COULD BE...
...IT LOOKS LIKE SOME KIND OF PARTY BALLOON FULL OF STRANGE SMELLING GLUE.

YOU DON'T WANT TO TOUCH THAT, YOUNG MAN...
EH!?!

IT LOOKS LIKE A USED PROPHYLACTIC SHEATH CONTAINING EJACULATE.
A WHAT!?!

IT'S A CONTRACEPTIVE DEVICE, A CONDOM IF YOU WILL, USED TO PREVENT A SPERM REACHING AND FERTILISING THE EGG...
...AND IT'S FULL OF JITLER.
EURGH!

THE STRANGER INTRODUCED HIMSELF. HE WAS MR. ORWELL, A TEACHER AT THE VILLAGE SCHOOL...
I'VE ONLY BEEN HERE A COUPLE OF MONTHS. ISN'T IT A LOVELY SPOT?
ANYWAY, I CAN'T STOP TO CHAT. I DON'T WANT TO BE LATE FOR SCHOOL.

AS MR. ORWELL LEFT, JACK'S MIND BEGAN TO RACE...
THAT MAN SEEMED TO KNOW AN AWFUL LOT ABOUT RUBBER JOHNNIES, DIDN'T HE, BOY?
HE'S BEEN HERE TWO MONTHS...MEG'S ABORTION BUSINESS DRIED UP TWO MONTHS AGO...I WONDER...
WOOF!

COME ON, SILVER. THERE'S DETECTIVE WORK TO BE DONE - UP AT GRUMBLEMERE SCHOOL.
WOOF!

JACK AND SILVER REACHED THE SCHOOL AND CREPT UP TO THE CLASSROOM WINDOW...
...SO THESE ARE THE THREE MAIN FORMS OF FAMILY PLANNING AVAILABLE...

...BUT EVEN WITH PROPER CONTRACEPTION, IT IS IMPORTANT NOT TO RUSH INTO A SEXUAL RELATIONSHIP...
SO THAT'S WHAT HE'S UP TO!

JACK HAD HEARD ENOUGH...
COME ON, SILVER. I'VE HEARD ENOUGH. LET'S GO AND REPORT THIS TO FATHER O'PLYWOOD!

FATHER O'PLYWOOD, I WENT TO FIND DONALD CAMPBELL BITS AND THERE WAS A DUNKY AND IT WAS FULL OF SPONGLE AND MR. ORWELL WAS THERE AND HE'S TEACHING THEM AND, AND...
WOAH THERE, YOUNG JACK! LET'S JUST CALM DOWN AND TAKE IT FROM THE BEGINNING, SHALL WE?

JACK EXPLAINED WHAT HE HAD SEEN AND HOW THE TEACHER WAS GIVING SEX EDUCATION LESSONS TO THE CHILDREN. FATHER O'PLYWOOD WAS HORRIFIED...
BLOOARGH!!

HOLY GOD JESUS MOTHER OF MARY H. CHRIST, JACK. WE'VE GOT TO PUT A STOP TO THIS BLASPHEMOUS MADNESS...
BUT HOW?

HANG ON, FATHER. YOU'RE A CATHOLIC PRIEST. WE COULD PLANT SOME OF YOUR PAEDOPHILE PORNOGRAPHY IN HIS DESK. THAT WOULD SORT HIM OUT.
GOOD IDEA.

HOW MUCH DO YOU WANT, JACK?
HALF A DOZEN HARDCORE MAGS SHOULD DO IT.

HERE YOU GO.
THANKS.
OH, AND JACK...

INSTALL THIS ON HIS HARD DISK JUST TO BE ON THE SAFE SIDE. IT'S RED HOT!
1001 CHOIRBOYS ARSES

THAT NIGHT, JACK AND SILVER VISITED GRUMBLEMERE SCHOOL TO CARRY OUT THEIR PLAN...

NEXT DAY...
MORNING EVERYBODY. NOW TODAY, WE'RE GOING TO TALK ABOUT LOVING RELATIONSHIPS AND OUR RESPONSIBILITIES TO...

CRASH!
WHACK!
AARGH!

SCUM OUT!
PAEDO FILTH!
KILL THE PEADOFILES
SAVE OUR KIDS FROM MR ORWELL
WHAT ON EARTH...?

THERE HE IS, PC BROWN! LOOK IN HIS DESK!
BUT...

AND IF YOU LOOK ON MR. ORWELL'S COMPUTER, YOU'LL FIND EVEN MORE EVIDENCE...
...IT'S IN A FOLDER IN 'RECENT DOCUMENTS' ON THE DESKTOP. YOU HAVE TO DOUBLE CLICK ON THE ICON.
ALTAR BOY ASS

RIGHT, JACK. I'LL JUST TAKE THESE...ERM...FOR EVIDENCE. AS FOR YOU, ORWELL, THERE'S A FRENZIED, MURDEROUS MOB OUTSIDE WOULD LIKE A QUIET WORD WITH YOU.
BUT...

A WEEK LATER...
WELL, AUNT MEG. IT LOOKS LIKE S-E-X EDUCATION IS OFF THE CURRICULUM
YES. AND I'M AFRAID CUMBRIAN BREAKFASTS ARE OFF THE MENU TOO.
NEWS OF THE WORLD
PAEDO SIR PULLED TO BITS BY BAYING MOB
EH!? WHY!?

I'M TOO BUSY DOING ABORTIONS.
HA! HA! HA!
NOW BE A LOVE, JACK AND NIP DOWN THE SHOPS FOR A BOTTLE OF GIN AND A NEW COAT HANGER.

AAAIIIEEEE!!!

SEX AND THE CITY-CENTRE CAR PARK

IF YOU'RE looking for sexy stars, you'd probably think of heading for Hollywood or trawling the topless beaches of St Tropez. The last place you'd expect to find them is in an NCP car park in northern England. But you'd be wrong. From Marilyn Monroe to Madonna, from Jayne Russell to Jordan, car park attendant *George Mintoe* has checked all their tickets.

And in his new book *'Multi-Story Star Park'* (Weetabix Books £12.99) 58-year-old George lifts the lid on the secrets of his celebrity-studded life at the sharp end of one of Newcastle's busiest multi-storey car parks. And his X-rated tales of saucy stars in their cars are set to raise more than a few eyebrows in the worlds of showbiz and car parks.

Early in the book, Goeorge reveals how he was expecting his first day working in the ticket booth to be dull. But his first visitor gave him the surprise of his life!

"It was the first day of my new job and I was feeling a little bit nervous. My mum had made me a flask of tea and I was just pouring a cup when I heard a tap on the window. When I looked out I couldn't believe my eyes. It was Hollywood sex goddess ***Marilyn Monroe***! She told me she was opening a pound shop nearby and was running a bit late. She wanted to know if she could use my ticket booth to change into her bikini.

"I was a 16-year-old lad and the world's most beautiful woman was asking if she could strip naked in my booth"

Just imagine how I felt. I was a 16-year-old lad and here was the world's most beautiful woman asking if she could strip naked in my booth. But deep down I knew that allowing non-company personnel into the booth was strictly against the rules, so reluctantly I had to refuse.

Monroe - almost stripped naked in George's booth

I often wonder what might have happened if I'd let Marilyn in through that door all those years ago. Perhaps she might have lost her balance whilst taking her knickers off and accidentally pushed her bosoms into my face. Who knows.

But I've got no regrets, believe you me. Those are the rules, and NCP car parks makes no exceptions for stars, no matter how sexy they are."

Marilyn was George's first brush with a glamorous celebrity, but she certainly wasn't his last. Later in the book, he reveals how a mix-up over coins very nearly led to a steamy encounter with a British sex siren:

"The Romps start when the engines stop" says attendant George

"It was December 1976 and the top deck of the car park was covered with snow. However, I was quite cosy in my booth as I had a chitty from NCP head office to turn on the second bar of my electric fire. Suddenly, there was a tap at the window. I looked up to see the gorgeous ***Susan George***. I recognised her immediately because I'd just been reading an article about her in Titbits.

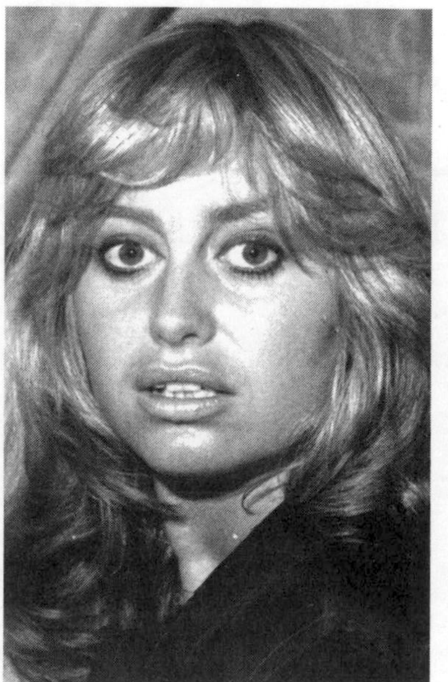

George - offered herself on a plate

I slid the glass partition back an inch or two. She told me she needed an 80p ticket, but she only had a pound coin. She wanted me to change her pound coin for five 20s. I explained I wasn't allowed to give change and pointed out the 'No Change Given' sign in the window but she was very insistent.

fingering

She started fingering the zip on her fur coat, telling me she would be "very grateful" if I would waive the rules this once. She certainly made it very obvious what she was offering in return for the change she wanted.

Believe you me, I'd be lying if I said I wasn't tempted. However just at that moment one of the other attendants came back from Greggs with some pasties and she went off to get some change in a sweet shop.

grateful

Susan George was offering me it on a plate and I often wonder what would have happened if my colleague hadn't returned at that moment. However, one thing's for certain. I should be grateful. If he hadn't come back when he did, I could have thrown away my whole career with NCP car parks for the sake of a few hours of unimaginable sexual ecstasy with one of the world's most desirable women."

Parking attendant George (above), yesterday and the multistorey car park (far right) where he worked for forty years. And the roof top CityGold Parking level (right) where the Sex In the City four-in-a-car lesbian show almost took place.

Most people have seen the film 'Body of Evidence', but few realise that the movie's notorious car park sex scene was shot not in Hollywood, but in Newcastle upon Tyne... right under George Mintoe's nose!

"I'm quite used to people making films in the car park, but it's usually small local productions like Spender, Catherine Cookson or When the Boat Comes In. So imagine my surprise when a stretch limousine driven by ***Madonna*** pulled up at my booth window, and she asked me the way to the set.

Madonna - almost had sex with George on car bonnet

I directed her to the third floor, and turned on my security monitor to see what was going on. Madonna was lying on a car bonnet in the rik, and everyone else was standing around looking at their watches.

sex

A few minutes later there was a tap on the glass. It was the director of the film. He explained that they were supposed to be filming a scene where Madonna had kinky sex with William Dafoe on the bonnet of a car.

The problem was, Dafoe's plane was late in from Hollywood. The director asked me if *I* would like to do the scene with Madonna. I couldn't believe my ears! Here was I, a middle aged car park attendant, being offered the chance to have it off on the bonnet of a Cadillac with the world's sexiest pop star. *What red-blooded englishman would refuse an opportunity like that?*

"Here was I, being offered the chance to have it off on the bonnet of a Cadillac with the world's sexiest pop star"

However, I had to say no. The other attendant had gone to Bakers' Oven for some steak bakes, and I couldn't leave the booth unattended. What would have happened if a customer had turned up wanting change and there was no member of staff there to refuse.

boots

In the end Dafoe turned up and did the scene. I watched it on the security video, thinking how it could so easily have been me. They say you only get one chance of having it off with Madonna in this life, and I guess that was mine. I often wonder how things would have turned out if my colleague hadn't nipped out to Bakers' Oven on that fateful morning. I could have been a household name like William Dafoe. Perhaps I'll never know."

Not all George's sexy encounters with stars have taken place in his booth. In his book, he recalls an episode when he went to investigate a case of illegal parking on the top floor...and nearly got more than he bargained for!

"I was sitting reading some pornography in the booth when I glanced at the CCTV monitor and noticed a car pulling into a space on the 7th floor. That level is reserved for CityGold Permit holders only, and I certainly didn't recognise this particular vehicle. It was definitely illegally parked, so I grabbed my book of tickets and went up in the lift to see what was going on.

When I got there I couldn't believe my eyes. It was an open-topped Rolls-Royce with ***Sarah-Jessica Parker*** and the ***other three from Sex and the City*** in it! They said they'd been unable to find another space on the lower floors. I told them I was going to have to give them a ticket unless they moved it, but they had other ideas.

treat

The girls told me they were going to put on a bit of a show for me. Sarah Jessica seductively began to unzip the front of her rubber dress, whilst the ginger one opened a carrier bag and took out a bottle of baby oil which she began squeezing onto her breasts.

kinkade

I have to admit, at this point I would have taken them up on their offer and let them park in the CityGold permit area. After all, I'm only flesh and blood, and here were four of TV's sauciest sexpots about to make my wildest fantasies come true.

Jessica-Parker - part of four way lesbian show that almost took place

However, I'd already written their registration number on the ticket. Because they're sequentially numbered there is no way I could just crumple it up and throw it away, no matter how much I was tempted. And I WAS tempted, believe you me. Sadly, I put the ticket under the windscreen wiper as the girls put their clothes back on.

Looking back I think it was the right thing to do. We have a saying in the car park business: Rules are rules, and I think that's very true. **"**

Next week: *How* **Sam Fox** *nearly took her bra off to fix a fanbelt, and the time a jammed ticket machine almost led to oral sex with* **Liz Hurley.**

FRU T. BUNN THE MASTER BAKER & HIS GINGERBREAD SEX DOLLS

CONTINUED OVER

AYE... Y'SEE, WHILE Y'WUZ AT THE SHOPS, SON... I BECAME A MORMON...
... AN' Y' KNAA WHAT THAT MEANS...
HOO, YEE! WHERE THE FUCK'S MY MUTHA'S DAY CARD?
AYE!... AN' MINE... Y'LITTLE CUNT
HOO... GOT THE WAY O' THAT FUCKIN' TELLY
ARE YEE GANNA MEK US, LIKE?

TRANNY MAGNET

...AND NOW ON BBC2, A SPECIAL TRANSVESTITE THEME NIGHT.
NOOO!

I'M OFF DOWN THE NAGS HEAD MUM.
HAVE A NICE TIME DEAR. DON'T DRINK TOO MUCH...
...OR YOU WON'T BE ABLE TO GET IT UP IF YOU GET THE CHANCE OF A FUCK.

TRANSVESTITE BAR
FORMERLY THE NAGS HEAD
UNDER NEW MANAGEMENT
GUINESS COCKTAILS 1/2 PRICE
SMART DRESSES ONLY
JESUS! IS NOTHING SACRED?

HEY-UP, WILLIE! HAVE YOU SEEN WHAT THEY'VE DONE TO THE NAGS HEAD?
I KNOW, ERNIE. THE LIKES OF US WOULDN'T BE WELCOME IN THERE NOW.
THAT'S WHY I'VE INVESTED IN THESE BEAUTIES! JUST FEEL THE FIRMNESS!
NYYAAAGH! GERROFF!

TRAVEL AGENT
COME TO IBIZA FOR A GUARANTEED SHAG WITH FIT BIRDS. ONLY £10 WITH CHEAPO AIRWAYS
WAHEYY! THAT'LL DO ME!
SCREEECH!

SO...
HANG ON! WE'RE FLYING PAST IBIZA! STEWARDESS! I'VE MISSED MY STOP!
Buh-Thumpa-thumpa-thumpa-thumpa-thumpa...

THAT'S RIGHT, SIR. SINCE WE TOOK OFF, CHEAPO AIRWAYS HAVE GONE BUST SO WE'VE GOT TO MAKE A ONE-WAY TRIP TO AN ALTERNATIVE DESTINATION.
ANYWHERE! AS LONG AS IT'S NOT TRANNY-OBSESSED ENGLAND!

Welcome to BANGKOK
HEY JOHNNY! YOU WANT A SURPRISE?
TRY SOMETHING DIFFERENT, MISTER?
I GOT A PRESENT FOR YOU, HONEY.
BAH!
© LEW STRINGER. 2003

NEW SETT BACK FOR GUTHRIE

"Tipton Chief Romped in Layby" ~ Claim

Guthrie: No stranger to scandal

A scandal-hit West Midlands councillor is once again clinging to his job, this time after a local newspaper published pictures of him apparently performing a sex act on a badger.

by our BADGER CORRESPONDENT
RUDOPLH HESS

The publication of the photographs forced Hugo Guthrie, deputy chairman of Tipton Borough Council's Civic Amenities committee, into a humiliating climbdown after he had earlier denied ever having visited Brockodale Woods where the incident took place. He now admits that he did go to the area, known locally as Badger Gobblers' Gulch, after one of his constituents reported a spate of illegal fly tipping in the area.

statement

Reading a prepared statement, Mr Guthrie's solicitor told reporters: "My client has now remembered that he did indeed park his car in the Brockodale Woods layby on Wednesday morning.

"He then went for a short walk amongst the trees to look for evidence of unauthorised rubbish disposal. During this walk he met a badger which he now admits he took back to his car."

manager

He continued: "In the car, the badger appeared to be experiencing some discomfort. Fearing that it was suffering a sudden attack of pancreatitis, Mr Guthrie decided to make an examination of the affected area. Unfortunately, he had forgotten his glasses, so he moved his head very close to the badger's lower abdomen."

robbery

"Upon realising the severity of the badger's pancreatitis attack, Councillor Guthrie opened his mouth to gasp in astonishment. It was at this moment that his picture was taken through the car window by a photographer from the Tipton Advertiser newspaper."

account

But this account of events was dismissed as nonsense by Tipton Advertiser editor Max Agincourt. He told us: "Councillor Guthrie is a bare-faced liar. We've got photographs which we couldn't possibly print in a family newspaper which clearly show him performing perverted sex acts on this badger."

adduke

Two years ago, similar circumstances forced Mr Guthrie to resign his chair as assistant treasurer of the Tipton Council Town Twinning subcommittee. Following what he described as a 'moment of madness' during which he climbed a tree in Tipton Park and performed an act of gross indecency with two grey squirrels, he was fined £400 plus costs by local magistrates.

Victorian Dad

SHORTLY...
SLAP!
OUCH!..
DFDS SEAWAYS
...BUT LUPIN... I DON'T KNOW WHAT HAPPENED TO THE LUGGAGE

NO MATTER! IN THE ABSENCE OF A BATMAN IT IS THE WIFE'S DUTY TO CATER FOR THE GENTLEMAN'S LOGISTICAL REQUIREMENTS
ALL MY EVENING WEAR WAS IN THOSE TRUNKS

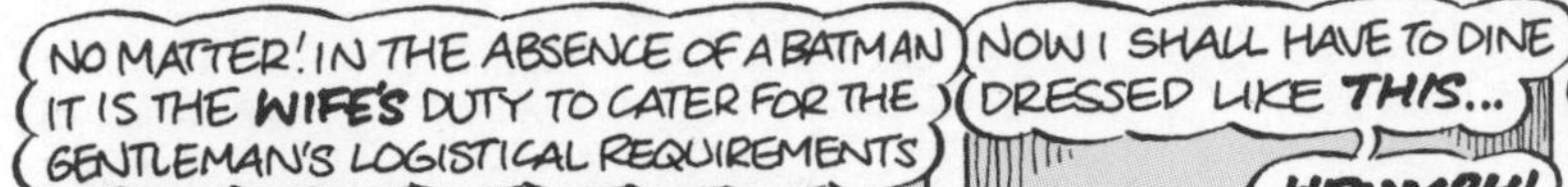
NOW I SHALL HAVE TO DINE DRESSED LIKE THIS...
HRUMPH!
PARTAKING OF DINNER IN A DAY COAT AND WALKING SPATS... OH THE SHAME!

IF MY CLUB WERE TO HEAR OF THIS OUTRAGE, I WOULD SURELY BE BLACKBALLED
THE 7 SEAS RESTAURANT

A TABLE MY MAN... I TRUST WE SHALL BE SEATED WITH THE CAPTAIN
ER... YOU JUST... SIT ANYWHERE
HEY LOOK, SIS... IT'S AN 'ALL YOU CAN EAT' BUFFET!
SWEET AS!
SLOBBER!

SHORTLY...
EGAD!
WHAT IN THUNDER!?
THAT BUFFET'S MINT!
I'M GOING TO GET SOME ICE CREAM NEXT!

WHAT VILE GLUTTONY IS THIS!? YOU HAVE COMMITTED ONE OF THE FOULEST OF ALL SINS!
BUT WHA...
?
HAVE I NOT TRIED TO TEACH YOU ALL THE BLESSINGS OF PARSIMONIOUS FRUGALITY?

A FULL STOMACH IS THIS QUICKEST WAY TO HELL'S DAMNATION
SCRAPE!
SCRAPE!

BUT, DAD... WE'RE STARVING!
HUNGRY OF BODY, REPLETE OF SOUL
BLESSED ARE THE FAMISHED, FOR THEIRS SHALL BE THE KINGDOM OF HEAVEN

SNI-I-I-I-IF!!
AAAH!

CLINK! CLINK!
WELL, I'D BETTER EAT MY PEA BEFORE IT GETS COLD
SNIGGER!

I HAVE NOT YET SAID GRACE, BOY!
THUMP!

THE DEVIL IS WITHIN YOU, CHILD, BUT DO NOT FEAR...
...I SHALL BEAT HIS SPAWN FROM YOUR SOUL

THWACK!
OW!

THWACK! THWACK! THWACK! THWACK!

THWACK!
HNNG!
GNNN!

RIGHT, BOY, NOW SIT DOWN AND I SHALL BLESS THE TABLE...
AHEM!
TUT!

OH, LORD, WRETCHED AS WE ARE, WE THANK THEE FOR THESE, THY BOUNTEOUS GIFTS OF WHICH WE ARE TRULY UNWORTHY, AND WE HUMBLY BESEECH THEE, O LORD...

TO TAKE US UNTO THY CARE, SHOULD THY SEE FIT IN THY WISDOM TO CHOKE US UNTO DEATH UPON THIS, OUR DAILY BREAD FOR WHICH WE GIVE THANKS

TO YOU, OH HOLY FATHER, THE SON AND THE HOLY GHOST. WHO MADE ALL THE CREATURES THAT CRAWL UPON THE LAND AND FLY UPON THE AIR AND SWIM UPON THE SEA. WHO MADE THE LION AND THE LAMB, AND THE OXON AND THE SWINE, AND THE CATTLE AND THE GOAT, AND THE CAMELEOPARD AND THE OSSIPHRAGE...

8 HOURS LATER...
...AND THE STAGBEETLE AND THE GRASSHOPPER, MAY WE FOREVER BESOIL OUR VESTMENTS IN FEAR OF THY TERRIBLE WRATH, NOW AND FOR EVERMORE
AMEN!
EH!?.. WASSAT?
SNORE!

ATTENTION, PLEASE.. WE HAVE DOCKED IN AMSTERDAM. WOULD ALL PASSENGERS MAKE THEIR WAY TO THE EXIT ON DECK 5
AH! NO TIME TO EAT...
LET US AWAY TO AMSTERDAM.
YAWN!

LATER...
COME ALONG, FAMILY... DO KEEP UP! ACCORDING TO TYNDAL, THE CLOG MARKET SHOULD BE JUST AROUND THIS CORNER HERE...
CHEESE WINKLE

GASP!
LIVE SEX SHOW 20€

GIRLS- OPEN
SEX
SALE
SEX 24 HOUR
PROS FROM 50€
GIRLS HAPPY HOUR 2 FOR 1

AWAY!.. AWAY!.. QUICKLY... AND AVERT YOUR EYES!
LET US GO BACK TO THE HOTEL!
PROS

THAT NIGHT...
I SHALL THROW THE BOOK AWAY... IT FAILED TO WARN ME I WAS WANDERING INTO A...A...SODOM!
TO THINK THAT THESE EYES HAVE GAZED UPON A SEETHING CAULDRON OF DEPRAVITY AND LUST

HMM... WELL, NO HARM DONE, EH?
DIS- GUSTING!
A VERITABLE SODOM AND GOMORRAH, I TELL YOU...

OH, LORD...
...THOSE STREET WHORES
...DISPORTING THEIR... PULCHRITUDINOUS FLESH

...SITTING IN THEIR WINDOWS... WITH THEIR BREASTS... THEIR FULL BREASTS AND LUBRICIOUS GENITAL REGIONS.. ON SALE
DID YOU SEE THEM?
HMM?
ON SALE TO ANY MAN TOO WEAK TO SPURN TEMPTATION. ...SUCH ABJECT LICENCIOUSNESS

OH MY.. I...ER...I'VE COME OVER.. SINGULARLY CHOLERIC. I THINK I'LL ER...GO OUTSIDE FOR A.. BREATH OF AIR
YES! THAT'S IT...
SNORE!
PERHAPS A WALK TO THE MIDNIGHT TULIP MARKET MIGHT... ER... RESTORE THE BALANCE OF MY VAPOURS

5 MINS LATER...
UHN! UHN! UHN! OH GOD FORGIVE ME... UNG! UNG!
OOH, JESUS, YEAH!
HEY! OFF THE TITS
IT'S FIFTY EUROS MORE FOR THE TITS!
NOW SERVING
31

HULA-HOOP EMERGENCY WARD

PANDA, 84, PUNCHED IN FACE

Xiang Xiang shows the bruises she received and (inset) an artists impression of the attacker.

...all for £2 OF BAMBOO

By our Zoo Crime correspondent
Capybara Palmer-Tompkinson

OLD age panda Xiang Xiang Robinson yesterday told how she was beaten black and blue in her own home by an intruder... all for just £2 worth of bamboo.

Xiang Xiang, 84 was awoken by someone knocking at the door of her enclosure in Bristol zoo in the early hours of Saturday morning. The caller asked for directions to the monkey house, but when Mrs. Robinson said she couldn't help, he pushed past her into the cage.

bamboo

Xiang Xiang said "I asked him what he wanted and he shouted 'where's your bamboo?'"

Mrs Robinson, who has arthritis, diabetes and lice said "I pointed to my tyre hanging from a rope at the far end of my pen where I keep all my bamboo.

bull and bush

I thought he would take it and go, but he didn't. He was convinced I had more bamboo hidden away in the panda house."

But Xiang Xiang never keep more than £2 worth of bamboo in her enclosure at one time ever since the elderly Chimpanzee next door had his live savings of bananas stolen whilst he was at a tea party.

The thug then laid into Xiang Xiang, punching her once in each eye, on the end of her nose and both ears. He then fled with the bamboo leaving her badly bruised. Though dazed and weak, she managed to attract the attention of a porcupine who raised the alarm.

grey whistle test

The incident has left Xiang Xiang afraid to leave the shelter in her enclosure. Zoo keeper Craig Driftwood said "This was a despicable attack on a frail and vulnerable panda. The fact that just £2 worth of bamboo was taken makes it even worse. The sooner the culprit is caught, the better."

The attacker is described as 6 feet in length, white with small black ears, black rings around his eyes, a broad black stripe over his shoulders and black legs. He was wearing a coat of long, close fur and spoke with a Chinese accent.

POPE-EYE the PONTIFF MAN

I'M GONNER TAKE THESE FLOWERS OVER TO SISTER OLIVE
BIBLE
THAT NUN IS THE SWEETEST PATOOTY IN TH' WHOLE VATICAN

THIS WAY, HOLY FATHER — YOU'RE DUE TO GIVE A PAPAL SPEECH FROM THE BALCONY
AW, POOEY!

BLESS YA, MY CHILDREN. I YAM GONNER TALK TER YA ABOUT TH' IMMORALITY OF COMPERACEPTIVE BIRTH CONTROL
THESE THINGS IS TOTALLY DISGUSTIPATIN' IN THE EYES OF TH' CAT'LIC CHOYCH

BLOW ME DOWN! IT'S CARDINAL BLUTO
HELP!
HE'S MAKIN' OFF WIT' SISTER OLIVE

BOROUGH OF REDCAR
—NO— PARKING
LERRUZ IN THIS F-FFUCKIN' W-WW F-FF-WINDBREK YER B-BB-BBB- BITCH!
KEEP YER FUCKIN' NOISE DAHN. YER FUCKIN' SHOWIN' ME UP.
WOT?!

DID YER F-FFUCKIN' 'EAR THAT, EH? SHE SEZ I'M F-FF-FFUCKIN' SHOWIN' 'ER UP... ME... FFUCKIN' SHOWIN' 'ER UP...
A JUSST WANT TER F-FF-FFUCKIN' MEK A F-FF-FFUCKIN' BIT CASTLE FER ME B-BBAIRNS... AN' THAT F-FF-FFUCKIN'...
BITCH!!
...WAIN'T LERRUZIN T'F-FFUCKIN' WINDBREK.

ALLREYT... A... A... F-FF FFUCKIN' BRAYED 'ER. A ADMIT IT... AN' A'M SORREH FERRIT...
BURRIT WOHN'T ME WOT DID IT. IT WOH THE FFUCKIN' ACE.

SO DUN'T YOO FFUCKIN' TELL ME A'M SHOWIN' 'ER UP... OR YOO'LL BE T'NEXT TER FEEL TH'WRATH OF TH'ACE.
OI! EIGHT!

YES MY LUV..? ARE Y'LERRINUZZIN TH'WINDBREK?... A PROMISE A'LL NOT KNOCK YER ABAHT THIS TIME...
A'M A CHANGED MAN, ME.

OH YER ARE, ARE YER? WELL 'ERE'S ONE FORTEH-NINE TER GET TH'BAIRNS SUM ICE CREAMS.

...AN' IF YER A CHANGED MAN LIKE YER SAY, AN' YER DUN'T SPEND IT ON ACE...
...A'LL LET YER CUM INTEH TH'WINDBREK FER A MINNIT.

REYT. THIS IS IT. THIS IS ME LAST CHANCE TER SHOW 'ER A'VE F-FF FFUCKIN' CHANGED. TER SHOW 'ER A'VE FINALLY BEATEN THE F-FFUCKIN' ACE.
ICES

THIS ONE FORTEH-NINE'S TH'KEYS OF A NEW FFUCKIN' LIFE FER ME AN' TH'MISSUS AN' THEM BBAIRNS.
ICES
THE WAY TO ICES

THE FF-FFUCKIN' ACE 'AS 'ELD ME 'OSTAGE FER TOO LONG. A'VE BIN TRAPPED IN ITS THRALL... WELL IT CAN F-FFUCKIN' FUCK OFF 'COS MY BBAIRNS IS SKRIKIN' FER CONES AN' A'LL NOT LERREM SKRIKE IN VAIN...
ICE CREAM
BUT...
PATEL'S BROTHER'S SEASIDE MINI MART
!?

GO ON - GET YERSELF SOME ACE! TREAT YERSELF - YER DESERVE IT!... GO ON... F-FF-FFUCK THE LORRO FEM! ...'AVE YER ACE!
B-BB-BUT...

DUN'T LISTEN TO 'IM, EIGHT. YOO 'AVE A RESPONSIBILITEH TO YER FAMBLEH!
...SO 'AVE THESE AN' MEK SURE THEH YER LAST EIGHT TINS... THEN DEFINITELY FFUCKIN' GIVE UP AFTEH THESE.

WHACK! WHAARK!
PATEL'S BROTHER'S SEASIDE MINI MART
ACE LAGER ON SALE HERE!
8 ACE.
YES BOSS. THAT'LL BE ONE FIFTY.
ONE F-FFUCKIN' FIFTEH!? YER F-FFUCKIN' BROTHEH AWNLEH CHARGES ONE F-FF FFUCKIN' FORTEH-NINE!

AH YES. BUT IT'S HIGH SEASON, BOSS.
AW GO ON... LERRUZ OFF TH'PENCE, EH?
SORRY BOSS...
...A PENNY TO ME IS LIKE A THOUSAND POUNDS.

'EY, PAL... YER'VE DUN US A F-FF-FFFUCKIN' F-FFAVOUR THEER.... THATS A WARNIN', THAT... THAT PENCE IS A F-FFFUCKIN' OMEN.

IT'S GOD GIVIN' US ANOTHEH CHANCE TER DO RECT BY ME F-FFUCKIN' FAMBLEH.
YES BOSS.
SNIFFLE

...SO FUCK YOO, FUCK THAT PENCE, AN' F-FF-FFUCKIN' FUCK THE ACE. ...A'M FINISHED WI' IT... FER GOOD!

THAT'S IT! THE LAST DROP O' THAT F-FFUCKIN' PISS 'AS PASSED THESE LIPS. THIS ONE FORTEH NINE'S GUNNEH PAY FER THE BIGGEST CONES THEM FFUCKIN' BBAIRNS 'AVE EVEH SEEN!
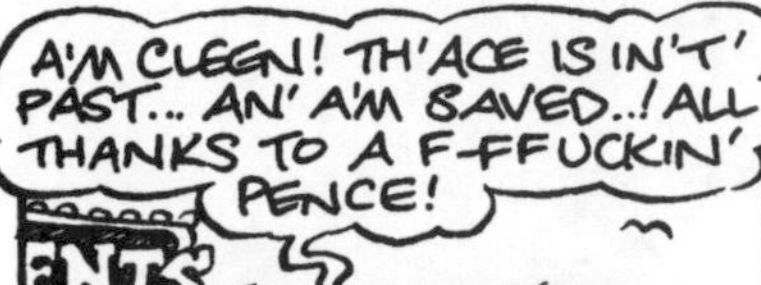
A'M CLEEN! TH'ACE IS IN'T' PAST... AN' A'M SAVED..! ALL THANKS TO A F-FFUCKIN' PENCE!

ENTS

IT'S LIKE A'M WALKIN' ON FFFUCKIN' AIR... THIS IS THE FFF-FFIRST FFUCKIN' DAY OF THE REST OF ME....
PENNY GRAB

PENNY GRAB
....LIFE.

PENNY GRAB
1p
CHANGE

CLUNK!
1p
PENNY GRAB

WHIRR! WHIRR!
GRAB

BOLLOCKS! WOT DO I WANT A FFUCKIN' ROLEX WATCH FOH? A KNAW WOT FFUCKIN' TIME IS...
IT'S F-FFUCKIN' TIME FER ACE.

CLUNK! WHIRR!

WHIRR!

WHIRR...

EVENTUALLY...
...WELL, YOU'RE ME LAST F-FFUCKIN' PENCE. IT'S ALL DAHN TER YOO. YOO STAND BETWEEN ME AN' THEM EIGHT TINS OF 'APPINESS...
DUN'T F-FFUCKIN' LERRUZ DAHN.

KISS!

1p
CLUNK
WHIRR!
GRAB!

LIFT!

DROP!
PENNY GRAB
!

HALLEH-F-FF-FFF-FFUCKIN' LOOYEH!

MAM! MAM! MAM! MAM! WHERE'S US DAD WI' US CONES?
WHERE THE FUCKIN' 'ELL IS 'EE? THE USELESS FUCKIN' CUNT.

'ERE YER ARE, LUV... THEH DIN'T 'AVE VANILLEH... SO A GORREM ....ERM.... SAND...

ERM... A'LL JUSST GO AN' SIT OUTSIDE TH' WINDBREK, SHALL A...?

BRITAIN'S FASTEST GROWING HOBBY!

ARE YOU SITTING QUUMFTABLY?

QUUMF!

THE MAG FOR MEN WHO SNIFF LADIES' BIKE SADDLES

INCORPORATING SNURFING GAZETTE AND Snudgers & Snudgemen

Britain's Best-Selling MOOMPHTY MONTHLY
Feb. £2.75

SADDLE DO NICELY!

Win a week working in Bike Maintenance at CenterParcs in our FANNY-TASTIC Competition!

MUSTY-HAVE!

We test-snudge Brookes' double-sprung Gran Turismo

BRITAIN'S UNLUCKIEST SNURGLAR

'I found Kylie's BMX chained to a railing – and I had *sinusitis*!'

TALKING SCENTS!

Celebrity Shniffle-Piffler JONATHAN ROSS reveals all

SADDLE SNIFFER'S A-Z

Overdose on the Odours of OXFORD

SWEAT PRODUCTION OR AROMA RETENTION?

The Great Leather/Plastic Debate Continues

ON SALE NOW!

SPOILT BASTARD...

SID the SEXIST

TYNESIDE'S SILVER-TONGUED CAVALIER

HOBOCOP

CHRIST SCHOOL
TEACHER ♡ MISS MAGDALENE

GOOD MORNING, CLASS
NOW SETTLE DOWN WHILE I TAKE THE REGISTER
HOLY GHOST PUPPET

LANKY CHRIST?
OMNIPRESENT, SIR
SPOTTY CHRIST?
OMNIPRESENT
FATTY CHRIST?

HAS ANYONE SEEN FATTY THIS MORNING?

PLEASE SIR, HE'S SCOFFED ENOUGH LOAVES AND FISHES TO FEED 5,000 PEOPLE, AND ISN'T FEELING WELL
GROAN
TSK

WHAT AN UNFIT BUNCH OF MESSIAHS YOU ARE
POOL
OFF TO THE SWIMMING POOL WITH YOU. A SPOT OF EXERCISE WILL GET YOU INTO SHAPE

NOW, WE'LL HAVE TEN BRISK LENGTHS OF FREESTYLE WALKING ON WATER
FOLLOW ME, CHILDREN

HUH! EXERCISE IS BORING
A QUICK MIRACLE WILL PUT A STOP TO THIS

WOW! ALL THE WATER HAS TURNED TO WINE
IT'S TOO STICKY TO WALK ON — I'M GOING TO...

...LOSE MY BALANCE
GLUB!
SPLOOSH!

HO HO! TEACHER'S SWALLOWED SO MUCH WINE HE'S DIED OF ALCOHOL POISONING!
IT'LL BE THREE DAYS BEFORE HE'S ABLE TO RISE AGAIN

LATER IN THE PLAYGROUND
BOO HOO! THAT FOURTH FORM BULLY BASHER CHRIST CHUCKED MY SCHOOL CAP OF THORNS IN A MUDDY PUDDLE
SNIFF! IT'S RUINED

WE'LL TEACH THAT BIG BULLY A LESSON
OINK! GIBBER!
PIGGERY
SQUEAL!
HM. LOOKS LIKE THE SCHOOL GADARENE SWINE ARE POSSESSED BY PLENTY OF DEMONS TODAY

I'LL JUST CAST THE DEMONIC SPIRITS OUT OF THE PIGS...
ABRACADABRA!

...AND THEN CAST THEM ALL INTO BASHER CHRIST
ALAKAZAM!
ERK!

MEANWHILE
AH, MR AND MRS ALMIGHTY. SO GLAD YOU COULD COME
PARENTS OPEN DAY
CHRIST SCHOOL
HEAD MASTER
WE'RE ALWAYS DELIGHTED TO SHOW PROSPECTIVE PARENTS AROUND THE SCHOOL

...YES, OUR PUPILS ARE THE MEEKEST AND MILDEST SAVIOURS THAT YOU ARE LIKELY TO MEET...
HEAD MASTER

YARRGH! GIBBER! DEMONS IN MY HEAD!
HEAD MASTER
WELL! I DON'T CALL THAT PARTICULARLY MEEK AND MILD

GRR! SHOW ME UP IN FRONT OF THOSE PARENTS, WOULD YOU? YOU'RE FOR IT NOW, BOY!
WHILE I'M PUNISHING BASHER, THE REST OF YOU ARE FREE TO DIE UPON THE CROSS FOR THE REDEMPTION OF MANKIND

WRITE OUT ONE HUNDRED TIMES, "I MUST NOT GET POSSESSED BY EVIL SPIRITS"
HO HO! TOUGH LUCK, BASHER — YOU COULDN'T "SAVIOUR" SELF FROM THAT PUNISHMENT!

Raggy Mag

Here it is!
Yor **FREE** 3-page
Raggy Omaar pullout!

In this issue

What *REALLY* scares the fearless Baghdad hack?

- find out in the A~Z of Raggy

PLUS

Quizzes, Crosswords and a FREE super pair of Raggy
SEX-RAY SPECS

THE RAGGY OMAAR STORY

The Raggy Omaar Alphabet

THE TV COVERAGE of the Iraqi war has been choc-full of stuff for the lads - guns, bombs, explosions, tanks and fighting. There's even been an impromptu football match! But unlike previous conflicts, the ladies have been glued to their screens too, thanks to the presence of Raggy Omaar, the BBC's hunky Baghdad correspondent.

Raggy's authoritative rooftop reports from the Palestine Hotel have set the news agenda, whilst his dreamy good looks have sent the nation's ladies into a spin. The coalition forces may have stormed right into the heart of Saddam's stronghold, but Omaar has stormed straight into the heart of every red-blooded British bird.

Unfortunately, now that the thrill-a-minute bombardment of the Iraqi capital is over we'll be seeing less of Omaar on our screens. So to keep the ladies going, here's the A to Z of Britain's best-loved bullet-dodging dreamboat.

A is for **ANTS**. Although bombs, shells and missiles hold no fear for Raggy, he's absolutely terrified of ants!

B is for **BREAKFAST**. Raggy gets up every morning and munches his way through TWO bowls of Golden Grahams!

C is for **CAMBRIDGE**. The posh university. But Raggy didn't go there. He went to Oxford.

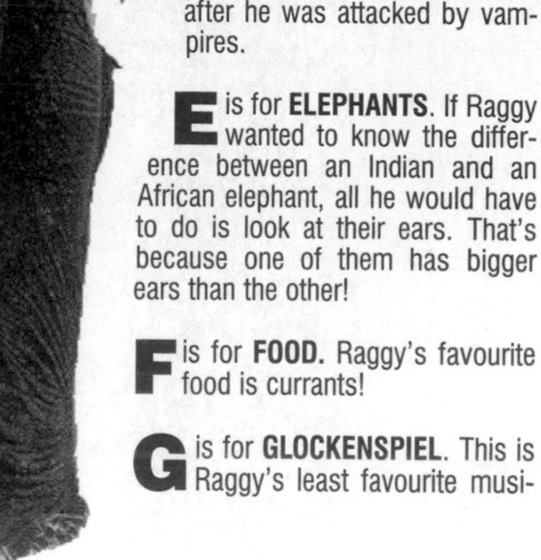

D is for **DRACULA.** Whilst a student, Raggy spent the night in a haunted house to raise money for charity. However, he fled halfway through the night after he was attacked by vampires.

E is for **ELEPHANTS**. If Raggy wanted to know the difference between an Indian and an African elephant, all he would have to do is look at their ears. That's because one of them has bigger ears than the other!

F is for **FOOD.** Raggy's favourite food is currants!

G is for **GLOCKENSPIEL**. This is Raggy's least favourite musical instrument. He hates its sound, after being forced to play it at nursery school!

H is for **HISTORY**. Want to know when the Battle of Hastings was, or how many wives Henry the Eighth had? Just ask Raggy - ***he's got a degree in history!***

I is for **INTERCOURSE**. Raggy's the proud dad of two lovely kids - which means he must have had sexual intercourse in a lady.

J is for **JUNGLE BOOK**. Raggy's favourite film is Disney's Jungle Book. *"I reckon I must have seen the Jungle Book over 500 times,"* he says.

K is for **KIPLING**. Raggy's favourite story by Rudyard Kipling is the Jungle Book *"I reckon I must have read the Jungle Book over 500 times,"* he says.

L is for **LIBERTY-X**. Raggy is the teen band's biggest fan. His favourite is Kelli.

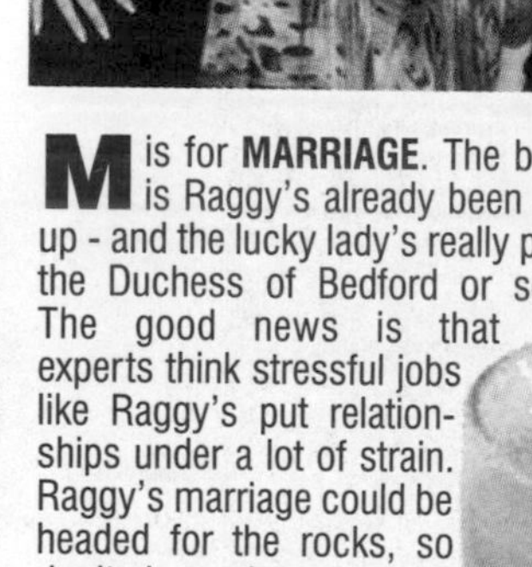

M is for **MARRIAGE**. The bad news is Raggy's already been snapped up - and the lucky lady's really posh, like the Duchess of Bedford or someone. The good news is that experts think stressful jobs like Raggy's put relationships under a lot of strain. Raggy's marriage could be headed for the rocks, so don't give up hope just yet, girls!

N is for **NUDE**. For a bet, Raggy once read the 9 o'clock news...stark naked! But don't get too excited, girls. It was on the radio!

O is for **ORANGE JUICE**. When he was 14, Raggy knocked a full glass of orange juice over on the kitchen table. His mum quickly mopped up the mess with some kitchen towels, and the whole incident was swiftly forgotten.

P is for **PRANKSTER.** Raggy once put a live crab down the back of Iraqi information minister Mohammed Saeed al-Sahaf's trousers!

Q is for **QUANTUM LEAP**. Raggy always mixes up the TV show 'Quantum Leap' with 'Sliders'. *"I can just never tell them apart"* he says.

R is for **RAISINS**. After currants, Raggy's second favourite food is raisins!

S is for **SULTANAS**. Strangely, although he loves currants and raisins, Raggy absolutely HATES sultanas. He says they look like rabbit droppings. Ugh!

T is for **TEASE**. Throughout the Gulf conflict, Raggy got the lady viewers hot under the collar by undoing the top two buttons of his shirt.

U is for **UNCLE**. Raggy has a famous uncle. Pint-sized veteran legless stand-up comedian Arthur Askey is married to his mother's sister.

V is for **VEST**. Raggy never goes out and about in war-torn Baghdad without his bullet-proof vest. But don't worry girls, he keeps his other vital organs well protected...in a sexy bullet-proof silk thong!

W is for **WAR.** Despite reporting on wars all over the world, Raggy is not a fan of armed conflict. He prefers peace!

X is for **XYLOPHONE**. It is not known whether Raggy has any particular feelings one way or the other about xylophones.

Y is for **YIKES!** Raggy once swallowed a drawing pin, and had to mash up his stools with a fork for a whole week to be sure it had come through his system!

Z is for **ZZZZZZZ.** When the Gulf War is over, Raggy's going home to catch up on his beauty sleep. Not that he needs it, eh girls?!

RAGGY TIME FUN PAGE

Raggy Crossword

Two sets of clues- but the answers are the same...

Cryptic

Across

2. Actor Sharif has got an extra 'a' (5)

Down

1. Madness's trousers, but with an 'r' instead of a 'b' (5)

Coffee break

Across

2. War correspondent Raggy's surname (5)

Down

1. War correspondent Omaar's christian name (5)

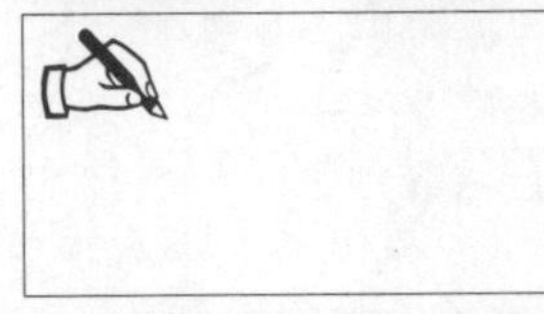

Who's That?

We've pixilated the face of this famous Iraqi war correspondent. Can you guess who he is?

Clue: Look to the roof in Baghdad

OMAAR WORDSEARCH

Hidden in the grid below are five words to do with Raggy Omaar. Can you spot them? They may read backwards or forwards, horizontally, vertically or diagonally.

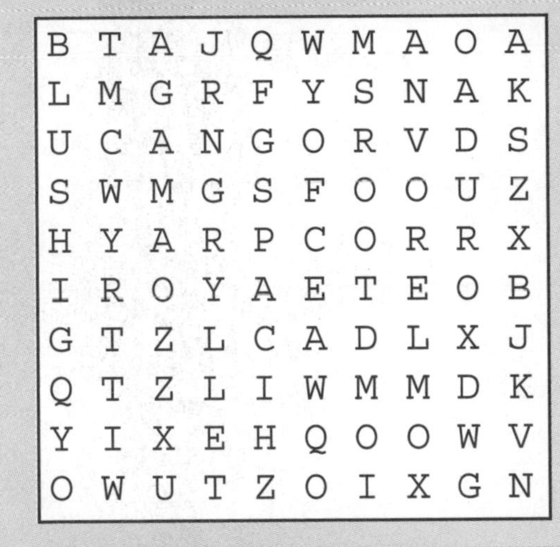

B	T	A	J	Q	W	M	A	O	A
L	M	G	R	F	Y	S	N	A	K
U	C	A	N	G	O	R	V	D	S
S	W	M	G	S	F	O	O	U	Z
H	Y	A	R	P	C	O	R	R	X
I	R	O	Y	A	E	T	E	O	B
G	T	Z	L	C	A	D	L	X	J
Q	T	Z	L	I	W	M	M	D	K
Y	I	X	E	H	Q	O	O	W	V
O	W	U	T	Z	O	I	X	G	N

Hidden Words

Raggy
Omaar
War
Roof
Telly
Lush

Crossword answers
Across: 2. Omaar **Down:**
1. Raggy

Raggy's Microphone Mix-up

Raggy is about to broadcast to Britain from the roof of a Baghdad hotel. But of, dear! ~ not only are his reports being monitored, but he's mixed up his his microphones too! Can you help him find out which one is plugged into the satellite dish?

Omaar, he's making eyes at me!

Raggy's 'come to Baghdad' eyes are an irresistible lure for any woman. Now we've harnessed their extraordinary power so you can share in the sexy BBC satellite dish's success with the ladies. Next time you go out, take these fantastic FREE Raggy Omaar Sex-Ray Specs with you, and you can rest assured you won't be coming home alone.

Before

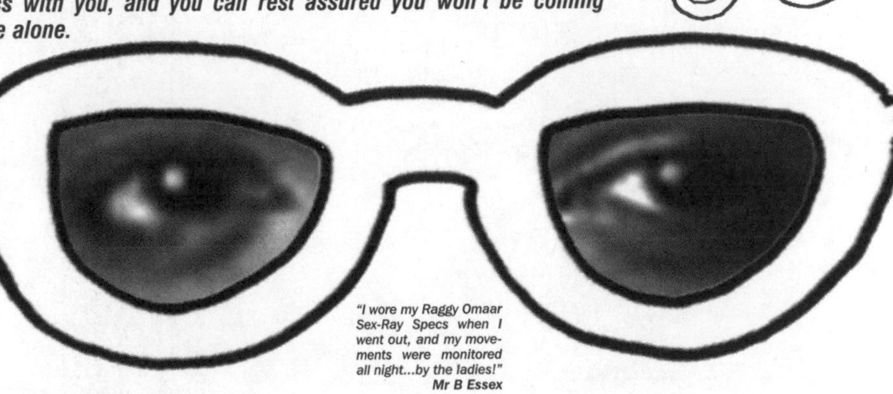

"I wore my Raggy Omaar Sex-Ray Specs when I went out, and my movements were monitored all night...by the ladies!"
Mr B Essex

After

OH, LORDY... IT'S THE

FAT SLAGS

SHORTLY...
FWISH!!

FUCKIN' 'ELL... I'VE GOT THROUGH ME BAIT! I 'AD A PINT OF MAGGOTS S'MORNIN' AN' I'VE ONLY GOT HALF A DOZEN LEFT.
MUNCH! MUNCH!.. MAGGOTS?

...I THOUGHT IT WAS RICE! MUNCH! MUNCH!.. EURGH! I'M NOT 'AVIN' ANY MORE
UGH! THAT'S DISGUSTIN'. THE THOUGHT OF A TINY PINK THING WRIGGLIN' AROUND IN Y' GOB

Y' DIDN'T SAY THAT WHEN Y' WAS NOSHIN' BAZ OFF LAST NIGHT. MUNCH! MUNCH!

LATER STILL...
JESUS! I'M BORED
FWIT!
T' THINK WE COULD BE AT 'OME WATCHIN' SOMEBODY 'AVE A SHIT OR SUMMAT ON BIG BROTHER INSTEAD OF WASTIN' TIME 'ERE!

HEY, LISTEN, DAVE... SAYS HERE FISH ARE STRONGLY ATTRACTED TO HORMONES THAT BIRDS GIVE OFF
ANGLING TIMES
MAN CATCHES
IT SAYS Y' SHOULD ALWAYS KEEP A PAIR OF Y' MISSUS' KNICKERS IN Y' BAIT TIN TO ATTRACT THE BIG FISH

'ERE, SAN... GIZ A LEND OF YER DUNGHAMPERS
WOT FOR?
A LITTLE EXPERIMENT

JESUS, SAN... 'OW LONG 'AVE YOU 'AD THESE ON?
A WEEK
ME OTHER PAIR GOT NICKED OFF THE LINE... SOMEBODY'S BIN 'GOIN' ROUND THE ESTATE

AYE... THE FILTHY FUCKIN' PERVERT
YOU'RE JUST JEALOUS 'COS HE DIDN'T NICK YOURS
AM NOT
WELL, I'LL TELL Y' WOT... ANY FISH THAT THESE SCUNS ATTRACT WILL COME OUT ALREADY COVERED IN BATTER

FWIF! FWIF! FWIF! FWIF

FWOOOF!
HEY! ME KNICKERS!
THERE!
THAT SHOULD DRAW 'EM IN.
PLOP!

IS IT ME OR IS THAT WATER TURNIN' A FUNNY COLOUR?

BLOIP!
BLOIP!

BLOIP! BLOIP!
BLOIP!
BLOIP!
BLOIP!
BLOIP!

FUCK ME, SAN... THEM WAS STRONG KNICKERS... LOOK!
HEH! HEH! YOU CAN COME AGAIN

THAT NIGHT...
...AND ENVIRONMENTAL SCIENTISTS ARE TRYING TO FIND OUT WHAT CAUSED THE DEATH OF THOUSANDS OF FISH ALONG A TEN MILE STRETCH OF THE RIVER TRENT. THAT'S THE END OF CHANNEL 4 NEWS. NOW, BACK TO BIG BROTHER

RIGHT! DOES ANYBODY WANT SOME MORE?... THERE'S CHUBS, CARPS, ROACHES AND DACE.
NOT ME, TRAY... I'M SURE THEY'RE NOT EDIBLE Y'KNOW
RUBBISH! THEY'RE LOVELY! 'AVE Y' GOT ANY MORE TENCH, TRAY?
DEE TWENTY FAWA IN THE BIG BROTHER HOOSE... AND SCOTT IS GANNIN' FORRA SHITE...
NAILS

Letterbocks

It's the page that's BRIGHTER than 10 HIROSHIMAS, BREEZIER than 10 EL NIÑOS and a HURRICANE ANDREW and PACKS MORE PUNCH than 10 LENNOX LEWISSES with 6 MILLION DOLLAR MAN ARMS ... ON 10 DRUGS!

STAR LETTER

I AM a fireman, and I recently met a woman who had a thing for men in uniforms. However, when we went back to her house she insisted that I took it off straight away. I wish women would make their minds up - either they like the uniform or they don't.

Rob Harris, Somewhere

Letterbocks
Viz Comic
P.O.Box 1PT
Newcastle NE99 1PT

In this space age you can electromail your letters and tips to letters@viz.co.uk

Alf awake

WHILST recently enjoying a friends reunion in Huddersfield, we returned from the pub and began a drunken wrestling match in the hotel where we were staying. At 2.30 am, we were interrupted by a knock on the door. To my surprise, standing in the doorway in his pyjamas was grumpy old Alf Garnett actor Warren Mitchell. He told us to 'cut it out' because he had to get up at 6 o'clock in the morning. Luckily, he didn't see that one of my friends was coloured, or we'd have been in a lot more trouble.

Alun Roberts, e-mail

I RECENTLY got a ten minute lecture from my ladyfriend simply because I got drunk with my mates on her birthday. As the lecture came to an end, she said '...and another thing.' Why do women do this? Men give you a lecture and finish; why must women always add something onto the end of lectures?

Rob Harris, Somewhere

I WORK in a library and I'm fed up of reading books all day. I fancy being a window cleaner so as I can look into people's houses, or maybe an undertaker so I can look at dead bodies. Would any *Viz* readers like to swap jobs?

Snowbeast, e-mail

Coy carp

WHY IS IT that in a lot of pornographic films I watch, many of the women have bikini tan marks? It seems a bit rich that whilst they are willing to let some bloke empty his sack on their face for worldwide consumption on film, they get all coy when they have to get their tits out on the beach.

Joel Young, Newcastle

ON A RECENT trip to Norfolk, I observed a sign in a layby which read 'Please take your litter home with you.' Imagine my dismay when British Airways charged me £327 for my excess baggage of two weeks worth of crisp packets, used contraceptives and chopsticks. Thanks very much Norwich City Council.

Kuddenzo John Chi, Shinjuku, Japan

THAT JK Rowling needs to fucking cheer up. She's about to trouser a cool 30 million quid from the latest Harry Potboiler, and she's still got a face like a smacked arse. If somebody gave me just a fiver I'd at least smile, the miserable bitch.

Fat Bloke, e-mail

PS. The same goes for Alan Shearer.

LAST Christmas, a Catholic Priest shat himself in my mate Bryan's back garden in Hartlepool. I want to know if any other readers have any similar tales of Holy Turd-laying or Priestly pant-pooing

Jay, e-mail

Doctor's orders

I ENJOYED reading Paul Evans's letter on page 50, in which he described the order in which he would enjoy each of Samantha Mumba's orifices should she visit him whilst his wife is out and demand a portion. However, as a medical practitioner, I feel I must point out that should he deliver the portion in the said order, ie arse, gob, arse, and if he has any left, arse again, the poor girl would almost certainly contract bum herpes, a serious viral infection.

Incidentally, in the unlikely event that Samantha Mumba, suffering from bum herpes, turns up at my surgery and demands treatment, this is the order I would examine her in: Arse, gob, arse. If I had any time left, I would examine her arse again.

Dr Roger Howard, Lincoln

LAUGH WITH "It is the way I am telling them" G. RAVISHANKAR

The funny fellow with English as his second language

There was a man who had a meeting in a different country. He met a woman and that night they had their own meeting. While they were having sex, she was yelling "TROU FAUX, TROU FAUX." He did not know what that meant, but assumed it to be some sort of praise.

The next day, he went to play golf with the men he had the meeting with. One of them made a hole in one. He yelled, "TROU FAUX, TROU FAUX!"

They looked at him and said, "What do you mean wrong hole?"

The confusion was because of American and Fenchman who did not bother to know the exact meaning!

That one was a cracker. More laughs next time!

Pig ignorant

I WAS recently stopped by a police officer for simply urinating in the road. The officer in question asked my name. As a well brought up young man, I gave it, then offered my hand to shake and asked his name. Can you imagine my disbelief when he ignored this and continued writing in his notebook. Are all police offficers ignorant, or was this just one 'bad apple'?

Rob Harris, Somewhere

Going spare

I RECENTLY paid £18 for a replacement Ford Mondeo fanbelt at my local Ford dealership. Imagine how cross I was when I went into Halfords and saw a non-branded but perfectly good alternative on sale for just £6. I bought one, and took my first fanbelt back to the dealership for a refund, but they refused. As you can imagine, I was absolutely livid by the time I got home. To cap it all, my wife then reminded me that we don't have a car.

Edwin Scott, Walsall

Bruce Springsteen & The E Street Band hear your employment grumbles

Dear The Boss,
I was recently sacked by OBSCURED ON LEGAL ADVICE, the UK's largest builders merchants. I was falsely accused of theft with no evidence, and my complaints were brushed under the beaurocratic rug. What a bunch of cunts.

Former OBSCURED ON LEGAL ADVICE employee e-mail

Dear The Boss,
Loyalty doesn't mean a thing these days, especially if you work at OBSCURED ON LEGAL ADVICE, Wetherby. I have just been made redundant after 20 years continuous service. I received the minimun redundancy payments (12 weeks notice, 20 weeks pay plus holiday pay entitlement). They have not only destroyed my livelihood, they have destroyed me emotionally, and my faith in the British employer. I will never forgive OBSCURED for what they have done to me and wouldn't recommend anyone to work there.

Anonymous, Wetherby

Bruce Springsteen and the E Street Band regret that they cannot answer any queries or arbitrate in work related disputes.

I JUST wanted to say that, whilst I find *Viz* often quite funny, the Christ School cartoon was not. I thought it was blasphemous - an offence, not against Christians, but against Jesus.

Mark Robinson, e-mail

FROM THE way he swaggers up to the despatch box, I wouldn't be at all surprised if 'more time with my family' Geordie MP Alan Milburn was hung like a donkey. And the looks he gets off lady MPs on Question Time makes me even more suspicious. I'd love to know if it was true.

G Windyarse London

**Are you a tailor who has made a suit for Alan Milburn MP? When you measured his inside leg, did you make a mental note of the size of his genitals? Write, in the strictest confidence, to: Stars Confidential, Viz Comic, PO Box 1PT, Newcastle upon Tyne, NE99 1PT.*

WHILST watching the BBC Wimbledon coverage recently, I was suddenly struck by the awful notion that British No1 Tim Henman may have had sexual intercourse with Sue Barker, probably in a seedy motel. I hope I am wrong, but so far nobody has come up with any evidence to the contrary.

Albert Hammer London

** Are you the manager of a seedy motel in the Wimbledon area? Have Sue and Tim ever checked in under false names and left a pile of spent contraceptives under the bed? If so, write and tell us, in the strictest confidence.*

Do YOU have a suspicion about a celebrity's private life? Write to Stars Confidential at the usual address and we'll do our best to confirm it.

TOP TIPS

PHILANDERERS. *Avoid the embarrassment of shouting out the wrong name in bed by only having flings with girls who have the same name as your wife.*

Russell Codd, Leeds

NEWCASTLE *United. Show your commitment to the "Show Racism the Red Card" campain by plastering posters all over the town, then employing Bowyer, Woodgate and Bellamy.*

Matt, Whitley Bay

THE NIGHT *after eating a real ring-stinger of a curry, put a dozen or so ice cubes down the bog. The splash-back caused when you have a shit will cool and soothe your burning ringpiece.*

Dan, Cambridge

HEROIN *addicts. Instead of getting up at the crack of dawn everyday to go shoplifting to raise money for smack, why not cut out the middle man and simply nick the heroin? Not only will this save time, but it will be much safer as drug dealers' homes don't usually have security guards and CCTV.*

Damian Marshall, e-mail

GENERATE *virtual after time drinking by simply setting your watch two hours fast and going to the pub two hours earlier. An added bonus is that when you arrive home pissed, yoiu can get two hours extra in bed by simply setting your watch back to normal.*

Andy Hill, (Professor of Drinking), Kingswinford

SAVE *money on tattoos by having a small one done over a muscle, then going to the gym until the muscle gets bigger. Hey presto, a big tattoo for the price of a small one.*

Ian Mainy, Bedford

MALES. *If stuck for something to talk about with other equally awkward males at social gatherings, simply pipe up about a random A road or motorway that you crossed on your journey and mention that it was 'quite busy.' This will spark off an exchange of similar road themed anecdotes that should last until hometime.*

Latchkey Wizzard, Canterspay

EXHIBITIONISTS. *Strain your eyes until they go numb before masturbating, then it will feel like someone else is watching you.*

John Budd, Reading

toptips@viz.co.uk

Benson & Hedges
ADAM ANT FAGS

Government Health Warning

SMOKING MAY LEAD TO PULLING A GUN ON SOMEONE IN A PUB AND THEN LOBBING A CAR STARTER MOTOR THROUGH THE WINDOW.

6mg Tar 0.5mg Nicotine 4mg Sex Music for Ant People

Have YOUR Say!

News that the Raelian Sect cloned two human beings over Christmas has set alarm bells ringing, not only in the scientific world, but in the wider community. Is it right that identical SADDAM HUSSEINS should be manufactured in their millions, or are we interfering with the balance of nature? We went on the street to find out your views...

NIGHTMARE VISION OF THE FUTURE: Would you like to live in a world like this?

...NOW THAT it is possible to produce babies by cloning, people will no longer have any motivation to have sexual intercourse. As the owner of a sex shop, I fear for my livelihood.

Sven Borgsdotir,
Shopkeeper

...THIS KIND of meddling with nature is very reminiscent of how the Nazis used to behave. Before we go any further down that road, I think we should round up both of these clones and gas them.

Beryl Harpie,
Housewife

...GOD MADE man and woman to propagate the species together. As a Christian, I find it deeply offensive that a woman should give birth to a child without having sex. That it should happen at Christmas time makes it doubly offensive.

Hazel Nutmonkbottle,
Secretary

...PEOPLE SAY that in the wrong hands, this technology could be used to create another Saddam Hussein. Frankly, I'm more worried about the prospect of there being two Ainsley Harriots in the world.

Francis Necromancer,
Builder

...THE SCIENCE of cloning has potential applications in the production of human body parts in the laboratory. I for one look forward to a world where dialysis machines are a thing of the past, and every man has Kylie's arse in a box under the bed.

John Sperm,
Postman

...CHANNEL 4 bosses should embrace cloning technology with open arms. In a few years time they could have enough Graham Nortons to achieve their aim of having him on TV 24 hours a day.

Rock Brazilliano,
Pirate

...ALTHOUGH it would now be technically possible to clone Saddam Hussein, I don't think we should panic. Scientists would first have to find a woman with a fanny big enough to give birth to a 16 stone man in full military uniform.

Frank Ladders,
Traffic Warden

...FOR YEARS I've been trying to suck myself off, but all I've got for my troubles is a bad back. I wonder, if I cloned myself, and I got the clone to suck me off, would it make me a pinch of snuff? If not, would it be okay for it to fuck me up the arse?

John Brown,
Publisher

...ONCE AGAIN, boffins go headlong into a project without thinking through the implications. What if, during the cloning process, a fly got into the test tube and got its D 'n' A mixed up with that of the clone? The resulting baby would be born with six wiggling legs and compound eyes that looked like tea strainers.

Hector Pozidrive,
Librarian

...MANY PEOPLE fear that clones may not live as long as the rest of us, but Dolly the sheep has proved that this is not the case. She's now seven years old, while the sheep on my farm never make it past six months.

George Tawdry,
Lamb Farmer

...IN ALL this talk about clones, people seem to be forgetting about the clones themselves. As children, they will almost certainly be picked on at school, what with their eerie, monotone voices and stiff, robotic movements.

Elmer Glutton,
Lollipop Man

...PEOPLE ARE worried about cloning upsetting the balance of nature, but this could easily be guarded against. Legislation could be put in place so that every time a scientist clones a tall, blue-eyed superman, he also has to make a clone of Jono Coleman.

Bertrand Tartrazine,
Horse Dentist

Paul Palmer

Mrs BRADY OLD LADY

MAJOR MISUNDERSTANDING

Third time lucky for Burton and Taylor

The world of show business is staring into its coffee and feeling slightly nauseous after the shock revelation that double Oscar-winning Dame, Dame Elizabeth Taylor is to exhume and remarry the late Richard Burton.

By our Gossip Columnist
Fanny Batter
in Hollywood

Hell-raising stage and screen actor Burton passed away in August 1984 and is currently interred at Celigny, Switzerland. Ex-wife Taylor now resides in Hollywood where she has suffered a string of serious health problems after which, she recently claimed, she was "feeling closer to dear Richard than ever before".

Cleaopatra

The tempestuous couple first married in 1964, not long after meeting on the set of long-winded epic Cleopatra. They divorced 10 and 12 years later, after a rocky relationship that had them dubbed the Amanda Holden & Les Dennis of their era. The pair went on to amass a staggering collection of approximately twenty discarded spouses between them, never managing to rediscover the magic they had once had with each other with anyone else.

needle

Former siren Taylor made her first cinematic impact playing Mickey Rooney in the 1944 movie National Velvet, and went on to appear in over two decent films. Readers of The Cock Snot Gazette voted her icon of the decade in 1959.

Sources close to Dame Elizabeth claim that she has been bored since she retired from acting in March this year after more than 60 years on screen, and has clearly felt the need for male companionship.

She is known to have been allegedly wooing the deceased Welshman for some months, sending him gifts of chocolates, flowers and 50-litre barrels of Scotch.

smack

Yank gossip columnists are greeting the news of the impending nuptials with cautious optimism; an article in the LA Enquirer suggested that the two celebrities would have learned from their past romances and that they would be determined not to rush into anything.

However, Burton's widow Sally said last week: "I'm not really sure if it's what he would have wanted, and I certainly wouldn't advise sexual relations in his condition."

The Eight Wives of Elizabeth the Taylor

Husband	Wed	Outcome
1 Conrad Hilton Jr	1950-51	Annulled
2 Michael Wilding	1952-57	Beheaded
3 Michael Todd	1957-58	Died in childbirth
4 Eddie Fisher	1959-64	Divorced
5 Richard Burton	1964-74	Went on loan to Manchester City
6 Richard Burton	1975-76	Retired
7 John W. Warner	1976-82	Beheaded
8 Larry Fortensky	1991-96	Survives her

GILBERT RATCHET
COO!
LOOKS LIKE THE LORD MAYOR OF FULCHESTER HAS INJURED HIS ARM

I'VE GOT REPETITIVE STRAIN INJURY FROM TAKING BACKHANDERS OFF LOCAL BUSINESSMEN, GILBERT
HOW CAN I FULFILL MY OFFICE AS MAYOR NOW THAT MY BRIBE-TAKING HAND IS OUT OF ACTION?

NOT TO WORRY MR MAYOR
MY CORRUPT-MAYOR-O-MATIC AUTOMATICALLY DISPENSES RUBBER-STAMPED PLANNING APPLICATIONS IN EXCHANGE FOR WADS OF CASH.

I'D LIKE PLANNING PERMISSION TO PUT UP A RADIO MAST, PLEASE
BLEEP THAT'LL COST YOU FIVE GRAND
I'LL LEAVE YOU IN CHARGE OF THE MACHINE, GILBERT. HERE'S A THOUSAND QUID FOR YOUR TROUBLE.

HOORAY! I'VE GOT THE GO-AHEAD TO BULLDOZE A SCHOOL FULL OF CHILDREN AND BUILD AN ASBESTOS SUPERMARKET IN ITS PLACE.
THINK I'LL CELEBRATE WITH SOME CHAMPAGNE

WOW!
TINKLE
POP
THAT FAT-CAT BUSINESSMAN HAS FIRED HIS CHAMPAGNE CORK INTO THE MAYOR-O-MATIC

BLEEP I HEREBY DECLARE THIS VICARAGE FÊTE OPEN
CRACKLE
UH-OH! THE MACHINE IS MALFUNCTIONING

WHAT A FRAUD! WE'VE JUST PAID YOUR MACHINE SEVEN GRAND FOR A PFI HOSPITALS CONTRACT, AND ITS AWARDED US FIRST PRIZE IN FULCHESTER'S BONNIEST BABY CONTEST!
1ST PRIZE BONNIEST BABY
IT'S A RIP-OFF!
WE'RE CALLING THE POLICE

AND SHORTLY
DEFRAUDING LOCAL BUSINESSMEN IS A SERIOUS OFFENCE, YOUNG MAN
YOU COULD GO TO PRISON FOR THIS...

..UNLESS YOU'D CARE TO BUY A TICKET TO THE POLICEMAN'S BALL FROM THIS BENT-COPPER-O-TRON I'VE INVENTED
BLEEP MIND HOW YOU GO, SIR
THE PRICE IS ONE THOUSAND POUNDS
BAH!

THE ADVENTURES OF RADIOHEAD
COLIN
JONNY
PHIL
ED
THOM
CHART-TOPPING POP BAND RADIOHEAD WERE STAYING AT THEIR MOUSE FARM, DEEP IN THE HEART OF THE DEVON COUNTRYSIDE

THE LADS WERE OUT IN THE PADDOCK, TENDING TO THEIR FURRY RODENT HERD
PHEW! THIS CHEESE SMELLS PRETTY RIPE, THOM!
CHEESE
HA HA! YES JONNY. THAT'S JUST HOW THE MICE LIKE IT!

SUDDENLY PHIL UTTERED A CRY
THOM, LOOK — IT'S COLDPLAY! THEY'RE SKULKING BY THE PERIMETER FENCE!
WHAT DO THEY WANT HERE?

WITH A SNEER, COLDPLAY EMPTIED A WRIGGLING SACK INTO THE MOUSE PADDOCK
RECKON THIS FELLOW WOULD LIKE TO GET HIS TEETH INTO YOUR MOUSE FARM, RADIOHEAD! HA HA!
A BIG SNAKE! IT'LL EAT ALL OUR MICE!
WE'LL BE RUINED!

THEN ED HAD A BRAINWAVE
WAIT A MINUTE — SNAKES CAN BE 'CHARMED' BY MUSIC, CAN'T THEY?
WHAT ARE WE WAITING FOR? LET'S GET OUR INSTRUMENTS OUT OF THE FARMHOUSE!

SOON RADIOHEAD WERE PLAYING A SELECTION OF THEIR HIT SONGS TO THE SCALY REPTILE
IT'S WORKING GUYS — THE SNAKE HAS GONE INTO A HYPNOTIC TRANCE

CATCHING THE DROWSY SNAKE OFF GUARD, COLIN FLICKED IT OUT OF THE PADDOCK WITH HIS GUITAR
'FANGS' FOR THE PRESENT, COLDPLAY — BUT YOU CAN HAVE IT BACK NOW
WAH! LOOK OUT!

WELL, THAT WAS A NARROW SQUEAK FOR OUR MOUSE FARM — EH THOM?
IT 'SERPENTLY' WAS, JONNY!
BUT I THINK COLDPLAY HAVE 'ADDER' ENOUGH OF PESTERING US FOR A WHILE!
HA HA HA HA!

TWO HOURS LATER...

...IF YOU HAVE SCRATCHED OFF THREE BELLS, THEN CONGRATULATIONS! ...YOU HAVE WON A TRIP TO FRANCE! (travel expenses not covered)

...IF YOU HAVE SCRATCHED OFF THREE LEMONS, THE-EEE-N CONGRATULATIONS! ...YOU HAVE WON A SHARE IN A DRAW TO WIN A TAPE DECK...

...IF YOU HAVE SCRATCHED OFF THREE CHERRIES, THEN

FOUR HOURS LATER THAN THAT...

...IF YOU HAVE SCRATCHED OFF SEVEN DWARFS, THREE BEARS, SANTA CLAUSE AND A TOOTH FAIRY THEN CONGRATULATIONS! ...YOU HAVE WON OUR £10,000 JACKPOT!

BOLLOCKS!

...AND IF YOU HAVE SCRATCHED OFF THREE POUND SIGNS THEN, WAIT FOR IT... WAIT FOR IT... WAIT FOR IT... STAY ON THE LINE A LITTLE LONGER... IF YOU HAVE SCRATCHED THREE POUNDS, THEN, BIG FUCKING DEAL! YOU'VE WON SOME FUCKING SHITTY PLASTIC NECKLACE OR SOMETHING, NOW, PISS OFF!

BASTARD! THAT'S THE SEVENTY THORD PLACCY NECKLACE I'VE WON THIS WEEK.

STILL, A COUPLE MORE AND THATS ALL ME BAIRNS' CHRISTMAS PRESENTS SORTED

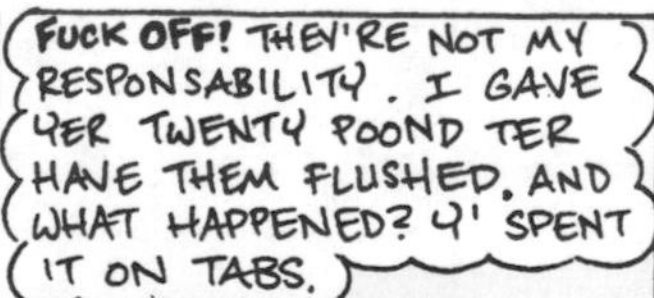

OH NO!! IT'S THE
PATHETIC SHARKS

"IT'S A NIGHTMARE HOLIDAY FROM HELL" SHOW ONE, SCENE ONE - ACTION!

SO WOULD YOU SAY THIS HOLIDAY IN BARBADOS ISN'T WHAT YOU EXPECTED?
RIGHT FROM THE START IT'S JUST BEEN A NIGHTMARE.
JUST A NIGHTMARE.
COULDN'T SMOKE ON THE FLIGHT... KIDS HAD NOWHERE TO PLAY ON THE PLANE. NOT A CHILD-FRIENDLY AIRLINE AT ALL!

WE GOT TO THE HOTEL, PENTHOUSE SUITE WITH A SEA VIEW, BUT THE TIDE WAS OUT!
THEY SAID IT WOULD BE BACK LATER LIKE BUT THAT AIN'T IT IS IT?
HOLD IT! CUT!

IT'S JUST NOT NIGHTMARE ENOUGH. LOOK, THERE'S SHARKS IN THE SEA. THIS COULD ADD SOME HUMAN DRAMA TO THE SHOW!
MUMMY! DON' WANNA MEET SHARKS!
YEAH? WHATEVER SUITS.
S'ALRIGHT POPPET. YOU'RE INSURED.

DUUUMM-DA.
DUUUMM-DA.
DUMDUMDUMDUM DUMDUMDUMDUM DUMDUMDUMDUM DUMDUMDUMDUM
DADDLADAA DADDLADAA...

SHARRRKS!
MY BABIES! IT'S A NIGHTMARE!

YES, WE KNOW WHAT WE ARE, THANK YOU VERY MUCH!
IT'S RUDE TO POINT.
IS THERE A LOO AROUND HERE? I'M DYING TO GO.
OOH. YOU'RE A SLAVE TO YOUR BLADDER, JUSTIN!

CUT! THESE SHARKS AREN'T SCARY. IN FACT THEY'RE CRAP!
AND SOMEWHAT CAMP TOO I EXPECT.

WE'RE NOT CAMP. WE'RE JUST WELL BRED.
STEADY NOW, RUPERT! REMEMBER YOUR BLOOD PRESSURE.

LISTEN. HELP US WITH OUR DOCUMENTARY AND I'LL FEED YOU ENOUGH SMALL MAMMALS FOR A FORTNIGHT.
URRGH! I'D RATHER HAVE A CROISSANT IF YOU DON'T MIND.
AND A NICE MILKSHAKE PLEASE.
NOT FOR ME! I HEARD THEY PUT CHICKEN FAT IN MILKSHAKES TO THICKEN IT UP!
WELL, THAT'S ME OUT THEN BECAUSE I'M A VEGETARIAN.

LOOK, - WILL YOU HELP OUT OR NOT?
THERE'S NO NEED TO SHOUT. SHARKS AREN'T DEAF Y'KNOW!
OR ARE WE? I CAN'T REMEMBER.

ALL YOU HAVE TO DO IS PRETEND TO TERRORISE THAT FAMILY. IT'LL MAKE GREAT TV!
OH ALRIGHT THEN.

REMEMBER, YOU'RE SHARKS! I WANT YOU TO SCARE THESE FOLKS! I WANT THIS FAMILY AND THE VIEWERS AT HOME TO SHIT THEMSELVES! BE BRUTAL ... BE TRUE TO YOUR NATURE!
ACTION!

HEY YOU! YOU SHOULD WEAR A HAT OR YOU'LL GET SUNSTROKE.
YES, AND A HIGH FACTOR SUN-SCREEN.
FACTOR IS AT LEAST!
AND DON'T DROP LITTER OR YOU'LL GET FINED.
YES, SOME CAT COULD SWALLOW A LOLLY WRAPPER AND CHOKE, SO THINK ON!
CUT! WHAT THE FUCK ARE YOU DOING?

WE'RE BEING SCARY LIKE YOU ASKED US TO BE.
YES, BY POINTING OUT THE DANGERS OF THE BEACH!
YOU'RE AS SCARY AS A FUCKING CHRISTMAS TREE FAIRY!
THERE'S NO NEED FOR THE EFF-WORD. YOU COULD SAY SUGAR INSTEAD.
THAT'S TWICE HE'S USED IT. ONCE AS A NOUN, ONCE AS AN ADJECTIVE. OR WAS IT A VERB?

LOOK! I'VE FOUND A BEACH BALL!
OOH! YOU LOOK JUST LIKE THAT OLD TV SERIES; THE PRISONER WITH PATRICK MACNEE!
IT WASN'T PATRICK MACNEE. HE WAS IN THE AVENGERS WITH DIANA DORS.
I LIKED STINGRAY XL5 THE BEST WITH CAPTAIN JIMMY KRANKIE.

YOU'RE TOTALLY SHIT SHARKS AND YOUR MINDS AREN'T ON THE JOB! FUCK OFF BACK TO THE SEA WHERE YOU CAME FROM!
WE'RE NOT STAYING WHERE WE'RE NOT WANTED!
THE EFF WORD! AGAIN!
I THINK IT WAS USED AS A NOUN THAT TIME.

WHAT A WASTED DAY!
WELL, WE COULD ALWAYS EDIT SOME BITS OF THE SHARKS WITH SOMETHING ELSE TO MAKE IT REALLY SCARY! REMEMBER, THIS IS BARBADOS...

AAGHH! SHARKS!
IT'S A NIGHTMARE!!

THANKS MRS. BLAIR. THE VIEWERS WILL BE CRAPPING IT.

DREAM CHE

Dree-ee-ee-ee-eam, dream dream dree-eam, dree-ee-ee-ee-eam, dream, dream dream. So sang the Everley Brothers in their song All I Have to Do (Is Dream).

But what are dreams, when do we have them and what exactly do they mean?

Psychologists believe that dreams are a sort of safety valve for our brains. They allow us to explore our deepest fears and desires whilst we're safely tucked up in bed at night. Scientists have proved that if we were unable to dream, we would go mental. In experiments snails were prevented from dreaming using paperclips and a 9-volt battery. They quickly lost their grip on reality and descended into depression before eventually shrivelling up, going hard and catching fire.

"Savoury snack produces sweetest dreams" ~*say scientists*

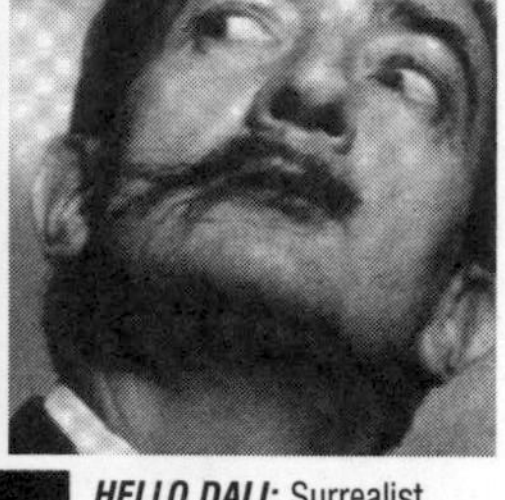

HELLO DALI: Surrealist Salvador painted dreams fuelled by cheese on toast nightcap.

Say Cheese

For hundreds of years it has been known that the best way to ensure a good night's dreaming is to eat some cheese just before bedtime. And today, thanks to the huge range of cheeses from around the world available at our supermarkets, this is truer than ever.

Here, poor man's Raj Persaud psychologist *OLIVER JAMES* and his Naked Chef palindrome reverse namesake *JAMIE OLIVER* team up to look at a variety of cheeses and analyse the sort of dreams they produce.

Gouda....................................

Gouda is a medium fat hard cheese from the North of Holland. It doesn't cook particularly well, but slices beautifully and is the ideal accompaniment for dry crackers or a tasty bit of fruit. This versatile and tasty cheese rightfully deserves its place as the most popular of the Dutch breakfast cheeses.

Holland is a country notorious for its relaxed attitute to windmills, hardcore sex, and cheese. Thanks to its hardness and this Dutch heritage, dreams after eating Gouda will almost certainly be of an explicit sexual nature. But be careful how much you eat before bed. Too much gouda could make you lose all inhibitions, and you could end up dreaming about getting up to things you wouldn't do in your wildest dreams!

Kraft Philadelphia......................

This is a very light, soft, spreadable cheese which is handy when you've got to make quick sandwiches for the kids, and is great on a Ritz cracker for a tasty snack in front of the telly. It's also useful in the kitchen for knocking up souffles and delicious cheese sauces.

Eating such a lightweight cheese as this at bedtime will usually lead to dreams about flying. Soaring above the landscape can be very exhilarating, but there is a risk. If you fall from a great height in your dream and you don't wake up before you hit the ground, you may die in real life. Consequently it's a good idea to eat a piece of dense cheese such as cheddar or haloumi to keep your altitude down to a safe level.

Camembert................................

Camembert is a soft, runny cheese with a distinctive flavour which gets stronger as it matures. One of the most popular French rinded cheeses, it's an essential part of any respectable cheeseboard. It should be served at room temperature, and is equally delicious with biscuits or served as an accompaniment to grapes or figs.

As it is a runny cheese, camembert causes dreams about running. If you eat this cheese you will have nightmares where you are running through the woods, chased by packs of wild bears or ravenously hungry wolves. It will be like running through treacle and no matter how fast you run, you will not be able to get away from your pursuers. You may even wake up to find that you have wet the bed with fear. Indeed, the word 'camembert' sounds like it could well mean 'the bears are coming' in French.

SE!

This wonderful dream cottage worth £300,000 could be yours to own... IN YOUR DREAMS!

From time to time everyone dreams of living in their own dream cottage in the country. With its picturesque thatched roof, roses round the door and a garden full of hollyhocks and foxgloves OUR £300,000 dream cottage is everyone's idea of a picture perfect place to live.

Your chance to win a DREAM COTTAGE!

Now we're offering one lucky reader the chance to dream about it *EVERY NIGHT* for the *REST OF THEIR LIFE* in our fantastic celebrity cheese competition. The winner of this fabulous contest will receive a lifetime's supply of *COTTAGE CHEESE,* one spoonful of which at bedtime will ensure a whole night dreaming about the dream cottage of their dreams.

To enter, simply use your skill and judgement to match up the 5 celebrities below with their favourite cheeses. Then send your entry to ***Viz Dream Cottage Draw, PO Box 1PT, Newcastle upon Tyne NE99 1PT*** before November 1st 2008. The lucky winner drawn out of our hat in 5 years' time will receive a single 150g tub of Tesco "value" cottage cheese every week until they die or ask us to stop sending them cottage cheese through the post.

1: Clint Eastwood: *What cheese makes his day?*

2: Paul Daniels: *He likes which cheese, but not a lot?*

3: Tommy Cooper: *He "just like that" sort of cheese.*

4: Cerys Matthews out of Catatonia: *Which cheese on her rarebit?*

5: Arnie Schwarzenegger: *He'll be back, but what cheese for?*

~~20~~ 7 things you never knew about DREAMS & CHEESE

1 A small piece of Wensleydale costing just 5 cents was responsible for the most influential dream of modern times. Civil rights leader Martin Luther King ate the savoury noggin on a ryvita just before turning in on 27th August 1963. "I'd never really thought about civil rights before eating that cheese," he said. "But that night I had a dream where children grew up in a world in which people weren't judged by the colour of their skin." 40 years later Dr King's dream has come true and our children now grow up in a world where racial hatred is a thing of the past and all people live together in harmony. And it's all thanks to a nickel's worth of crumbly cheese.

2 The most holes ever in a piece of cheese was 2348, in a 2lb piece of Jarlsberg produced at the Magnusson dairy, Stavanger on 4th September 1974. According to witnesses, there were so many holes and they were so close together that there wasn't any cheese there...just the rind!

3 Amazingly, you don't have to be fast asleep to have a dream. A 'daydream' is a sort of twisted sex fantasy experienced by schoolboys, commuters and bored office workers.

4 Nobody thought about the meaning of dreams until beardy Austrian psychoanalyst Sigmund Freud decided to interpret them at the turn of the century. His dirty ideas outraged polite society and his family was ostracised. Even 70 years later his grandson Clement Freud was reduced to selling dogfood on commercial television.

5 Wet dreams aren't, as you might imagine, dreams about swimming. They are nocturnal emissions of semen experienced by 13-year-old schoolboys, popes and 63-year-old Peter Pans of pop.

6 Wet Wet Wet dreams aren't, as you might imagine, three dreams about swimming. Neither are they three nocturnal emissions of semen in a row. They are actually dreams about an 80s pop group fronted by a grinning heroin addict.

7 "I like it! I like it!" So sang 60s Merseybeat combo Freddie and the Dreamers. But ironically lead singer Freddie Garrity didn't like cheese! "I can't stand the stuff," the star told us from his 75 pence a night bed at the Birkenhead Salvation Army Men's Palace.

Hypochondriac chuckles with

SHERIDAN POORLY

AYE-AYE, REG. YOU'RE LOOKING WELL...

EEH! YOU WOULDN'T WANT THE WEEK I'VE JUST 'AD!

BEEP! BEEP! BEEP! BEEP! BEEP!

In Britain, a telephone call centre operative is paid an average of £7.23 per hour.

In India, a person doing exactly the same job gets £9 per *month.*

That's why our call centres are in Bombay and Calcutta.

At HSBC, we never underestimate the importance of local knowledge

I want to talk to you about planning for the future...

Black Frank Windsor, Scourge of the Seven Seas

I want to talk to you scurvy dogs about plannin' for the future.

We don't like to think about when we might get the black spot, but won't it make 'ee feel a little more at ease to know everything's taken care of? That'd certainly make me swing easier in my hammock at night.

For as little as two pieces of eight a day, you can buy yourself peace of mind. That's all your final expenses covered for slightly less than the price of a dockside slattern.

And whoever you want to leave your fortune to, we'll make sure your wishes are taken care of. Whether the loot goes to your crew, your parrot, or the cabin boy, we'll draw up fully accurate maps covered in skeletons which will lead them to your buried treasure after ye be gone.

And if you apply today, we'll send you this beautiful carriage clock absolutely free.

08999 546 546

ADMIRAL BENBOW PIRATECOVER

So don't put off making your plans for Davey Jones' locker. Call our number now for a free no-pressgang quote. You won't regret it.

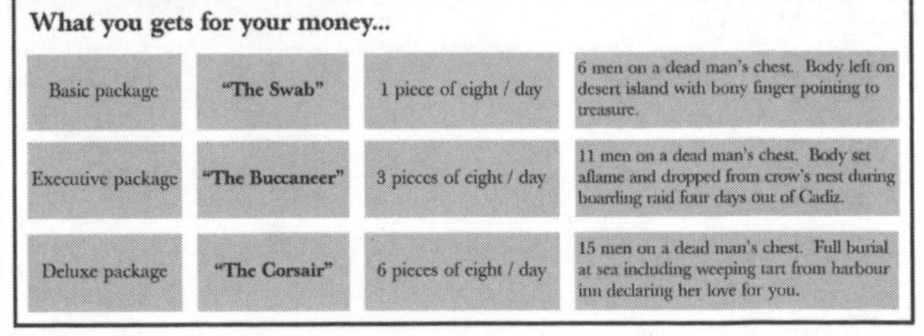

What you gets for your money...

Basic package	"The Swab"	1 piece of eight / day	6 men on a dead man's chest. Body left on desert island with bony finger pointing to treasure.
Executive package	"The Buccaneer"	3 pieces of eight / day	11 men on a dead man's chest. Body set aflame and dropped from crow's nest during boarding raid four days out of Cadiz.
Deluxe package	"The Corsair"	6 pieces of eight / day	15 men on a dead man's chest. Full burial at sea including weeping tart from harbour inn declaring her love for you.

Registered member of the British Association of Pirate Insurance Brokers. And don't ee listen to that son of a shark Christopher Timothy who be hawking his wares round these parts. If I catch him I'll slit him from chin to gizzard.

2 HOURS LATER...
IT'S HALF THREE GRASSY. ARE YOU COMING HOME? IT'S CHUCKLEVISION TONIGHT.
HOME!? HOME!? I CAN NEVER GO HOME!! I KNOW TOO MUCH!
WHAT?
I'VE WORKED IT ALL OUT!

THE SEMOLINA PUDDING I USUALLY EAT AT LUNCHTIMES COMES IN PACKS OF TWO, RIGHT?
ERM... I SUPPOSE SO...

YOU STILL DON'T GET IT, DO YOU? IT'S STARING YOU IN THE FACE! "TUPAC" SHAKUR FAKED HIS OWN MURDER, LIKE JFK, MARILYN MONROE AND THE LINDBERGH BABY, AND INFILTRATED THE GROCER'S IN LUTON TO WARN ME THAT THE CIA HAD ME IN THE FRAME TO BE THE FALLGUY IN THE ANNAN ASSASSINATION!

WELL, THEY'VE PICKED THE WRONG PATSY THIS TIME. WHEN ANNAN STOPS THAT BULLET TOMORROW, I'M GOING TO BE SAFELY IN DETENTION, WHERE THE MILITARY-INDUSTRIAL COMPLEX CAN'T PUT THE FINGER ON ME.

SO...
NO FOOTBALL ON THE SCHOOL FIELD.

HEY! YOU!
ACE! IT'S THE CARETAKER!

ARE YOU PLAYING FOOTBALL ON THE GRASS?
YES! AND LOOK. I'VE GOT MY TOP BUTTON UNDONE... AND I'M WEARING MY INDOOR SHOES.

RIGHT. STRAIGHT TO THE HEADMASTER WITH YOU. IT'LL BE A DETENTION FOR SURE.
GREAT! I'LL TELL HIM EVERYTHING I KNOW, RIGHT FROM THE TOP!

I'M GOING TO NAME NAMES AND BLOW THIS WHOLE SINISTER GLOBAL CONSPIRACY WIDE OPEN! THEY'LL WISH THEY'D NEVER...

BANG!
..GAGH!

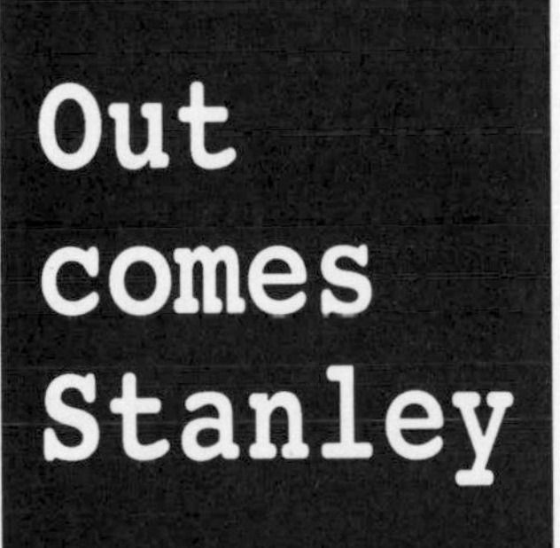
Out comes Stanley

Shops and shopping.
SIMS HARDWARE

Right, so that's a big pack o' tacks, two gross screws, and a box of nubbins.
CLOSE

£8.76.
£8.76!? For these bits?
I'll give you four!

Look mate, I only work here. I can't haggle the odds.
If the till says £8.76 then it's £8.76.
KLIK

- two, three, four!
Hee hee! Grand doing business with you sonny!

FISH MONGERS
Nice bit of halibut for me tea I think...

H MONGERS FRESH FISH DAILY
OPEN

Cheeky beggar!
£10 a pound?
I said, I'm not paying that!

KEEP BRITA TIDY

Hi there laddie! Just you get yourself back here and put that rubbish in the bin!
Squat on this Gramps.

There, see?
That didn't kill you did it?
Gurgle...

Letterbocks

Letterbocks
Viz Comic
P.O.Box 1PT
Newcastle NE99 1PT

STAR LETTER

I SENT an e-mail to you a few days ago explaining the meaning of 'Plumpkian'. After a bit of investigation, I have just found out that the word is 'Blumpkin'. Sorry for any inconvenience.

Tim, e-mail

Plumb Crazy

I RECENTLY had a burst pipe, and was flicking through the Yellow Pages when I noticed an ad for the snappily named 0.0.0.0.0.0.0.0.0.0.0.1.1.1.A Aqueous plumbers. Has anyone spotted a more contrived and desperate attempt to be first in the phonebook?

A Collier
Newcastle

PS. It didn't even work, as the typesetter with a sense of humour stuck it under O rather than under zero.

Pollen Off

THANK God for the hay fever season. Now my mother will think that all the tissues in my bin are from sneezing rather than spirited masturbation as she usually does.

Nadrew Glassberg,
South Woodford

IF I had my way, Channel 5 weather girl Lara Lewington's front would definitely be occluded with a torrent of cumulus. Or something.

John Wigton
e-mail

EARLIER this year, I downloaded Bob Dylan's 'Blonde on Blonde' album off the internet. I have recently discovered that I have infringed international copyright and unknowingly performed an illegal act. I was wondering if any of your readers know Bob Dylan's personal banking details, account number, sort code, etc, as I wish to make a deposit of thirteen pounds, the retail cost of the album. I have contacted his record company on numerous occasions but have found the staff rude and unhelpful.

Kym Sansovini
e-mail

IMAGINE my surprise when my birthday surprise was a copy of 'Imagine' by John Lennon.

Russ Petcher
e-mail

In this space age you can electromail your letters and tips to letters@viz.co.uk

I THINK the funniest joke I have ever heard was the one where the man shit in the cowboy hat. Class.

Jeff Rogers
e-mail

**What's your favourite joke? Don't send the whole joke, just a brief resume of the plot. We'll print a selection of what sound like they should be the funniest in the next annual.*

Bone Idol

MY MISSUS loves Gareth Gates and this calendar she bought from Woolworths took pride of place in the dining room until we noticed just how pleased he was to have his picture taken. Maybe he should have a cold shower before photo shoots in future.

Andy and Terri,
Surrey

His Mumba's Up

I WAS very amused to read Paul Evan's (page 50) letter about the order in which he would do Samamtha Mumba (arse, gob, arse. If he had any left, arse again.) After consulting with my solicitors I would like to advise that this is the order in which I would do him: House, pension, the secret bank account he thinks I don't know about. If he's got any left, I'll have that too.

Mrs Evans
e-mail

I AM dismayed at the way the once gorgeous Phillipa Forrester has let herself go. At one time you would have gladly eaten your dinner off her minge. These days, however, she'd probably beat you to it.

Andy Dewhurst
e-mail

Lend a Hand

IT OCCURED to me that fundamentalist cleric Abu Hamza may be unable to masturbate due to his hook handedness. This would cause him a large amount of frustration, which may explain his fanatical outlook on life. As a working prostitute I normally charge £20 for hand relief, but as a service to the nation I am willing to give Mr Hamza this service at a special rate of £15.

Dawn Knight
Manchester

THE BBC reports that Saddam Hussein had a $25million bounty on his head. You'd think that with a bar of chocolate that size on his swede they would have spotted the cunt a bit quicker.

Pete, Rob and John
e-mail

Invitro Veritas

CONGRATULATIONS to Dr Patrick Steptoe on the 25th anniversary of the birth of the world's first test tube baby. However, I can't help but notice that she's now a bit of an old minger. Come on, docs, have a look at Angelina Jolie or Halle Berry, and try to spot where you're going wrong.

Raymond Dunthorne
St Albans

I'VE JUST learned that you cannot make someone love you. All you can do is stalk them and hope they panic and give in.

M Clitorina
Hull

UPON moving to Canada last year, I was shocked to find that their fag packets are covered in pictures of discoloured teeth and unsightly lung cancers. Haven't these people heard of Saatchi & Saatchi? Even I know that pictures of puppies or fit birds would sell more tabs.

Dave Lucas
Nova Scotia

Sweet Memories

I'LL NEVER forget the day my grandfather gave me my first Werther's Original. I remember well being whisked upside down by my dad, and the hearty cheer that went up after several smacks on the back finally dislodged the leathal little fucker from my windpipe.

Jed Wokkit
Armistit

COULD you please forward this to Cyril Fletcher twenty years ago? Thanks

Cheeseworm
The Black Country

16. Prawn Crackers........

SOUPS

17. Crap Meat and Sweet Corn Soup........
18. Won Ton Soup........
19. Hot and Sour Soup........

IF, as Jodie Marsh says, Jordan's breasts aren't real, then I must have just dreamt that she's got beautiful big tits. Have any readers had the same dream?

Stuart Robertson,
Blackburn

FATE IS indeed a cruel mistress. Had Davros, the leader of the Daleks been born with a Dalek top half and a human bottom half, at least he could have had a wank. Maybe that was the source of angst that in later

LAUGH WITH "It is the way I am telling them" G. RAVISHANKAR

The funny fellow with English as his second language

I would like to frankly share my funny personal experience.

When I was walking on the road, a drunkard person asked me, "What is the time?".

I told him, "It is 9:00pm".

The crazy drunkard person laughed at me.

"Your watch is too slow. See, having drunk lots of liquor, my watch is fast. It is now midnight."

I said to myself, "The crazy fellow must have too much alcohol to forget the real world!"

That one was a cracker. More laughs next time!

life drove his desire to conquer the universe.

Dave Anfield, Reading

THERE'S never been a better time to visit your Ford dealership' said an advert I watched last night. Imagine my dismay when I rushed down at 1am on Sunday morning only to find them closed. Have any other readers been duped by misleading adverts?

Otis Goldsmith
Northampton

THE authorities would have us believe that the Nazi menace was over in 1945, but only last week, our newsagent told my 10 year old son that his papers were not in order. We must all be vigilant.

NL Sedated,
York

IN ORDER to impress on a 1st date, I took a lady friend out for a drink and a curry. Back at my place, a two-in-a-bed romp ensued. In the morning, I slipped out of bed to evacuate an enormous fart that had brewed up. To muffle the sound I used her dress. The fart was a controlled blockbuster, but as I went to replace her dress I discovered that I had followed through badly. Can you recommend a good Indian restaurant whose food will not have this effect on my bowels? Also, do you have a lonely hearts section?

Name and address withheld.

LAST WEEK I couldn't find my favourite pen. I searched all over the house but I couldn't find it anywhere and eventually I gave up. yesterday whilst looking for my glasses, I found the pen. perhaps the Americans should take a leaf out of my book and start searching for Saddam Hussain's bicycle clips. Sod's law will surely take effect and they're bound to find his weapons of mass destruction.

Phil O'Mara
e-mail

Dutch Crap

I HAVE just come back from Amsterdam. I was in a pub full of Holland people and it sounded like a Stanley Unwin convention. When will they learn to speaken correction?

Big Jugs
Hull

FOLLOWING the death of Ayrton Senna, Murray Walker said that he would be horrified if he thought that F1 viewers watched the races just to see the crashes. This being the case, all viewers of ITV's F1 coverage should close their eyes during the opening titles of the show which feature an end-to-end montage of the most exciting pile-ups of the previous season.

Michael Curry,
Whitley Bay

TOP TIPS

toptips@viz.co.uk

PENSIONERS. *Get to the bus stop 30 mins before your bus pass starts. That way you can spent half an hour whingeing that the driver wouldn't let you on the bus. You will especially enjoy this if the driver is black.*

Simon Drugs, Walsall

MAKERS *of Anchor Spreadable Butter. Save time and printing ink by simply calling it 'Anchor Butter.'*

Richard Daw, Hereford

FELLAS. *Caress your girlfriend's back and arms occasionally to give the impression that you are not just interested in her sexual parts.*

James Broom, Paris

SMOKERS. *If using chewing gum as part of your effort to kick the habit, check that the packet does not say 'Contains a source of phenyalanine. Excessive consumption may produce laxative effects' before chewing your way through three packets in one day.*

Mr Shittypants,
Edinburgh

PEOPLE *who don't like eating breakfast. Sit on your cornflakes until they go numb and, hey presto, it feels like someone else is eating your breakfast.*

Jason Knight, Reading

SAVE *money on expensive CDs by simply cutting circles of cardboard from an empty cornflakes packet and covering them with foil.*

Jamie McKenzie
West Drayton

HOUSEWIVES. *When washing clothes, pop a couple of teabags in the washer instead of soap powder, milk where the fabric conditioner should go and put it on a boil wash. Hey presto, when the clothes are washed you can enjoy a nice cup of tea.*

Adam Smith,
Bradford

SAVE *money on your water bill. Every time you flush the toilet, piss into the cistern. It all goes down the same way and you'll save approximately £1.56 over a lifetime.*

Albert Shortfish
West Midlands

SKY TV *viewers. Avoid repetitive strain injury by holding down the 'prog+' button on your remote control and Sellotaping your finger in place.*

Herman Grout, e-mail

YOUNG *mothers. Calm hysterically crying children in the supermarket by firmly slapping their legs and then tugging them along by the wrist.*

Jamie McKenzie
West Drayton

MOTORISTS. *Park for free in any city centre by smashing the windows, pulling out the radio and attaching a 'Police Aware' sticker to the front windsreen. Long term parkers may wish to burn their vehicles out for greater effect.*

Rob Chingford
e-mail

POTENTIAL *suicidees. Increase your chances by taking more than 10 tablets, locking your front and back doors and not phoning close family friends threatening to 'do something stupid'.*

James Shaw, e-mail

VISITORS *to the Argyll Wildlife Park near Inveraray. Avoid paying the entrance fee by simply walking down the lane at the rear of the establishment. Here, 4 of the 6 animals can clearly be seen.*

Richard Anke, e-mail

FORMULA *one teams. Inject a little excitement into fuel stops by employing 'Carry On' character Alf Ippatitimus as your pit 'lollipop man.'*

Morris Otis
Northumberland

CRAIG *David. Avoid having dog shit smeared all over the bonnet of your Porsche 911 in the Royal Well car park by not saying "My minders will fucking muller you if you bump into me again" to drinkers in Time Nightclub, Cheltenham.*

Brown Hands
Cheltenham

Viz Factz

UNLIKE *monkeys, dogs and teachers, rabbits have never been used in any NASA space programme. That's because the cute, long-eared, shit-eating vermin are the only animals that don't become weightless in space. Scientists believe it may be something to do with the fact that in normal gravitational fields they hop. "It's bunny peculiar", quipped electric-powered Major Morgan-voiced egghead Stephen Hawking. "But it's probably just one of those things."*

OH, LORDY! IT'S...
THE FAT SLAGS

CHRISTMAS EVE, 11·30...
... AN' WHEN SHE UNWRAPPED IT ON CHRISTMAS MORNIN'.. BARP! IT WERE THE BOTTLE OF THAT KNOCKED OFF PERFUME I GOT OFF BIG TED...
XMAS STRIPPER TONITE
HSBC
...AN' I'D GIVE ME MUM THE FUCKIN' JAPANESE LOVE EGGS

REMEMBER THAT, SAN?.. WHEN I GIVE ME MUM THEM JAPANESE LOVE EGGS I GOT YOU, EH?
AYE. SHE'S NEVER GIVE 'EM BACK AN' ALL
HEH! HEH!

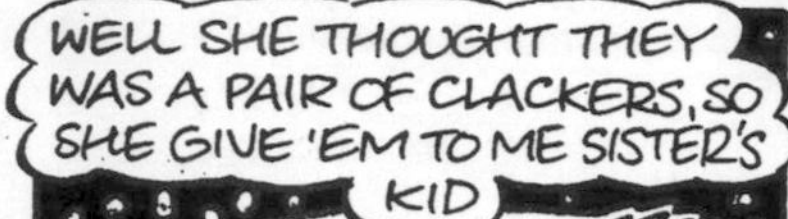
WELL SHE THOUGHT THEY WAS A PAIR OF CLACKERS, SO SHE GIVE 'EM TO ME SISTER'S KID

NA-AA-AA!

ANYROAD, I'D BEST BE OFF. I'VE GOT T' DO ME CHRISTMAS SHOPPIN
EH?
THELMA'S GOT ME A PLAYSTATION 2. SHE'LL GO FUCKIN APESHIT IF I DON'T GET HER A PRESSIE, LIKE

WHAT Y' GOIN' T' GET 'ER THIS TIME O' NIGHT, BAZ? CHRIMBO EVE AN' ALL.
I'LL GO TO THE ALL-NIGHT GARAGE AN' GET HER A BOX OF FERRERO ROCHES

I'D BEST HOPE THEY SELL EM. IT'S THE ONLY CHOCOLATES SHE EATS. SHE MIGHT END UP WI' A FUCKIN' ROAD ATLAS AN' A TIN O' DUCKHAMS
HEY, DON'T GO YET, BAZ

COME BACK TO OURS... I'VE GOT A SPECIAL PRESENT FOR YER
SPECIAL, EH?
WOT IS IT?

DON'T TELL 'IM, RIGHT...BUT I'M GOIN' T' LET 'IM FUCK ME
EH?

WELL...WHAT'S SPECIAL ABOUT THAT? HE FUCKS Y' EVERY NIGHT... EXCEPT DARTS NIGHT
YEAH, BUT THIS TIME IT'S DIFFERENT... I'VE SHAVED ME CLOPPER. SHHHHHH!

EEH! YOU'VE NEVER!
YEAH! HE'S BIN GOIN' ON AT ME FOR AGES T' DO IT...
I'M GOIN' T' WRAP IT UP WHEN WE GET BACK... I CAN'T WAIT T' SEE 'IS FACE WHEN HE OPENS IT

SO...
NOW, I CAN'T STOP LONG, GIRLS... FIVE MINUTES AT THE MOST.
THAT'S PLENTY LONG ENOUGH F' YOU, BAZ... YOU'LL BE ABLE T' SORT YER PRESSIE OUT AN' STILL HAVE TIME T' BOIL YERSELF AN EGG.

SHORTLY...
C'MON SAN... TELL US WOT IT IS
YOU'LL FIND OUT IN A BIT. WE'RE JUST GOIN' T' WRAP IT UP

GIZ A CLUE, THEN... CAN I WEAR IT?
SORT OF
WOULD IT FIT ON ME HEAD?
NO BOTHER

DOES IT SMELL NICE?
NA-AA-AA!
CAN I EAT IT?
NA-AA -AA!

IN THE KITCHEN
RIGHT! 'OW WE GOIN' T' DO THIS, THEN?
DUNNO...
...I HAVEN'T REALLY THOUGHT ABOUT IT

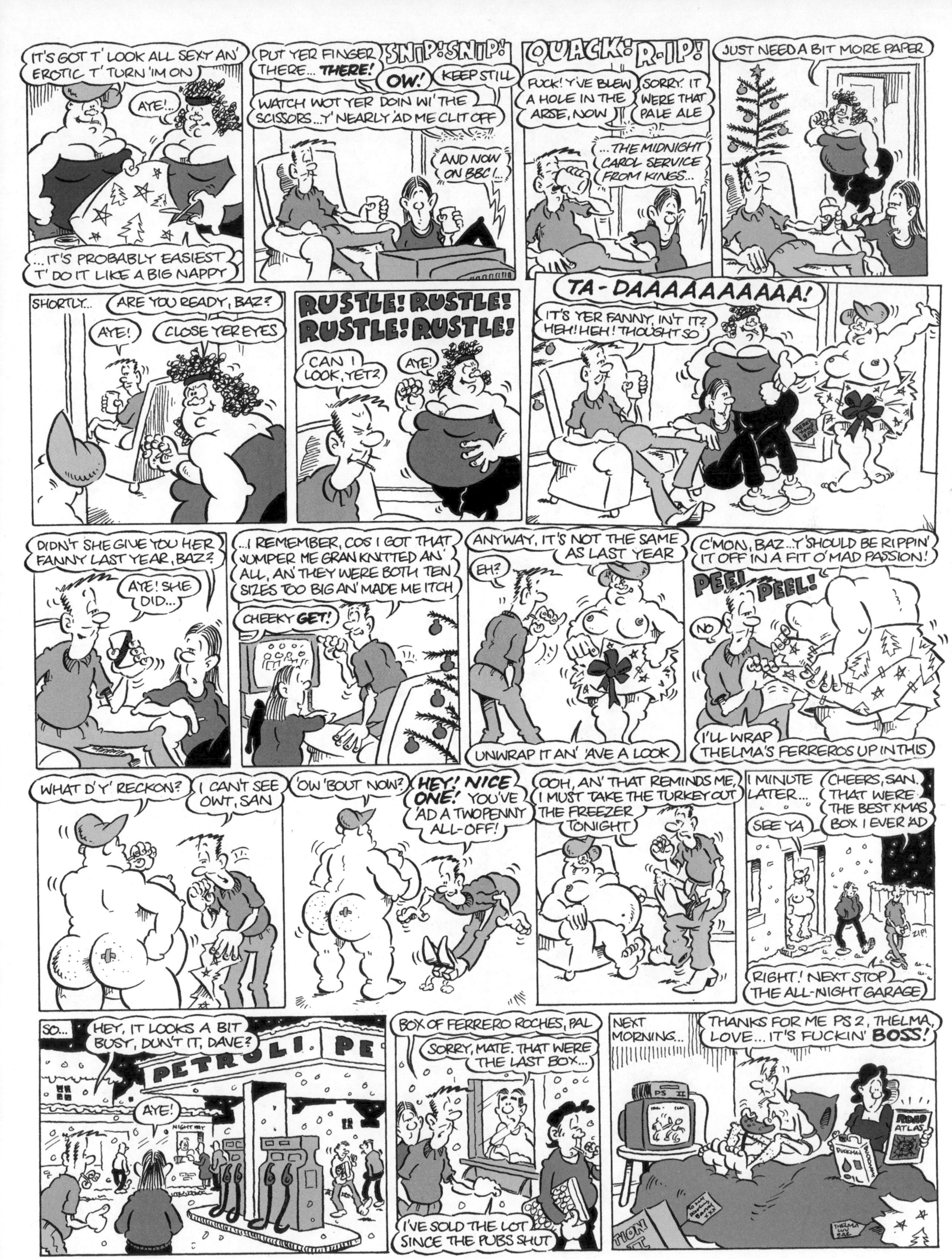
IT'S GOT T' LOOK ALL SEXY AN' EROTIC T' TURN 'IM ON
AYE!...
...IT'S PROBABLY EASIEST T' DO IT LIKE A BIG NAPPY
PUT YER FINGER THERE... THERE!
SNIP! SNIP!
OW!
KEEP STILL
WATCH WOT YER DOIN WI' THE SCISSORS...Y' NEARLY 'AD ME CLIT OFF
AND NOW ON BBC!...
QUACK! R-IP!
FUCK! Y'VE BLEW A HOLE IN THE ARSE, NOW
SORRY. IT WERE THAT PALE ALE
...THE MIDNIGHT CAROL SERVICE FROM KINGS...
JUST NEED A BIT MORE PAPER
SHORTLY...
ARE YOU READY, BAZ?
AYE!
CLOSE YER EYES
RUSTLE! RUSTLE! RUSTLE! RUSTLE!
CAN I LOOK, YET?
AYE!
TA-DAAAAAAAAAA!
IT'S YER FANNY, IN'T IT? HEH! HEH! THOUGHT SO
DIDN'T SHE GIVE YOU HER FANNY LAST YEAR, BAZ?
AYE! SHE DID...
...I REMEMBER, COS I GOT THAT JUMPER ME GRAN KNITTED AN' ALL, AN' THEY WERE BOTH TEN SIZES TOO BIG AN' MADE ME ITCH
CHEEKY GET!
ANYWAY, IT'S NOT THE SAME AS LAST YEAR
EH?
UNWRAP IT AN' 'AVE A LOOK
C'MON, BAZ...Y'SHOULD BE RIPPIN' IT OFF IN A FIT O' MAD PASSION!
PEEL! PEEL!
NO
I'LL WRAP THELMA'S FERREROS UP IN THIS
WHAT D'Y' RECKON?
I CAN'T SEE OWT, SAN
'OW 'BOUT NOW?
HEY! NICE ONE! YOU'VE 'AD A TWOPENNY ALL-OFF!
OOH, AN' THAT REMINDS ME, I MUST TAKE THE TURKEY OUT THE FREEZER TONIGHT
1 MINUTE LATER...
CHEERS, SAN. THAT WERE THE BEST XMAS BOX I EVER 'AD
SEE YA
ZIP!
RIGHT! NEXT STOP THE ALL-NIGHT GARAGE
SO...
HEY, IT LOOKS A BIT BUSY, DUN'T IT, DAVE?
AYE!
PETROL PE
BOX OF FERRERO ROCHES, PAL
SORRY, MATE. THAT WERE THE LAST BOX...
I'VE SOLD THE LOT SINCE THE PUBS SHUT
NEXT MORNING...
THANKS FOR ME PS 2, THELMA, LOVE... IT'S FUCKIN' BOSS!
ROAD ATLAS
OIL

GORDON BLEURGH!

Hot-headed, ginger-headed chef Gordon Ramsay is putting his reputation on the line with his new restaurant venture.

The award-winning martinet has opened the swanky The Courgetterie with a challenge to all customers.

Ramsay

"If you come to my restaurant and you tell me that you're a fucking vegetarian you WILL get eaten," bellowed Ramsay at nervous diners on the opening night of his Edinburgh eatery.

Black-shirted waiting staff applauded and saluted their ex-footballer boss as he led a table of six corduroy-clad schoolteachers from St Andrews to an uncertain fate behind the kitchen doors.

This is not the first time that the foul-mouthed millionaire has courted controversy with his attacks on fussy eaters.

Bobby Moore

In January 1998 Mrs Janet Best complained to the Board of Dining Control when she was forced to eat her lightly poached husband, Enoch, after he had notified the maître d' at Les Cinq Saisons in Aberdeen that he suffered from a nut allergy.

Mrs Best: *Complained after she was forced to eat husband.*

's tackle against Brazil in Mexico '70

The controversial chef remains unapologetic for upsetting his patrons. "If they don't like meat then they can fuck off," he told us from his Glasgow home.

Suck your *OWN COCK* in just *TWO WEEKS?...*

It can't be done!

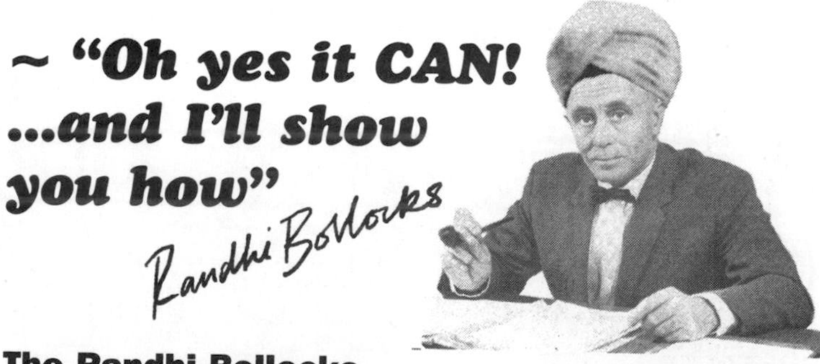

The Randhi Bollocks SCHOOL OF YOGA

Nostradamus in Pyjamas

Jeremy
PAXMAN
THE BRAINBOX OF THE BBC
BIG LONG WORDS
CLEVER THINGS
SMART STUFF

HERE ARE THE QUIZ QUESTIONS FOR YOU TO ASK ON TOMORROW'S 'UNIVERSITY CHALLENGE' MR PAXMAN
STUDIO B.
BBC
LET ME SEE — TCHOH! LOOK AT THIS

"WHICH POP GROUP REACHED NUMBER ONE WITH THEIR 1977 HIT 'SO YOU WIN AGAIN'?"
TSK! THIS ISN'T PROPER KNOWLEDGE ~ IT'S JUST COMMON TRIVIA ABOUT POP MUSIC

I'M FAR TOO INTELLIGENT TO BE INTERESTED IN PLEBBY KNOWLEDGE LIKE THAT
BBC CENTRE
MY MIND CRAVES MORE SOPHISTICATED LEARNING, LIKE STUFF ABOUT GREEK MYTHS AND POSH CLASSICAL MUSIC

SHORTLY
I'LL JUST LEAVE MY BIG BOOK OF BRAINY FACTS ON THE WINDOWSILL TO COOL DOWN
PROF. GREYCELLS
BIG BOOK OF BRAINY FACTS
IT'S SO JAM-PACKED WITH CLEVER WORDS THAT IT HAS GOT QUITE OVERHEATED

DROOL! THAT PROFESSOR'S BOOK WILL FEED MY RAVENOUS INTELLECT
PROF GREYCELLS
BIG BOOK OF BRAINY FACTS
I'LL SNAFFLE IT WHILE HE'S NOT LOOKING

OOPS! MY BRAINBOX IS RUMBLING WITH INTELLECTUAL HUNGER
GURGLE
RUMBLE
UH? WHAT'S THAT NOISE?

GRR! TRY TO PINCH MY CEREBRAL TOME, WOULD YOU?
YIKES! TIME TO SCARPER!

LATER, IN THE PARK
OHO! IT'S LORD EGGHEAD OF BRAINSTORM MANOR ~ AND HE'S FEASTING ON A HIGHBROW RADIO 4 PROGRAMME ABOUT MEDIEVAL POETRY
..WELL, QUENTIN, IT SEEMS TO ME....
I'LL SNEAK UP AND HAVE A CRAFTY LISTEN

ARF ARF! I CAN ALREADY FEEL MY MIND CHEWING OVER THAT HIGH CLASS INTELLIGENT DISCOURSE
TIP TOE
..WELL CLAUDIA, IT SEEMS TO ME...

OH CRIKEY!
WHEEEEE
WHINE
CRACKLE
THE EXTRA-POWERFUL BRAINWAVES COMING OUT OF MY HEAD ARE INTEFERING WITH THE RADIO SIGNAL

YEOW!
YOU'RE LISTENING TO RADIO ONE
NOW IT'S TUNED TO SOME MINDLESS POP STATION

SHORTLY
..YES, THE OWNER OF THIS BRAIN MANAGED TO GET THREE DEGREES AT CAMBRIDGE
POST-MORTEM LAB
COO! HE MUST'VE BEEN CLEVER

HEH HEH! I'LL HAVE THIS CHAP'S BRAIN TRANSPLANTED INTO MY HEAD, AND ABSORB ALL HIS ACADEMIC KNOWLEDGE

QUICK! STICK THIS TOP-NOTCH GREY MATTER INTO MY SKULL, PRONTO!
TRANSPLANT SURGERY
TRANSPLANTS ON REQUEST
RIGHTO, GUV'NOR

SOON
SMASHING! NOW MY HEAD WILL BE ABSOLUTELY BURSTING WITH BRAINY THOUGHTS
TRANSPLANT SURGERY
PULSATE
EXCUSE ME ~ A BRAIN HAS GONE MISSING FROM OUR LAB. HAS ANYONE SEEN IT?

IT'S OWNER HAD BEEN AN OBSESSIVE FAN OF THE 1970'S POP GROUP "THE 3 DEGREES." HE ONCE MANAGED TO BOOK THEM TO PLAY AT CAMBRIDGE SPEEDWAY CLUB
ERM..
THAT POP GROUP WAS HIS LIFE. HE KNEW NOTHING ABOUT ANYTHING ELSE AT ALL.

NEXT DAY
..AND YOUR NEXT QUESTION: "WHAT WAS THE TITLE OF THE 3 DEGREE'S TOP TEN CHART HIT OF 1975..?"
UNIVERSITY CHALLENGE
OOH! OOH! I KNOW THIS ONE! I KNOW THIS ONE!

20 things you never knew about ELTON JOHN & spiders

SIR ELTON JOHN. Loathe him or hate him, you just can't ignore him. Whether he's bubbling at one of his pal's funerals, mincing off a tennis court because someone called *"yoo-hoo"* at him or suing himself for spending a million pounds a month on flowers, the fat puff's flamboyant antics are never far away from the headlines. We think we know all about him, but do we really? *What's his real name? What's his favourite colour? How many legs have they got?* Here's 20 *Captain Fantastic* Facts you never knew about Elton John and Spiders.

1. Elton John's real name is Reginald Hercules Dwight. He took his stage name from two childhood heroes - ITV football commentator Elton Welsby and 70's Welsh rugby player Barry John. *"I tossed a coin to see if I should be Elton John or Barry Welsby,"* he told Rolling Stone magazine in 1994. Luckily for the world of pop, it came up heads!

2. Elton cannot swim - and it's all down to a 4th century Greek mathematician. Archimedes discovered that a floating body displaces its own weight in water, yet due to an anatomical quirk which leaves scientists scratching their heads, the pint-size star displaces three times his weight. As a result he sinks like a stone each time he jumps into his luxury swimming pool.

3. The smallest ever Elton John was only three inches tall. Tiny Calvin Phillips performed *Candle in the Wind* at his pet mouse's funeral...on a grand piano made from a matchbox!

4. The lake surrounding Princes Di's funeral island has a leak in it, and the water level constantly drops. Each month, the bespectacled singer-songwriter makes a bizarre pilgrimage to Althorp House where he spends four of five hours grieving at the lakeside until his tears have topped up the water level.

5. Despite being homosexual, Elton is very keen on football. In the seventies, he even had his own team, Watford FC! At half time, the effeminate chairman would don a French maid's outfit and serve the players fairy cakes and Earl Grey tea in bone china teacups.

6. Already famous for his piano-shaped glasses and piano-shaped swimming pools, John fell foul of the FA in 1974 when he unveiled plans for Watford United to play on a piano-shaped football pitch! Lancaster Gate bosses refused to allow the change, sending the singer into one of his hissy-fit strops that lasted 18 months.

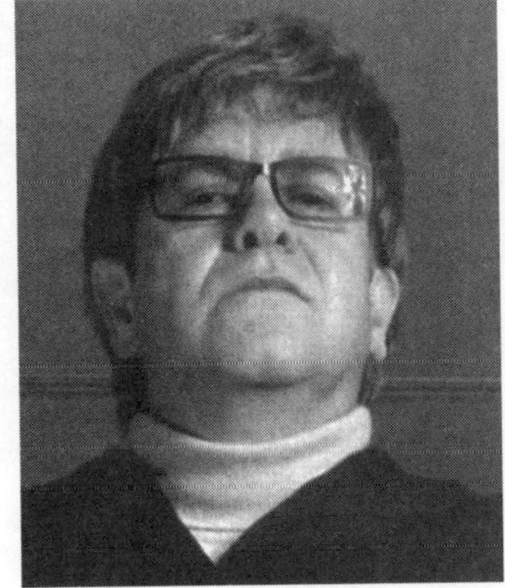

Zany ~ Elton larks about for the camera

7. Elton owns no less than 12 houses around the world. As a result, each time he visits the supermarket he has to buy 12 of everything: 12 packets of biscuits, 12 pints of milk, 12 toilet ducks etc. His weekly food shopping bill can easily top £200.

8. Elton John is synonymous with a crazy rock and roll lifestyle. In fact, he is so zany that *his wife is actually a man! Called David!*

9. John has spent the past four years searching Beverley Hills for a plastic surgeon willing to perform a delicate operation. So obsessed is he with piano-shaped things, that he plans to have his anal sphincter re-shaped so that he is able to excrete 'piano stools'!

10. Elton has written countless songs about the weather, including *Candle in the Wind* and *Don't let the Sun Go Down on Me.*

11. And *Cold as Christmas.*

12. And *Through the Storm* with Aretha Franklin.

13. When not penning chart-topping pop hits, Elton also likes to dabble in chemistry. In 1986 the scientific community granted him the ultimate accolade when an element he'd invented - *Eltonjohnium*, a dense semi-metallic halide - was accepted for inclusion in the periodic table between potassium and calcium.

14. Despite writing hundreds of songs about the colour blue, such as *I Guess That's Why they call it the Blues, Blue Eyes* and many more, Elton's favourite colour is actually green! *"I hate the colour blue,"* he told MTV in 1997.

15. John courted controversy recently when he tried buy the misshapen skeleton of seventies piano playing freak Mrs Mills from the British Museum.

16. At the height of his 1980's excesses, nutty Elton had his teeth replaced with piano keys. Now, instead of a 6-monthly check up at the dentist, he goes twice a year to have his gnashers tuned by a blind man.

Creepy crawly ~ A spider (above) with 8 legs yesterday and Elton (left) fighting to keep his emotions in check as he performs 'Pinball Wizard' at the funeral of Princess Diana in 1997.

17. The smallest spider in the world is the money spider *Arachnidae numismatans*. An example was recently found running up and down a bath belonging to the world's smallest man, Calvin Phillips.

18. *"I haven't got eyes in the back of my head"* is not an expression you'll ever hear a spider say. That's because spiders *have* got eyes in the backs of their heads! And because they can't talk anyway.

19. All spiders have eight legs, the same number of legs as pop group the Beatles, whose songs such as *Lucy in the Sky with Diamonds* and

I Saw her Standing There have been recorded by Elton John. So this one counts as two so that's 20.

OH, LORDY... IT'S THE FAT SLAGS

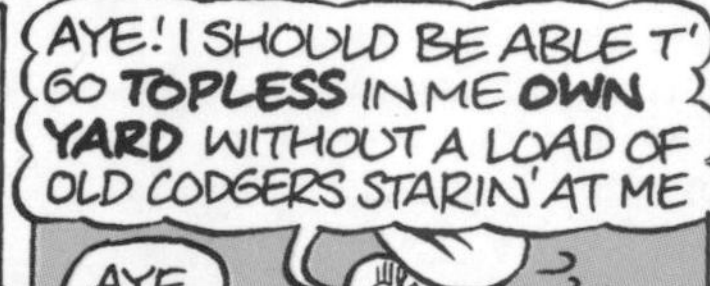

ROGER MELLIE

THE MAN ON THE TELLY

MONEY MAKING PETS

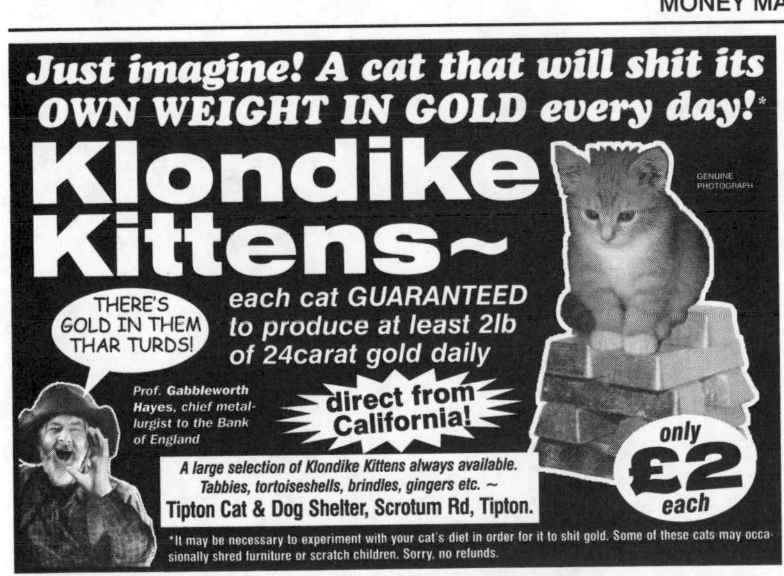

MRS. CARDEW! THERE'S BEEN A LITTLE MISTAKE. YOU SEE, GOLDFISH BOY WASN'T FOR SALE. HERE'S YOUR 10P., IF I COULD JUST...

I'M SORRY, FATHER, BUT THIS GOLDFISH BOY IS MINE. I BOUGHT HIM FAIR AND SQUARE

BUT I'VE HAD HIM FOR YEARS, MRS. CARDEW. HE'S THE ONLY COMPANY I'VE GOT. AND I LOVE HIM. I LOVE ALL GOD'S CREATURES

THAT'S AS MAYBE, FATHER. BUT A PURCHASE IS A PURCHASE AND MY STATUTORY RIGHTS ARE NOT AFFECTED...

...GOOD DAY

I'M NOT LETTING THE OLD COW GET AWAY WITH THAT. GOLDFISH BOY IS MINE AND I'M GOING TO GET HIM BACK...

...ONE WAY OR ANOTHER!

LATER...
THERE YOU GO, FATHER. YOU WOULDN'T HEAR A BOMB DROP THROUGH THESE. YOUR HOUSE WILL BE AS QUIET AS THE GRAVE...
...THAT'LL BE £500, PLEASE
GREAT!...

...I'LL TRY THEM OUT LATER. I'M JUST GOING FOR A LITTLE WALK FIRST...ERM... TO THINK ABOUT TOMORROW'S SERMON. DO YOU MIND IF I BORROW THESE?

SHORTLY...

DON'T WORRY, GOLDFISH BOY. I'LL HAVE YOU HOME IN A JIFFY
EH!?... WASSAT!?!

EEEEK! RAPE!! MURDER!! POLICE!!
CLICK!
ERM!...I...ERM! LET ME EXPLAIN...

HEURGH!
YOU SEE... ERM... OH, DEAR!

I THINK I'VE SCARED HER TO DEATH, GOLDFISH BOY...
...BUGGER!

'ELLO! 'ELLO! 'ELLO! WHAT'S GOIN' ON 'ERE THEN?
ERM...OH, AH! YES. WELL!...

...ERM, I WAS WALKING PAST THE HOUSE, ERM, CARRYING A LADDER...AND, ERM... A CROWBAR WHEN I HEARD MRS. CARDEW DYING...
...SO I, ERM... ENTERED HER BEDROOM TO ADMINISTER THE LAST RITES
AH, WELL DONE, FATHER BROWN. IT LOOKS LIKE YOU GOT HERE JUST IN TIME

YES, SHE'S DEAD ALRIGHT
OH, LOOK. THERE'S HER WILL...
...LET'S HAVE A LOOK, SHALL WE?

WELL, IT SAYS HERE THAT SHE WAS SO TOUCHED BY YOUR LOVE OF ANIMALS THAT SHE'S LEFT HER GOLDFISH BOY TO YOU...
HOW MARVELLOUS!

...IN FACT, TO KEEP YOU COMPANY, SHE'S LEFT YOU ALL HER PETS
EH!?!
8 DOGS, 14 CATS, 9 PARROTS, 3 SCREECH OWLS, 6 HOWLER MONKEYS, 2 GEESE AND A KOOKABURRA
JESUS!

LATER...
TWIT! TWOO!
TWITTER! TWITTER!
CHIRRUP! CHIRRUP!

WELL ZEN, MAH EENGLEESH CHURMS, ZAT'S ALL FROM EUROTRASH FOR ZEES WIK... SALUT MAINTENANT!
SNARL!
SQUAWK! SQUAWK!
HONK! HONK! HONK!
HONK!
WOOF!

CILLA BLACKBEARD

THE BLOODTHIRSTY EARLY EVENING TELEVISION PRESENTER OF THE SEVEN SEAS

Open the Floodgates!

Water rats: *A filthy tide of humanity that may grow gills and fins for an aquatic-based invasion on the UK.*

Thousands of unkempt East European immigrants are set to surf into Britain's lovely beaches on a TIDAL WAVE of effluent, following EU expansion next spring.

It is feared that as soon as countries such as Poland and Hungary are accepted into Europe, other aquatically trained migrants may FLOOD the Thames

Barrier by leaping upstream like salmon on the capital's great river.

think tank

Top think tank Immigrant Watch, run by Mrs Beryl Walsh and her son Mordred, have exclusively revealed what many commentators have feared for some time now; that asylum seekers have developed gills and fins in order to seep unnoticed into Britain by our country's soft touch river systems.

The Walshes also warned that others who are unable to transform themselves into fish-like form may instead use a disguise in order to get into the country. Mrs Walsh reported that people traffickers in Eastern Europe are already selling hundreds of surfing outfits to unshaven benefit hungry Slovaks, Poles, and Ruritanians in preparation for Common market expansion in 2004.

think bike

The kits are freely on sale for up to $500 US on the streets of Budapest and Moldova and include a surfboard, a bleach-blond wig and a map showing the locations of housing offices in Newquay and St. Ives.

Newquay seekers: *Swarthy immigrants disguised as surfers prepare for their invasion on Bulgaria's Black Sea Coast.*

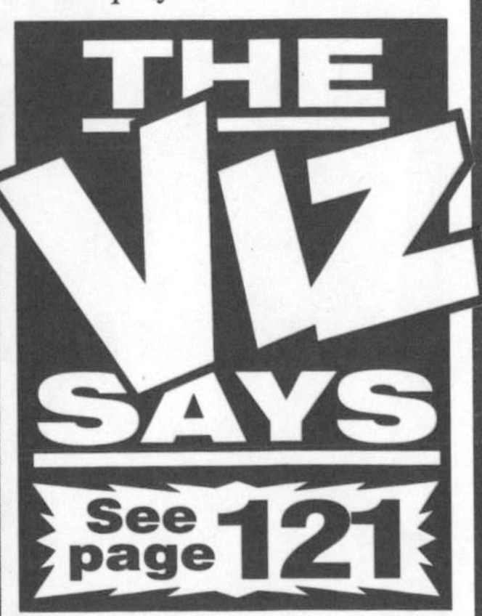

Letterbocks

£50 STAR LETTER

A LETTER of mine about Warren Mitchell was published in Viz 127. It was a funny, true story and I received nothing. 20 years ago my sister sent a letter to Bunty, lied and received £5. That's the last fucking letter I ever send you.

Alun Roberts, e-mail

Letterbocks
Viz Comic
PO Box 1PT
Newcastle NE99 1PT

In this space age you can electromail your letters and tips to letters@viz.co.uk

WHAT A nicer place the world would be if the police took a leaf out of swimming pool attendants' books and simply peeped their whistle at people they spotted breaking the rules.

Anon, Somewhere

YOUR T shirts are rubbish. They fall apart after just 10 years, even with light farm/garage use.

Louise Lear-Jones Scotland

TERRORIST group Al Qaeda have on three occasions attempted to assassinate former Iraqi president Saddam Hussain. Assuming that they eventually succeed in killing him, will they qualify for the $25 million bounty put on his head by George Bush? If they do, then what on earth are the Americans doing funding Osama Bin Laden and his cohorts? If not, can we ever trust a man like Bush who fails to keep his promises? Whatever the outcome, the hypocrisy of it will sicken me.

G Heffer Antrim

For the Record

THE LATE Roy Castle would have us believe that all you need to become a record breaker is a little dedication. What nonsense. I need 53 double decker buses, an Aston Martin and a disused airfield.

Ryan Marshall Belfast

MY LOCAL hospital has a sign which reads "This way to accidents and emergencies". Haven't people in hospital got enough trouble already, without going looking for further misfortune and misery?

Paul Wilde Stockton on Tees

Poetic Justice

I RECENTLY noticed that celebrities who are prosecuted for underage sex offences tend to have names that rhyme with slang terms for the arse, eg. Gary Glitter - shitter & Jonathan King - ring. Using this formula, my money's on Michael Stipe (Pipe) as the next one to get pulled in by the cops.

Matthew Edwards Email

Saw Point

I WAS reading about these people moaning about the colour of their false limbs not matching the colour of their skin. With the state of the NHS, they should count themselves fucking lucky the surgeon cut the correct limb off.

Jon Chesham

I HAVE an Aunt Hilda and an Aunt Matilda, and that's just fine by me. But the day can't be far off when a half-heard conversation on the street - maybe with a wagon passing by - is going to leave the wrong one being blamed or praised for something.

M. Macdonald Email

IF WE blokes don't mind wearing socks with holes in them, how come birds kick up such a fuss about split-crotch panties.

Millward Brown Leamington Spa

Fertility Wrongs

I'M SICK and tired of hearing politicians wringing their hands about the ethics of experimenting on women's eggs. Millions of my tadpoles die every morning and afternoon, yet does anyone care? I think not.

Oliver Cameron Email

Top Tart

LAST Sunday (24th September) I persuaded my bird to buy my drinks, drive me 200 miles home and then have sex with me. Later on, she cooked my tea and mended my shirt. Can any readers do better than that?

Adam Zerny London

Blind Fate

HOW prophetic that Cilla sang the lyric "Surprise, Surprise. The unexpected hits you between the eyes." Perhaps if her son had paid some attention to these words his terrible ordeal at the hands of robbers could have been averted.

I. Bell Email

UP THE ARSE CORNER

Top Tips

HOUSEWIVES. Before attempting to remove stubborn stains from a garment, circle the soiled area with a permanent pen so that when you remove it from the washing machine you can easily locate the area to check the stain has gone.

Dean Saville, Email

MAKE sure you get good service at the McDonald's Drive-thru by pasting a big yellow 'M' to your windscreen and ticking a clipboard as you place your order.

Rosslynman, Email

PEOPLE in Cheltenham. When smearing dogshit on Craig David's Porsche 911 in the Royal Well car park, make sure you get plenty under the door handles and not just on the bonnet.

I. Purdy, Email

COUNCILLORS. Next time you and your 'personal assistant' travel to somewhere sunny abroad on a factfinding tour why not pack some holiday clothes? You won't be inspecting civic amenities all the time, so you may as well take the opportunity to enjoy yourselves. After all, you are giving up your spare time in the service of the public.

Tony Pease, Email

RECREATE the smell of farts by opening a pack of Iceland's diced chicken.

Grant Warner, New Malden

DIABOLISTS. For the full effect when photographing Satan, make sure to switch off your camera's red-eye reduction feature.

Paul Bradshaw, Email

Smiles per Galleon

IT'S A shame you're not still doing insincere smiles, because these two grimaces (below) in the current Norfolk Line cross-channel ferry brochure would have been perfect.

Talbot Clark
Gainsborough

SO WOULD this one.

Patrick Wright
California

Collection Point

WHY DO these big charities always focus on eradicating stuff like blindness which only affects a small percentage of the population? Maybe if they looked at eradicating something that affects all of us such as wasps they'd get alot more support from the public.

Chingford Rob
e-mail

Do You Know Who I Am?

LAST week I saw Loadsamoney star Harry Enfield on Oxford Street trying to avoid getting a parking ticket on his moped by asking the traffic warden "Do you know who I am?". When the balding thesp threw a poncy showbiz hissy fit, a humorous passer-by shouted "Now I don't believe you wanted to do that."

Neil Hawes
Finchley

**Have you seen a "celebrity" asking people if they know who they are? Write to the usual address and let us know. Mark your envelope "I've seen a celebrity asking people if they know who they are". There's £10 for the first person to send one in that isn't Alan Davies.*

TRAVEL NEWS

A64 Leeds - Woman waiting to turn right on Lower Briggate into Boar Lane. Traffic tailing back to Carlton Street, Castleford.

A55 St Asaph - Woman primping hair in rear view mirror at the junction of the A552, Llandudno turning. Police advise seeking an alternative route.

A610 Nottingham - Gillian Taylforth relieving a man's pancreatitis on the northbound lane at Derby Road. Rubber neckers causing long tailbacks.

A392 Reading - A woman in a Renault Clio attempting to park between two cars on Queens Road since Monday. Delays expected for at least another four days.

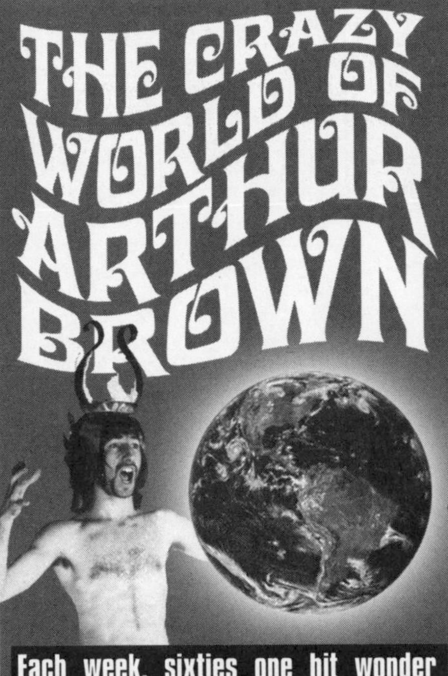

Each week, sixties one hit wonder Arthur Brown sets fire to his hat and looks through the world's papers in search of quirky news items.

The Colombian capital Bogota was thrown into chaos last week when gravity went into reverse for nearly a minute. Members of the public watched in amazement as everyday items floated up into the air, before diving for cover as pots, pans, cars, hammers, dustbins and apples rained down. Government meteorologists blamed a large glittery cloud which had been seen behaving strangely in the sky and making mysterious tinkling noises earlier in the week. "It was like something from a science fiction film," said city mayor Boco Perez.

Source: Bogota Herald & Advertiser

Henry Kissinger was last night back at work less than half an hour after being eaten by a snake. The former US foreign secretary was on a diplomatic visit to Java when he slipped on a roller skate and was pitched into the waiting jaws of a forty foot annaconda. Speaking from the beast's stomach via a mobile phone, the Nobel prizewinner calmly reassured his aides that he was safe and well whilst Javanese government officials dosed the snake with liquid paraffin. Two minutes later the steely-nerved diplomat was shat out onto a tarpaulin, and completed his fact-finding tour as if nothing had happened.

Source: Java Telegraph & Argus

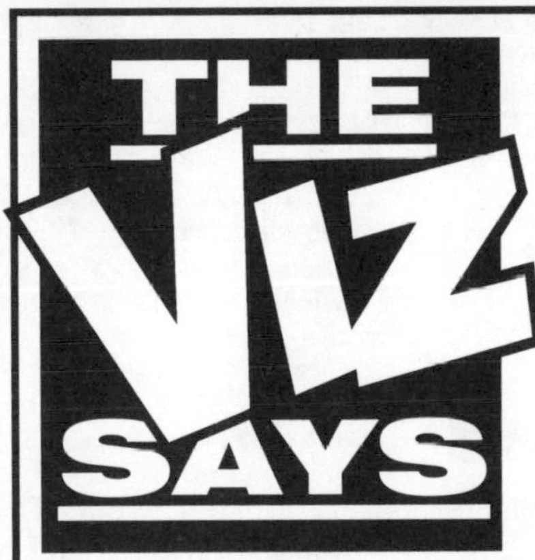

We don't want 'em, Guvnor

IT'S TIME to put the wind breaks up and take down this government's knotted hankie of a white flag to illegal immigrants.

A family magazine like this doesn't want to whip up a storm by using inflammatory words that will indirectly encourage gangs of baseball cap-wearing estate pikies to beat up foreign visitors to our nation.

But enough is enough. Just when will this filthy tidal wave of vermin-like effluent cease?

Wave upon wave of rat-like illegal immigrants are ready to surf into Newquay and other beaches on the South Coast. Others could soon be leaping upstream like salmon, over the Thames Barrier and into a fairytale land of fat benefit cheques and free council houses.

But thousands of ordinary decent work avoiding white British scum will be left high and dry without the single mother community centres and drug addict relapse organisations that normally look after them.

Is that what we want to happen?

Should we deport tabloid journalists?

YES	CALL 09932 9321341
YES, DEFINITELY	CALL 09932 9321342

Britain's brightest drawer chat page

I AM an artist, and I keep my underpants in a retractable, sliding, rack-mounted storage tray on runners. That is to say I am a *drawer*, and I keep my *drawers* in a *drawer!!!* How my wife and I laugh every time I make this observation.

T. Dangerfield, London

MY WIFE does the football pools each week, and one Saturday afternoon, she came running into the kitchen screaming that eight draws had just come up. I was about to open the champagne when I discovered that she had bought two chests of drawers (each containing four drawers), and that they had just ascended in the lift to our home on the tenth floor of a block of flats!

H. Willis, Reading

When is a Drawer Not a Drawer?

I WAS recently in Ikea, and was appalled to see that they were selling a set of 3 pine storage boxes in a frame unit in the drawers section. Furthermore, the same item was listed in their catalogue as a 'Kroll 3 Drawer Unit'. Call me old fashioned, but a lidless wooden box with a handle is not a drawer. I told one of the assistants that in Britain a drawer has runners, otherwise it is a wooden box in a frame. She refused my request to relocate the item to the general storage section of the shop and remove it from the catalogue.

P. Smith, Gateshead

Stick to the Rules

IT MAKES my blood boil when I hear young people complaining about their drawers sticking. I've got a set I've been using day in and day out for sixty years and they've never stuck once. I always say that it's not the sticking drawer that's at fault, it's the owner. A drawer, like a car or television set, needs regular maintenance to keep it in tip-top condition. If these people would only take the trouble to follow this five point drawer care plan they'd enjoy trouble-free drawer use for years to come.

1. *Always site chests of drawers well away from sources of humidity, excessive cold and excessive heat.*
2. *Never attempt to pull a drawer out at an angle. It could twist in its runners, damaging the sliding mechanism.*
3. *Never overload a drawer. As a rule of thumb, if you have to press the contents down in order to get the drawer back in, it is too full.*
4. *Open and close every drawer at least five times a day. This will ensure that the moving parts don't seize up due to lack of use.*
5. *Remove every drawer from its housing twice a year to oil or wax the runners.*

Brigadier Y. Lewerthwaite, Cumbria

PAEDOPHILE PRIESTS!

Caught with your fingers in the choir?

Nobody gets you safely out of the parish quicker than us.

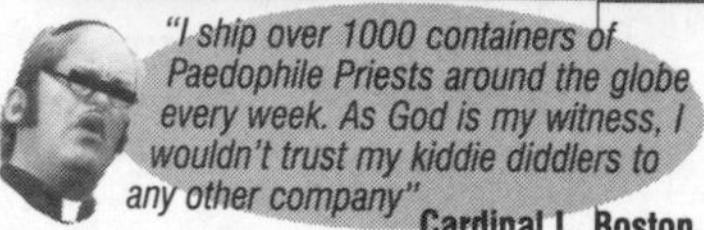

Cardinal L, Boston

Reservations and furter info:
Pederast Shipping Co.
Pederast House,
Port Bumlight, PB1 6RR
☎ 08002 333 55899
Email: sales@pederast.net

Miriam

DRAWER HELP WITH MIRIAM STOPPARD

LETTER OF THE DAY

Dear Miriam...

My husband left me after putting teaspoons in the dessert spoon compartment of the cutlery drawer.

I'm 32 and my husband's 35 and we've been married for 11 years. He always used to put the spoons in the correct compartments of the drawer, but about a year ago he started mixing them up. When I tried to talk to him about it, he would just fly off the handle and say he didn't want to discuss it.

Then one day he put a knife in the fork compartment. We had a blazing row and he ended up sleeping on the sofa. The next morning, the row started up again. He stormed out of the house and I set about putting my cutlery drawer back in order.

I didn't see him for six months, but now he has been in touch and he wants to come back. He says that things will be different and that he will put the cutlery back in the correct place.

I still love him, but the trouble is I have met another man. He is wonderful, and not only does he replace the cutlery in the right compartments, he makes sure they are all the right way round. He even has a separate drawer for best.

I'm afraid that if I take my husband back he'll revert to his old ways. Please help me, Miriam.

Mrs EB, Belfast

Miriam writes...

Wake up and smell the coffee, girl. Your husband thinks he can mix up the utensils in your cutlery drawer and then just breeze back into your life as though nothing has happened. He may say things will be different, but a leopard will not change his spots. My postbag is full of letters from women like you who have given their fellas a second chance to keep the cutlery tidy, and it never works. Your new man sounds like a gem. Hold onto him.

Dear Miriam...

I have recently started having trouble opening my sock drawer, and it's driving a wedge between me and my wife.

I am 48 and she is 32. We've been married for 12 years and I have never had any difficulty opening the drawer. Lately, however, I have found it increasingly difficult to get it open when I want to take socks out and put them in. My wife tells me it doesn't matter, but I can tell it is starting to bother her as well. There is a big age difference between us, and I am afraid she may find a younger man who has no trouble in the sock drawer department. I don't want to lose her. What can I do?

Miriam writes...

Every man has difficulty opening his sock drawer now and again. And worrying about it will only make the problem worse. Just relax and take it easy. Nine times out of ten the problem will cure itself. In the meantime, why don't you and your wife experiment with other places to store your socks, such as your underpants drawer, or a drawer in the kitchen? Or even her underwear drawer! After all, it is 2003.

Dr Miriam Stoppard

The Drawer lines you can trust

STICKING DRAWERS	000 8181 188881
LOOSE HANDLES	000 8181 188882
WON'T STAY CLOSED	000 8181 188883
VAGINAL DRYNESS	000 8181 188883

ON THIS DAY IN DRAWER HISTORY

25 years ago

Elton John was forced to call off a concert at Blackpool Tower after he trapped his fingers in a drawer at his guest house. Fans were offered a choice of a refund or tickets to a rescheduled show.

50 years ago

The first plastic drawer was unveiled to an amazed public at the 1953 Paris Expo. An early buyer was film star Zsa Zsa Gabor, who ordered three for the bedroom of her Hollywood mansion.

100 years ago

The first drawer ever to fly took to the air at Kittyhawk Beach, Oregon. The six inch drawer, containing Orville Wright's pipe, sunglasses and a box of Tictacs was airborne for twenty-three seconds and later bequeathed to the Smithsonian Institute in Washington.

TINRIBS
ANTI FREEZE
11-YEAR OLD TOMMY TAYLOR HAD A FANTASTIC ROBOT FOR A PAL

AT SCHOOL ASSEMBLY
TONIGHT IS HALLOWE'EN, CHILDREN
HEAD MASTER
IT'S THE TIME OF YEAR YOUNG CHILDREN CELEBRATE THE SATANIC MAJESTY OF BEELZEBUB BY DRESSING UP AS GHOSTS AND SKELLINGTONS.

AND THIS YEAR I WILL BE AWARDING A HAMPER FULL OF FIREWORKS AND PORNOGRAPHY TO THE PUPILS WHO SUCCEED IN MAKING MR SNODWORTHY SHIT HIS TROUSERS WITH FEAR.
HEAD MASTER
NUDEY LADIES
RAZZ
HAPPY HAUNTING, EVERYONE!
HUNH?

DON'T WORRY MATES — WITH MY ROBOT PAL ON OUR SIDE, MR SNODWORTHY'S PANTS ARE AS GOOD AS SHITTED
HI. I'M BARBIE. I LOVE YOU VERY MUCH.

TCHOH! YOU BRATS HAVEN'T A HOPE OF FRIGHTENING ME
BARGE
I'VE GOT NERVES OF STEEL, AND AN ANAL SPHINCTER OF IRON.

THAT EVENING
MR SNODWORTHY WILL DO A BUNDLE IN HIS KNICKERS WHEN HE SEES TINRIBS IN THIS SCARY GHOST COSTUME
M. SNODWORTHY ESQ.
DING DONG
GET READY TO MAKE SPOOKY NOISES, EVERYONE

WOOOOOO!
WURRRRR!
WOOOOOO!
HI. I'M BARBIE. I LOVE YOU VERY MUCH.

WHAT A FEEBLE EFFORT
M. SNODWORTHY ESQ
BOOT
YOU CAN TAKE YOUR PATHETICALLY UNSCARY ROBOT AND GET OFF MY PROPERTY.

AH, MR SNODWORTHY. I SHOULD HAVE THE RESULTS OF YOUR MEDICAL CHECK-UP ANY DAY NOW.
HUH? OH, ER, THANK YOU DOCTOR SMITH.

I KNOW HOW WE CAN SCARE MR SNODWORTHY.
FIRST I'LL ADJUST TINRIBS'S SOPHISTICATED COMPUTERISED VOICEBOX SO THAT HE DOES A PERFECT IMPERSONATION OF THAT DOCTOR SMITH

NOW, PRETENDING TO BE THE DOCTOR, TINRIBS CAN PHONE UP MR SNODWORTHY AND TELL HIM HE'S GOT CANCER.
M. SNODWORTHY ESQ
BLEEP BLEEP BLEEP
HE'LL SOIL HIS TROUSERS IMMEDIATELY, AND WE'LL WIN THE HAMPER.

DRING! DRING!
THE PHONE'S RINGING, TINRIBS
M. SNODWORTHY ESQ.
REMEMBER — TELL MR SNODWORTHY THAT HE'S GOT CANCER, AIDS AND NECROTISING FASCITIS.

THERE'S SOMEONE ON THE PHONE WHO SAYS HIS NAME IS BARBIE, DEAR. HE CLAIMS TO LOVE ME VERY MUCH.
TSK. IT'LL BE THOSE KIDS AGAIN, TRYING TO MAKE ME DEFECATE IN MY TREWS.

PERHAPS MY DOG ROLLINS CAN TEACH YOU A THING OR TWO ABOUT BEING SCARY.
SIC 'EM, ROLLINS!
SNARL!
WOW! RUN FOR IT!

LATER
MR SNODWORTHY HAS POPPED OUT TO THE POST BOX, LEAVING HIS WIFE ALONE IN THE HOUSE
FOLLOW ME, PALS — I'VE GOT A PLAN.

SHORTLY
AH, HELLO DEAR. GONE TO BED EARLY, HAVE YOU?
I'LL JUST GET MY JIM-JAMS OUT OF THE WARDROBE

WAH! MY WIFE'S BODY — WITH THE FACE ALL HACKED OFF!
B-BUT WHO'S THAT IN THE BED?

HO HO! WE KILLED YOUR WIFE AND CUT HER FACE OFF USING A JAGGED SOUP TIN FROM TINRIBS'S VERTICAL SUPPORT
AND NOW TINRIBS IS 'WEARING' HER FACE, JUST LIKE HANNIBAL LECTER. PRETTY SPOOKY, EH SIR?
HI. I'M BARBIE

YARRRGH! HELP, MUMMY!
PTTHHHBP!
I SAY! JOLLY GOOD WORK, CHILDREN. YOU'VE SCARED MR SNODWORTHY ABSOLUTELY SHITLESS

THREE CHEERS FOR TOMMY'S FANTASTIC ROBOT CHUM
HOORAH!
BAH!
HI. I'M BARBIE. I LOVE YOU VERY MUCH.

COPPER KETTLE The 'PC' who LOVES his 'PG'

BUT...
WAHEY!! LOOK AT ALL THAT TEA...! I MUST GET A CUP AND SAUCER!
HOT TEA
BULK HOT TEA
50,000 GALLONS OF TEA WITH
GLUG!
GUSH!
GLUG!

FORTUITOUSLY JEWISH
CUP & SAUCER SHOP
OPEN!
OPEN XMAS DAY DUE TO BEING FORTUITOUSLY JEWISH
AHA! LOOKS LIKE MY LUCK'S CHANGING AT LAST!

GOOD MORNING, SIR... WHAT CAN I...?
I'LL HAVE THIS, PLEASE!
£5

CERTAINLY, SIR. I'LL JUST WRAP IT FOR YOU.
IF YOU MUST- BUT PLEASE HURRY!
OKAY. NOW... WHERE DID I PUT THAT SELLOTAPE? HMM... LET ME THINK...
GLUG! GLUG!

20 MINUTES LATER...
RIP! RIP! TEAR!
GURGLE! GURGLE!

YES! YES! YES!
DRIBBLE!

BLOIP!
WHA..?! OH NO!
LAST DROP OF TEA.

BAH. THIS IS THE WORST CHRISTMAS DAY EVER.

HELLO- WHAT'S THIS?
AYUP, KETTLE. THERE'S BEEN ONE OF THEM "JONATHAN CREEK" STYLE MURDERS.
POLICE CRIME SCENE
FANCY COMING IN FOR A WARM?

IT'S A REAL PUZZLER. THE BODY WAS FOUND IN A ROOM LOCKED FROM THE INSIDE, LYING BY THIS CUP OF TEA...
TEA!?

SLOOP!
WE SUSPECT THE TEA WAS LACED WITH POISON.

5 MINUTES LATER...
...LET ME SEE NOW... KETTLE... KETTLE... AH, YES. HERE YOU ARE. YOU'RE IN.
ACE!
PEARLY GATES RECEPTION

WELCOME TO PARADISE!
BETTER GET A NICE BREW ON, THEN, ST. PETER EH?

A BREW ON!? WHATEVER FOR? WE DON'T ALLOW TEA OR COFFEE UP HERE, YOU KNOW. WE'RE ALL MORMONS.

SO...
NO TEA ALLOWED BY ORDER

AN ETERNITY LATER...
P-THOO! PTH! PTH!

Altarboy Chastity Pants

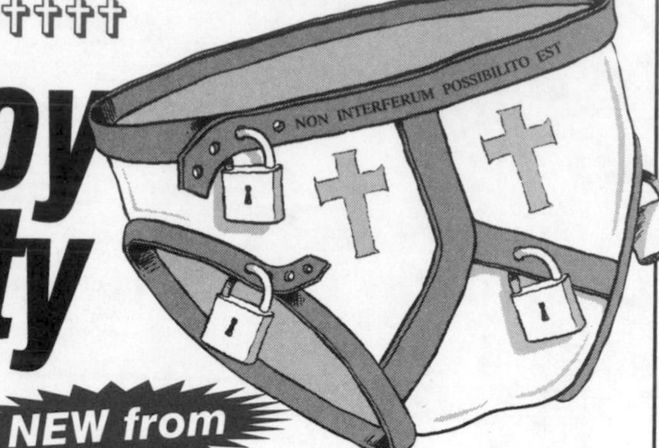

NEW from

Cath-o-Lock

Stops diddling priests IN THEIR TRACKS!!

-You can never 'altar' a priest's behaviour, but now you can keep his 'Roamin' Catholic' hands off YOUR son's genitals

- Steel-reinforeced waist and leg bands give flexibility whilst offering protection from priests' fingers.

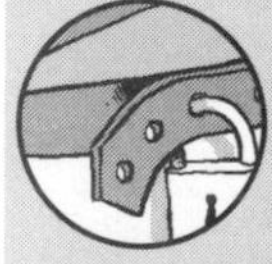

- Fully adjustable straps allow the Chastity Pants to be used on choirboys of all ages and sizes, from soprano to alto.

- Tempered steel locks on all 4 finger entry points give total security and parental peace of mind.

Prevents:-

- overfamiliar touching
- inappropriate fondling
- feeling-up

"I must confess, it would be a sin if junior got felt up for want of a pair of Chastity Pants. I holy reccommend them."
Cardinal B., Essex

Keep your kiddies' bits 'undies' lock & key for just £19.99 -per pair (inc 2 spare keys)

Now thwart even the most bothersome priests with the scent of a woman...

Father Begone™

priest repellant spray

£1.99

One spray, and your son will smell like an adult woman for up to 8 hours - enough to see him safely through even the longest mass

Effective on • priests • bishops • choirmasters and all manner of bothersome clerics.

NB: May require two applications in areas of high catholicism

Available in all good pharmacists

INFLATABLE

Decoy Priests

Stand him behind YOUR chiorboy son, and priests will simply move onto the next boy! It's THAT simple

£29.99 each

"Give him a surprise he'll not forgive and forget"

Powerful Spring Loaded

Surplice Traps

Worn under the choirboy's surplice clipped to the back of the underpants, these powerful, modified rat traps will make him think twice the next time.

Only £1 each or £10 per dozen

For when sopra-no MEANS no!

10,000v Priest Stun Guns

Send for our catalogue - *the widest range of electric priest deterrants available.*

Cathol-Prod Ltd
Box 90, Hull

Web meltdown horror! EXCLUSIVE!

FEARS OF A GLOBAL INTERNET COLLAPSE are growing this week, after the shock announcement that the man who runs the worldwideweb is to retire.

Lionel ~ tinkering with a bit of the internet, yesterday

Lionel Thruxton, 63, has admitted that the job is getting too big for his ageing shoulders. Speaking from the converted shed in Frampton-upon-Severn from which he runs the internet, he told reporters, "It's all a bit much for me at my age.

HOBBY

"I started the internet as a hobby in 1989. I got the idea from my model railway set, with trains taking things from station to station, so I connected all the stations together and had a working protoype in a couple of weeks.

"I thought it might be a cult fad, like CB radio or blowing spit meth up your arse, but it's turned into a worldwide phenomenon. The internet is bigger than Christ right now."

Pipe-smoking Thruxton thinks his invention might be worth up to £300,000 and is currently looking for a buyer to take the shed full of equipment off his hands. B&Q, Pete Waterman and Sewage France are thought to be amongst the bidders.

HUBBY

"Whoever gets it will have to have plenty of get-up-and-go," says Thruxton. "When I started, I used to pass a few e-mails from sender to recipient a week. These days, I'm passing on 14 billion a day. Some days I'm still sitting here at my desk at 9 o'clock at night! The missus is furious."

But the worlds of government, commerce, defence, media, entertainment, sport, charity, religion and terrorism have been flapping like hysterical swans at the news.

The Home Office is secretly drawing up plans for a state of emergency if Mr Thruxton cannot find a buyer for the internet and has to turn it off – something he hasn't done in over 15 years.

HIPPIE

A draft version of the survival strategy, *Operation Holy Shit*, was leaked to reporters. The plans include making every computer user print off at least TWO copies of the internet and keep one under lock and key.

There will be emergency bright blue e-mail boxes on every street corner, church and school halls will be requisitioned and turned into chat rooms, roadside pop-up adverts will appear on every motorway, and trained volunteer staff will help start conversations in offices and cafés.

"I don't think it'll come to that," says Thruxton, casually tossing another sackful on spam on the compost. "What with all the spin-offs – internet mugs and scarves and the like – I think it'll be an attractive proposition for the right sort of enthusiast."

Mrs BRADY OLD LADY

JOHNNY FARTPANTS
QUAK!
SEW A BUTTON ON THAT!
THERE'S ALWAYS A COMMOTION GOING ON IN HIS TROUSERS!

HELLO READERS! I'M OFF TO THE CHURCH FÊTE. IT'S ALL FOR A GOOD CAUSE!

HELLO JOHNNY. THANKS FOR COMING. WE HOPE TO RAISE ENOUGH MONEY TO BUY A BIG ROCKET TO TAKE OUT THE TOWEL-HEADS IN BAGHDAD

ST. THERESA'S HAVE HAD A BRING & BUY SALE AND HAVE BOUGHT A MOAB. BOMB.
SQUEAK! SQUEAK!
WE MUSTN'T BE OUT-DONE BY THE LEFT-FOOTERS, JOHNNY.

BAH! I'VE FORGOTTEN TO BRING A PUMP FOR THE BOUNCY CASTLE! THE LADY MAYORESS OPENS IT IN FIVE MINUTES!

DON'T WORRY VICAR, I'VE EATEN STEAMED LEEKS AND TIZER, I'LL GET IT INFLATED IN NO TIME!

SO...
I DECLARE THIS BOUNCY CASTLE WELL AND TR...
STILETTO SHOES

BOING! BOING! BOING! BOING!
BOING! BOING!

QUACK!
ERK!
POP!

OH NO! THE PUMP GASSES HAVE MELTED THE SKIN OFF THE LADY MAYORESS'S FACE! HER MEDICAL BILLS WILL TAKE A CHUNK OUT OF OUR PROFITS ... WE MUST GET BUSY IF WE'RE TO HAVE ANY CHANCE OF NUKING THE AY-RABS!
EEEK!

SHORTLY...
BAH! NOW I CAN'T REACH THE SOCKET TO PLUG IN THE CANDY-FLOSS MACHINE. THIS WILL REALLY HARM TAKINGS! WE'LL NEVER MAKE ENOUGH TO BOMB THE CAMEL JOCKEYS NOW!
CANDY FLOSS

DON'T WORRY, VICAR! I CAN HELP YOU THERE!...

THERE. I'VE UTILISED THE POWER OF FLATULENCE TO CREATE A HOT WHIRLWIND IN THE BACK OF MY SHORTS... SIMPLY TIP IN SOME SUGAR, AND HEY PRESTO!... YUMMY CANDY FOSS!
WHRRR!

GREAT JOHNNY! WE'RE DOING FANTASTIC TRADE!
ME NEXT!
YUK!
WHRRR!

DADDY! MY CANDY-FLOSS TASTES OF EGG!
OH NO! WE'VE RUN OUT OF SUGAR!
!
SUGAR
WHRRR!

I TELL YOU WHAT, I'LL GIVE YOU THAT ONE FOR HALF PRICE, SON.

JUST THEN...
I'M FROM THE COUNCIL. THERE ARE STRICT LAWS GOVERNING HOW MANY WINNITS CAN BE PRESENT IN ANY CONFECTIONARY. THIS CANDY-FLOSS EXCEEDS THAT LIMIT BY 50% ... I'M GOING TO HAVE TO CLOSE THIS FÊTE DOWN AND CONFISCATE ALL THE PROCEEDS!
FOOD HYGENE OFFICER

WELL JOHNNY, ALL OUR FUNDS ARE GONE AND IT'S ALL YOUR FAULT. THERE'S ONLY ONE WAY WE CAN DELIVER A TRULY DEADLY PAYLOAD TO EVIL SADDAM'S BAGHDAD...

AND...
WELL JOHNNY, WITH THAT T.N.T. AND DEPLETED URANIUM STRAPPED TO YOUR BOT, YOU MAKE AN IDEAL WEAPON OF GAS DESTRUCTION!
BAGHDAD 4,000 miles
HA! HA!
HO! HO!

RUSS ABBOT'S
DORMOUSE
MADHOUSE
DORMOUSE PSYCHIATRIC HOSPITAL

COO! LOOK AT THE TIME
DORMOUSE PSYCHIATRIC HOSPITAL
ELEVEN O'CLOCK ALREADY...

... IT'S MEDICATION TIME IN MY ZANY DORMOUSE MADHOUSE!

ONE BY ONE THE WACKY LITTLE RODENTS SHUFFLED UP TO RECEIVE THEIR DAILY DOSES OF PROZAC, LITHIUM, THORAZINE AND LARGACTIL

WOW, LOOK! THAT DORMOUSE IS SUFFERING FROM SCHIZOPHRENIC CATALEPSY
AND THIS ONE HAS BORDERLINE PERSONALITY DISORDER
IT'S THE BARMIEST DORMOUSE LOONY BIN WE'VE EVER SEEN!

CORKS!
LOOKS LIKE THE POWER SUPPLY FOR MY DORMOUSE ELECTRO-CONVULSIVE THERAPY APPARATUS IS RUNNING LOW

I'D BETTER GET A NEW 9-VOLT BATTERY
HARDWARE SHO
WITHOUT REGULAR ECT, THE CRAZY ANTICS OF THESE FURRY LITTLE FRUITCAKES WOULD BE NUTTIER THAN EVER!

STOP THIEVES!
HARDWARE SHOP
LOOT
THOSE CROOKS HAVE ROBBED MY TILL!

DORMOUSE MADHOUSE TO THE RESCUE!
A SPOT OF HIGH-SPEED OCCUPATIONAL THERAPY WILL FOIL THOSE CROOKS

MOVING AS SWIFTLY AS THEIR MEDICATION ALLOWED, THE MENTALLY-ILL RODENTS SET TO WORK....

...WEAVING A LARGE WICKER WASTE PAPER BASKET

NICE WORK, GUYS — THAT'S WHAT I CALL A REAL "LOONY BIN"!
NOW LET'S GET THOSE ROBBERS!

GOTCHA!
WHAT TH-?!
LOOT
LEAP!
YOW! WHO PUT OUT THE LIGHTS?

AND YOUR BONKERS DORMICE HAVE SAVED THE DAY. HELP YOURSELF TO ANYTHING FROM MY HARDWARE SHOP AS A REWARD
LOOT
DORMOUSE PSYCHIATRIC HOSPITAL
HMM — IN THAT CASE, I'LL TAKE ONE OF THOSE PINS, PLEASE...

JUST THE JOB FOR PERFORMING FULL FRONTAL LOBOTOMIES ON ALL MY DORMOUSE PATIENTS
DORMOUSE PSYCHIATRIC HOSPITAL
JAB
POKE
HO! HO! THIS'LL CURE THEM OF THEIR MADCAP TOMFOOLERY PERMANENTLY!
HA HA HA!

D.I.V.O.R.C.

Widower seeks split from wife after death

A HENPECKED Lincolnshire man is finally set to divorce his wife - *even though she has been DEAD for 18 years!*

EXCLUSIVE

Unemployed shopfitter Arthur Poindexter says he's so fed up with his late wife's nagging from beyond the grave that he's hired a MEDIUM to start legal proceedings to end his marriage in the afterlife.

Arthur, 58, wed his childhood sweetheart Renee in 1965 but almost immediately things started to go wrong. He told us: "She started nagging me before we even left the reception, and it carried on throughout our marriage."

Henpecked Arthur put up with Renee's constant carping for twenty years, until she was killed by a bus on her way home from the bingo. "I was a bit upset at first, but it was a new lease of life for me," he told us. "At last I was free from her giving it that in my earhole all the time. I was looking forward to finally getting a bit of peace and quiet." But Arthur's peace was short-lived.

TILL LIFE AFTER DEATH US DO PART: *Hen-pecked Arthur today and* (inset) *in happier times with wife Renee 38 years ago yesterday.*

"After the funeral, all the family came back here for a drink and a few sandwiches," he told us. "By the time everybody had gone home I'd had a few sherries and was feeling a bit emotional, so I decided to go upstairs for a lie down." But in his bedroom, Arthur got the shock of his life.

"I hadn't been in bed two minutes when the room went icy cold. Suddenly, a shadowy figure floated through the wall. It was Renee's ghost, and she wanted me to go downstairs and do the dishes. I tried to hide under the covers but it was no use; she just kept going on and on in an unearthly voice about the state of the sink, so in the end I went down and did them just to shut her up."

Sure enough, as soon as the dishes were dried and put away, the apparition disappeared. Arthur thought it was the end of his troubles, but as it turned out they were only just beginning.

"The next day I was sitting reading the Racing Post with my feet up on the coffee table. Suddenly, what I can only describe as an unseen force seemed to kick my legs to the floor. Then the hoover switched itself on. I tried to turn it off but nothing seemed to work.

"Then suddenly Renee's disembodied head appeared, floating above the mantelpiece. It was ashen-white and transparent. She told me to get off my lazy backside and vac the stairs.

"I was petrified, but I did as I was told. It was only when I'd done the stairs, including the half landing, that the machine switched off as mysteriously as it had switched on."

Over the last eighteen years the visitations have become more and more frequent. Now Renee's ghost materialises up to thirty times a day to bend Arthur's ear. Amongst her bizarre hauntings, she has

*** *WRITTEN* 'clean this now' in the dust on Arthur's TV screen**

*** *MANIFESTED* in the back of his car, telling him a traffic light was red**

*** *CREATED* havoc with poltergeist activity, causing brillo pads to whirl round the kitchen whilst the oven door slammed open and shut**

Arthur put up with Renee's ghostly carping until this Christmas, when she finally went one haunting too far.

"It was Christmas eve and I was popping out to the local for a pint with some friends. Renee manifested as usual, just as I was leaving the house. The phantasm warned me to be back in by ten or there'd be hell to pay. Unfortunately, there was a lock-in and I didn't get back till after one.

"I was hoping to sneak in without raising my late wife's vengeful spirit, but it was no good. As I turned the corner I could see her apparition hovering above the step. She had her head under her arm and a face like thunder. As I reached the front door, her ghostly voice asked me what time I called this, but before I had a chance to answer she hit me over the head with a

EEK!

see-through rolling pin.

"I certainly had some explaining to do in casualty."

Arthur decided enough was enough, and contacted Doris Stokes-Taylor-Joynson-Garrett, Britain's top spiritualist solicitor, and instructed her to begin legal proceedings to bring his marriage to an end.

"Doris got on the case straight away, and her red indian spirit guide Chief Billy Two Rivers served divorce papers on Renee straight away," said Arthur. "My late wife's solicitor then contacted me via the Ouija board to arrange a hearing seance next Tuesday.

"Basically, the judge will explain to Renee's spectre that I'm seeking the divorce on the grounds of her unreasonable paranormal behaviour. She has to rap on the table twice or make the lights go dim to accept the decree absolute."

But Arthur isn't celebrating his freedom just yet. He told us: "I can't see her giving up that easily. I'll not break out the champagne until I've got that piece of paper in my hand. I know my Renee only too well. I might get the vicar round to exorcise the house anyway, just to be on the safe side."

NAG WATCH U.K.

ARTHUR POINDEXTER isn't the only man to suffer his wife's nagging from beyond the grave. Amazingly, the British Isles are riddled with cases of dead fishwives making their husbands' lives a misery from the other side.

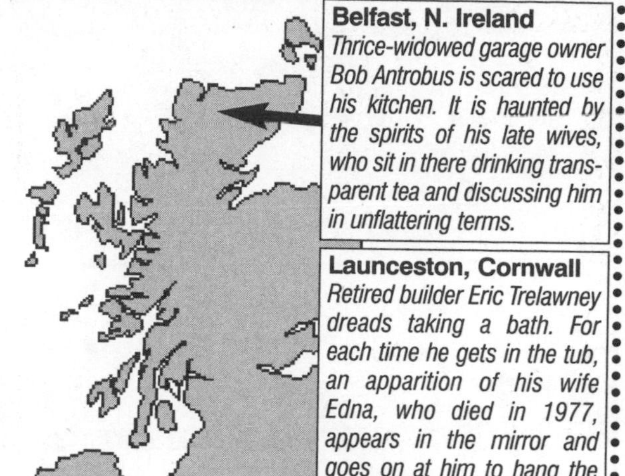

Belfast, N. Ireland
Thrice-widowed garage owner Bob Antrobus is scared to use his kitchen. It is haunted by the spirits of his late wives, who sit in there drinking transparent tea and discussing him in unflattering terms.

Launceston, Cornwall
Retired builder Eric Trelawney dreads taking a bath. For each time he gets in the tub, an apparition of his wife Edna, who died in 1977, appears in the mirror and goes on at him to hang the bath-mat up.

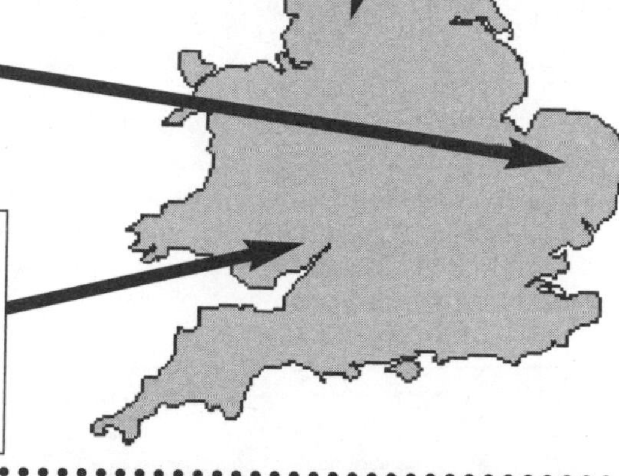

Oban, Sutherland
Each year, on the anniversary of his wife Morag's death, crofter Hamish McTavish is woken at midnight by a strange grey figure, who tells him she cannot rest until some shelves he bought in 1982 are put up.

Braintree, Essex
Since dying in 1973, Edna Bartram has visited her husband Jack every night. Her ghostly figure sits purse-lipped, pointedly refusing to speak to him, uttering a ghostly tut each time he asks what he's done wrong.

Is there anybody there?

Find out with our fantastic henpecked widower's Ouija Board

Don't keep your late missus waiting till the witching hour. Find out what the old battleaxe wants any time of day with this fabulous Cut Out & Keep Widowers' Travel Ouija Board.

Instructions

Cut out the board and stick it to a piece of stiff card. To summon the old trout's restless spirit from the other side, simply put an upturned Night Nurse cup on the central pentangle, place your right finger on it, and ask in a quavery voice if anybody is there. Once she has made her presence known, sit back and get nagged at, occasionally saying "yes, dear."

The Diary of Samuel L. Pepys

Thursday September 17th

1. I did arise by five, before day, and went to market to buy fowle and lamprey for dinner with Rear Admiral Kempthorne, his lady and his young cozens this night. Sweet bitches alright.

2. At market I had cause to speke roughly with one trader. Near twenty shillings for a sack posset and a dish of anchovies! Had to stand on the motherfucker's head so he could hear me better.

3. To the admiralty, there to attend a court martial of Captain Middleton. Lord, to hear of his rogueries and wretched doings! Popped a cap in his knee for his cheeke.

4. Thence home. And cooke come to prepare of dinner. Fat-assed motherfucker did reeke of wines and ales such that I caused to teach him his misgivings by boyling his unrighteous head.

5. Evening, and Rear Admiral Kempthorne come with his wife and, to my great content, his two cozens, whom I found to be of excellent discourse with titties to beat the motherfucking band.

6. Dinner was noble enough and my lady Emma did sing most finely so as to ravish us. Young Rose put her hand beneath the table to rest on my britches and therein, my dick.

Samuel L. Pepys was a highly respected member of court and government in 17th century London. He rose to become secretary of the Admiralty, and even did some time up the big house for alleged complicity in a plot to whack the Pope, surviving to become president of the Royal Society. A Bad Motherfucker, Pepys' diaries have supplied historians with the word on what shit went down with the highlife and lowlife of the capital in turbulent times - the plague, the great fire, the dope drought of '59 - all are documented in his faithful journal, giving us a true flavour of the situation around being a society brother in the big bad city. However, it wasn't all whores with sores and crap floating in the damn street. There was some fine pussy and grade A shit to be located if a brother kept himself on the good foot and looked after his moves.

7. The Admiral and his wife and I did withdrawe for port and to eat of fruits. Rose and Emma sat to sew and I to join them. To my great content, they smoke the bone with my barely asking.

8. Rear Admiral Kempthorne did spoil our mirth in bare five minutes. Red like a Kentish strawberry the brother chances to roar at my countenance and utter such words as are rarely heard!

9. Afore I could calm myself, I have ventured my flintlock into the old man's mouth. Thence to teach him of his rough ways and how he should not push his face to mine thusly.

10. The fat man's heart gives out presently. The Rear Admiral expires. His wife comes thither to find a scene and becomes shrill and undone. I need to slap some shush into her ugly face.

11. My Lord enjoys a moonlit swim from the chamber window. My lady continues in disarray wailing and lamenting of her late husband. I shoot the bitch out of God-damned principle.

12. My ladies Rose and Emma seem saddened, but are content once more on learning my lordship's legacy will make them the richest bitches in Southwark. And so to bed.

ABDUL LATIF'S Letterbocks

Brought to you by www.rentalord.com

I recently went along to the cinema to see *Calendar Girls,* but having done so, I advise your readers not to waste their money. Calendar 'Girls'? I don't think so. There wasn't a woman under 50 in it. The makers should have set it in the 6th form of a girls' school. That would have made it a much better film. Maybe they could have kept Helen Mirren in as the headmistress to cane any naughty schoolgirls, but the rest of the old boilers would have to go. It's no wonder our film industry is always in the doldrums.

Derek Coster, e-mail

So I'm not allowed to wear my hat in church, yet 'Sir' Elton John is allowed to keep his wig on whilst he sings at Lady Di's funeral in Westminster Abbey. And while I'm on the subject, the bishop doing the service left his titfer on as well.

T. Holliwell, Leeds

On Sunday morning, I borrowed my flatmate's 'Fido Dido Hangover Heaven' bubblebath which claims to make you feel better the morning after a night on the town. I fail to see, however, how a bottle of girly foam bath could ever remove the shame of pissing in the centre pocket of the pool table, being thrown out by the doormen for 'not being able to see', getting undressed in the kebab shop and shitting the bed, the stain of which will remain with me for some time to come.

Sean 'Magiclord' Scholfield, Penge

I recently ran a marathon for charity whilst bitterly hung over. After a dramatic sprint finish, watched by about a hundred people, I ate my chips backwards over Bob Holness who was handing out the medals. I think I got some on his wife's shoes as well.

Olly, London

Letterbocks
Viz Comic
P.O.Box 1PT
Newcastle NE99 1PT

In this space age you can electromail your letters and tips to letters@viz.co.uk

£50 STAR LETTER

***WHY ALL** this fuss about David Blaine getting in a box without food for forty days? British magician David Nixon did that when I was a kid, and as far as I know he's still in there, without food OR water. But does our press report this? Once again the Americans get all the glory.*

William Budd, e-mail

I love the stories and articles in *Viz,* but how about more pictures of bushbabies jumping onto sausage dogs' backs?

Edna Lamprey, Dover

* *Okay, Edna, just for you.*

In this day of modern communications, I find it unbelievable that although the terrible September 11th attacks on New York took place at 9.00am, we didn't find out about them until halfway through the afternoon.

Jake, Catford

When the Pope travels from country to country on his visits, does he have to go through customs like everyone else, or do the airport authorities make an exception? If, as I suspect, they do, then it is just another example of one law for the rich and one law for the rest of us. If, however, he is subject to the same border checks as everyone else, then what a disgraceful slur on the honesty and integrity of this great religious leader. Either way, the hypocrisy sickens me.

T. Holliwell, Leeds

This morning I went to the toilet as usual. When I had finished, I casually glanced into the pan to look at my deposit and noticed there was an apple sticker stuck to one of my turds. Can any of you readers beat that?

Mr Tumnus, Cardiff

On a recent visit to my mother's, I passed a supermarket called *Sainsburys Local,* but it is at least 10 miles from my house.

Kevin Larder, e-mail

Brendan Foster's Jigsaw Corner

Dear Brendan,

Last week I finished a 500-piece jigsaw of some kittens in a pint mug. Next week I'm going to start one of some lovely shire horses... with 750 pieces!

Mrs Edna Weltsmertz Dundee

Dear Brendan,

The things kids say! Whilst I was doing a 5000-piece jigsaw of a thatched country cottage, my five year old grandson looked over my shoulder and piped up: "Granny, why are you wasting so much of what's left of your life doing something so utterly, utterly futile?"

Una Emptyness Dundee

Dear Brendan,

I was once doing a 2000-piece jigsaw of some yachts, and I spent hours looking for a bit with 3 innies and an outie that was mainly blue with a bit of red at the top. In the end, I asked my husband to help. 'Do you mean this bit?' he asked, picking it up straight away. That was 26 years ago, and there isn't a day goes by when he doesn't remind me of it.

Mrs Ada Pointless Dundee

Dear Brendan,

I recently bought a puzzle of an Alpine scene. The box said that there were 4000 pieces, but when I counted them there were only 3998. I counted them four or five times, but each time came up with the same number. I am puzzled.

Mrs Ena Despair Dundee

**Don't worry, Mrs Despair. The number of pieces on the box is just a rough guide to give you an idea as to the complexity of the puzzle. There may be one or two pieces fewer or greater that stated.*

Dear Brendan,

I last saw my son 10 years ago when he emigrated to New Zealand. He married out there and had three lovely children. He recently sent me a photgraph of them, which I have had enlarged and made into a 1000-piece jigsaw. When I do this puzzle, I feel like they're almost in the room with me. When it's finished, I give them all a kiss, have a little cry, then break it up and start all over again.

Mrs Ida Tragic Dundee

Dear Brendan,

Has anyone lost this piece of jigsaw puzzle that I recently found on Muir Street in Dundee?

Yootha Sad Dundee

** Is this piece of what looks like mainly grass with a bit of snow or perhaps sky and a brown bit missing from YOUR jigsaw? If so, simply cut it out from the magazine and stick it onto a piece of cardboard from the back of a cornflakes packet.*

Are **YOU** missing a piece from **YOUR** jigsaw? Write in, giving as detailed a description as possible, and Brendan's army of eagle-eyed spotters will keep an eye out for it.

I Spent a Pony on Crap

After being in the pub all Saturday afternoon, me and the missus decided we'd better do a munchie run in preparation for the long night's drinking binge. We staggered off to our local convenience store where we sensibly asked for a receipt (below) for our purchases. Can any of your readers beat this awesome acquisition of comfort food?

Phil Wills, Exeter

DAWN TIL DARK
CONVENIENCE STORES
1A PRINCES STREET EAST
EXETER EX2 9ES
TEL NO 01392 667810

Item	Qty	Unit price	Price
SMITHS SCAMPI FRIES 27GR	7 @	£0.32	£2.24
SMITHS CHEESE MOMENTS 28G	17 @	£0.32	£5.44
FLAPJACKS 6'S			£0.95
BOBBYS BACON STREAKS 50G PM.30	2 @	£0.30	£0.60
WALKERS FRENCH FRIES CHEESE &	6 @	£0.32	£1.92
WALKERS FRENCH FRIES FISH & CH	11 @	£0.32	£3.52
SPACE RAIDERS CRISPS SALT & VI	4 @	£0.10	£0.40
BOBBYS PORK CRACKLES 50GR			£0.55
BOBBYS PORK CRACKLES 50GR			£0.55
STARBURST JOOSTERS LARGE BAG 2			£1.25
TOMS SWEET 'N' SOUR JELLY BAB			£0.99
MISCELLENEOUS			£1.00
HARIBO GOLD BEARS 175G			£0.99
CADBURY FLAKE CONE STRAWBERRY			£1.10
BOUNTY ICE CREAM LOLLY			£1.10
STARBURST STRAWBERRY ICE CREAM			£1.00
BOUNTY ICE CREAM LOLLY			£1.10
SNICKER ICE CREAM CONE 70GR			£1.00
CADBURYS ICE CREAM FLAKE CONE			£1.10
CADBURY. CARAMEL BAR			£0.39
CADBURY CARAMEL BAR			£0.39
CADBURY'S FRUIT & NUT 49G			£0.41
GALAXY CARAMEL SWIRL			£1.10
CADBURYS FLAKE DESSERT 100GR	3 @	£0.67	£2.01
CADBURY TWIN O			£-0.67
PORK FAM INDIVDUAL PORK& PICKL			£1.19
PORK FAM INDIVDUAL PORK& PICKL			£1.19
TIA LUSSO CREAM LIQUEUR 700ML			£13.99
H S CHOCOLATE MILKSHAKE 500ML			£0.69
H S BANANA MILKSHAKE 500ML			£0.69
HEINZ TREACLE PUDDING 320G			£1.29
KINDER SURPRISE EGG			£0.49
KINDER SURPRISE EGG			£0.49
Total:			**£50.45**
Vat:			£4.86

VAT ANALYSIS

** Can YOU better Phil's admirable shopping basket of junk, (slightly let down by the flapjacks, which are also available in health food shops)? Send your receipt to Comfort Food Blowout, Viz Comic, PO Box 1PT, Newcastle upon Tyne, NE99 1PT.*

All the women at work think I'm just trying it on when I tell them that my wife doesn't understand me. But it's true. She's a fourteen year old mail-order Thai bride who speaks no English.

A Newens, Isle of Skye

The manager of this souvenir shop in Holland would be very happy if any readers (female probably) would come round and inspect his goods.

Peter Hicks, Cleethorpes

What on earth is the matter with these people who keep banging on about bringing back hanging? Surely if capital punshment is to be reintroduced, we should think of a new method of executing prisoners, such as throwing them to sharks, or microwaving them.

Mrs J Scrotum, Ipswich

Last week I was listening to the classic Beatles song *A Hard Day's Night,* when I started thinking about the line 'I've been working like a dog'. has any reader actually seen a dog do any work except lick its own balls? If anyone happens to see Sir Paul McCartney in the street, could they please point this out to him.

The John Jakson, Wallington

They say you always hurt the one you love. If that's the case, I saw these four pissed up Geordies on the Quayside last Saturday night who had a pretty solid relationship with a southern student.

Simon Smedley, Newcastle

I saw an advert on the telly showing a film called the *Greatest Story Ever Told.* This is indeed some boast, as it would need to be one hell of a tale to beat the one my mate Baz told me about him and two strippers last Friday after doing tequilla shots and some coke.

Marty Morrissey, e-mail

Whilst stuck in a siding on a Virgin train, it occurred to me that the phrase 'Whatever you say about Hitler, at least he got the trains running on time' is especially pertinent today. I propose that when the Americans finally track down Saddam Hussain, who has often been compared to the late fuhrer, they hand him over to Network Rail and let him sort out the mess on our railways. They could chuck in the Queen Mum's old palace as part of the deal.

Simon Teabag Cacafuego, A siding somewhere

ME AND my mates all subscribe to satellite porn channels, and we were wondering which, if any, of the Spice Girls share our viewing habits. Our money is on Baby Spice, Emma Bunton. We would love to know one way or another. If only any of your readers worked for a TV company and had access to conclusive information one way or the other.

Name and address lost Sorry

**Do any readers have acces to this confidential information? Write in the strictest confidence and let us know.*

ONE MP has, by definition, got the smallest penis in Parliament. I've got a hunch, and it's nothing more than that, that it is foreign secretary Jack Straw. I know this will never be asked at Prime Minister's question time, so how can I find out?

Mrs Compton Leicester

** Are you an MP, or work in the Houses of Parliament? Do you ever go in the lower ground floor gymnasium at the same time as Jack Straw? If so, write and let us know, in the strictest confidence, how tiny his honourable member is.*

Do YOU have a suspicion about a celebrity's private life? Write to Stars Confidential at the usual address and we'll do our best to confirm it.

AFTER a hard night's drinking, eat two heaped spoonfuls of Bisto granules before going to bed and 'stir' by gyrating your waist. The following morning's inevitable bum gravy will be nicely thickened.

Andrew McGuigan, Stanley

OIL COMPANIES. Buy twenty quid's worth of groceries at Safeway and you'll be given a voucher for 20p off a litre of petrol. Send one of your tankers and fill it up with 20,000 litres and save 4 grand. Then sell it at your own petrol stations at the normal price. Safeway are in some disarray at present and are unlikely to work out your scam, and you won't have to rob your employee's pension funds to shore up your profits.

Terry Leahy, e-mail

AMERICANS. Save valuable time by not appending the words 'God Bless America' to your every fucking sentence.

John Terry, Newcastle upon Tyne

FOOTBALL fans with a lisp. Support Barcelona so as you can shout for your team without appearing stupid.

Welly Gogster, Kidsgrove

DON'T buy your sister-in-law a thong for her birthday then expect your wife to be pleased, particularly if you comment on how nice her arse looks in it.

GMK, e-mail

TOWN Councils. Reduce litter problems by issuing blind people with pointy sticks.

Rich, Ilford

BREAD knives can also be used to cut cheese.

Benjamin Gardner, e-mail

HORSE riders. Guard against your horse getting fat by giving it Hermesetas instead of sugar lumps.

Tracy Chitty, Hastings

WHEN visiting a Moto service station for a cup of tea and a slice of cake, make sure you arrange your bank loan or second mortgage before you get to the tills, saving time and embarrassment.

Russell Dundee, e-mail

ALCOHOLICS. Instead of hiding cans of cider from your wife in the laundry basket, or using Chlorets to disguise the smell of vomit from your boss, use your deviousness and intellect for greater financial reward by becoming a criminal mastermind like Lex Luther or Ernst Blofeld.

Dave Storey, e-mail

TOBACCO manufacturers. Be more positive in your packaging by pointing out that your customers may be able to star in their own TV commercial.

Tracy Chitty, Hastings

IF YOU want your mother-in-law never to come back to your house, buy her a razor for Christmas.

Dave Oxendale, York

CYCLISTS. Avoid getting a sore arse by simply placing a naan bread over your saddle. This will comfort your ride and when you return home, hey presto! A warm snack.

Chris Pearson, Southampton

Have YOUR say...

Comedy terrorist Aaron Barschak's gatecrashing of Prince William's 21st birthday bash has highlighted how vulnerable the Royal Family is to attack. On this occasion, they were merely subjected to 60 seconds of an embarrassing comedy routine. Next time it could be much, much worse. We went on the street to ask how YOU would protect Britain's V-est IPs.

...I think everyone in Britain who is not a member of the Royal Family should be forced to wear a collar with a bell on it. This would prevent anyone from creeping up on Royals unawares and attacking them from behind. Though I daresay the politically correct lobby will moan about civil liberties as usual.

Mrs Audrey Murphy, Housewife

...I work as a pest control officer, and I think terrorists could be caught in the same way as wasps. The government should build an enormous trap shaped like Buckingham Palace and bait it, not with jam, but with that woman who looks like the Queen. When the terrorists are trapped inside, they could be swatted with a giant rolled up newspaper on a crane.

Jim Nicelybig, Pest Control Office

...During the last war, the country's art treasures were evacuated to the relative safety of the inside of a Welsh mountain until hostilities were over. Since we are now at war with terrorism, and the Queen is our more priceless national treasure - valued at £7 billion - is there not now a case for entombing her many hundreds of feet under Wales until the battle against the axis of evil is won?

Mrs Anniseed Balls, Secretary

...The Royal Family would be much safer on the streets if everyone in Britain were forced to wear a muzzle at all times like a mad dog. It would be an end to some things we now take for granted, like drinking in pubs and eating out, but it would be a small price to pay for their Majesties' safety.

Mrs Audrey Murphy, Housewife

...Once again, the royalists want to have their cake and eat it. They claim that the one of the main functions of the Queen and her family is to help the tourist industry by attracting foreigners into the country. Then when foreigners do turn up to attack her, they start whingeing. I wish they'd make their minds up one way or the other.

Eric Tiletissue, Fluffer

...Terrorists such as Aaron Barschak and Osama Bin Laden will literally stop at nothing. I am concerned that they may attempt to plant dynamite up the anus of one of the Queen's beloved horses. To safeguard against such an outrage, the security services should superglue their bottoms shut.

Anton Karas, Zitherist

...The Queen should take a leaf out of cross-channel swimmers' books, and keep herself greased head-to-toe with goose fat. That way, when a terrorist attempted to grab her and make off with her, she would slip easily out of his evil clutches. It would cost the taxpayers a small fortune to keep our monarch coated with the high quality fat her position demands, but it would be money well spent if it prevented her being stolen.

B. Two Rivers, Indian spirit guide

...It's a farce. When Al Quaeda finally do succeed in wiping out our Royal family in a terrorist outrage, they'll probably just get a few hours' community service, and an apology from the Prime Minister for the distress they suffer being arrested. They'll walk away with tens of thousands of pounds in compensation ... and who'll be footing the bill? Joe Muggins here.

Joe Muggins, Builder

...The tyres on Michael Knight's car in Knightrider were bulletproof. Why not make the Queen a Michelin Man-style all-over bodysuit out of tyres - complete with a rubber gimp mask in case Bin Laden decides to go for a head shot? McCloud actor Dennis Weaver lives in a pile of tyres and he's not been murdered by terrorists yet.

Hazelnut Monkbottle, Beautician

...The only way to protect the Royal family from unwanted acts of aggression is for the entire population of the world except them to be castrated. This will make an unprovoked attack on the monarch and her family much less likely.

Mrs Audrey Murphy, Housewife

...The rot set in when Michael Fagan was allowed to sneak into Buckingham Palace and feel the Queen's breasts. He should have been hung, drawn and quartered, with his head set up on a pole at Traitors' Gate as a warning to Aaron Barschak and his terrorist ilk.

Bartram Shoelace, Meteorologist

ROGER MELLIE - THE MAN ON THE TELLY

LORDY, LORDY!... IT'S THE FAT SLAGS

BLACKWOOD 'LEAST FAMOUS MAN IN WORLD' say scientists

BBC spokesblack *Richard Blackwood* is the least famous man in the world according to a team of top boffins from Cambridge University.

Blackwood - not famous, yesterday

The eggheads' findings are published this week in New Scientist magazine and TV Quick following four years of research into the career of the almost successful comedian and singer. The conclusions ought to deliver a shattering blow to Blackwood's ego, although this is unlikely.

The blue-cross-week Will Smith, currently on our screens as the one no-one can recognise under John Simpson's rubber face, continues to confound researchers with his ability to masquerade as a top celebrity despite never having done anything anyone has given a hoot about ever.

Insignificance

Team leader Dr Horst Bucholdz used state of the art techniques in order to calibrate Blackwood's indistinguishability from millions of ordinary people.

"We employ a scale called the Bedingfield Index to measure the difference between how successful, fulfilled and talented a person believes themselves to be and the actual, grim truth of their anonymity and desperation. Richard scored over 108 points, putting him firmly in the 'who?' camp."

Don't Look Now

The shock figures show that Blackwood is slightly less famous than the man who does the night-shift in the Texaco StarMarket near Gordano Services at Junction 19 of the M4.

"I have examined the evidence thoroughly, and I am convinced even Mr Blackwood's mother would have some difficulty picking him out of a queue of people in Homebase," said Dr Bucholdz. "Several times during our work, we were forced to pin large, labelled photographs of Mr Blackwood on the laboratory wall to remind ourselves whom we were meant to be studying. He's really nothing special."

Walkabout

Undaunted by the findings, Blackwood is due to appear in over a dozen television projects and advertisments in the coming year, none of which, the researchers predict, will have any tangible effect on his fame whatsoever.

Flavoured condoms

NEW! duos

a taste of luxury for him...
...and for her!

one flavour OUTSIDE for the lady...
another flavour INSIDE for the gentleman!

MODEL	OUTSIDE, the lady loves...	INSIDE, the big man taste of...
BEAULIEU XL	Chocolate	Chili
MARLBOROUGH	Pie	Peas
RISE&SHINE	Egg	Bacon
DUOBASIC	Spunk	Fanny
THE DeVERE	Fruit Pastilles	Bella Emberg
BIG NIGHT OUT	Onion Bhaji, Chana Dhal, Lamb Rogon Josh, Pilau Rice, Banana Kulfi and a pint of Kingfisher please and a mint and a hot towel	Bella Emberg
EL DOLCE VITA	Bananas and Custard	Hot Custard
LA DOMINATRIX	Marigold Washing-Up Glove	Garden Hose

Yes! I want to experience the shared pleasure of DUOS™ with my partner! Please send me the following in a plain, brown, lasagne / murray mint flavoured wrapper:

BEAULIEU XL ☐ BIGNIGHTOUT ☐
MARLBOROUGH ☐ EL DOLCE VITA ☐
RISE&SHINE ☐ LA DOMINATRIX ☐
DUOBASIC ☐ BOLLARD ☐
THE DeVERE ☐ HESELTINE ☐

NAME ....
ADDRESS ....
.... POSTCODE ....
I enclose a cheque or luncheon vouchers for £2 per pack of DUOS.
Allow 28 days for delivery, slightly longer at lunchtimes.

SUPER-SAFE! SUPER-DELICIOUS!

LATEXCELLENCE Ltd
Unit 477, Bulgaria Buildings, Moth Street, Whitby

DUOS can only help prevent unwanted pregancies and sexually transmitted disease as part of a calorie-controlled diet.

He's a Celebrity - *Get Him Out of There!*

Frank finds Ant in chocolate egg

A SHOCKED office worker who bit into a Cadbury's Creme Egg got more than he bargained for when he found *Ant out of Ant and Dec* inside feasting on the filling!

Trainee invoice clerk Frank Liar bought the 35p treat from the office tea trolley, but when he munched on it he felt the tiny telly star wriggling about in his mouth. He immediately spat him out, and fellow workers screamed when they saw Ant out of Ant and Dec squirming in the egg's sticky fondant centre.

vomited

Frank told us: "I thought it tasted a bit odd, but I didn't expect to find Ant out of Ant and Dec inside. I used to love Cadbury's Creme Eggs, but I'll never buy one again. I nearly vomited when I realised how close I'd come to swallowing Ant out of Ant and Dec."

Sources close to Dec out of Ant and Dec last night maintained that Dec out of Ant and Dec had no explanation for how his partner Ant out of Ant and Dec could have got into the egg. They told us: "It's a complete mystery."

urgent

Meanwhile, a Cadbury's spokesman promised that an urgent investigation was underway. He said: "As Britain's leading chocolate manufacturers we strive to maintain the strictest hygiene standards throughout our operation. However, with such a large operation it's unavoidable that Ant out of Ant and Dec will occasionally end up in our products."

GILBERT
RATCHET
INVENTION PLANS

I'M OFF TO SCHOOL TO IMPROVE MY EDUCATION, READERS.
SCHOOL
WHIRR
WHIRR
AND THESE "HANDS-OFF-O-MATIC" METAL PANTS WITH ROTATING KNIVES SHOULD PREVENT ME GETTING MOLESTED BY P.E. TEACHERS IN THE CHANGING ROOM

COO! WHAT'S UP WITH THE HEADMASTER?
SCHOOL
HE LOOKS GLUM

I'M AFRAID OUR SCHOOL BULLY ISN'T EFFECTIVE ENOUGH, GILBERT
ERM... GIVE ME YOUR DINNER MONEY... SOMEONE...
THERE ARE SIMPLY TOO MANY YOUNGER CHILDREN FOR HIM TO COPE WITH

I'M CONCERNED THAT MY PUPILS AREN'T RECEIVING A PROPER ROUNDED BULLYING
LOOK - EVEN THESE SPECKY FOUR-EYED KIDS ARE DISPLAYING SOME VESTIGES OF SELF-ESTEEM.

NOT TO WORRY HEADMASTER
NAILS
I'LL INVENT A MACHINE WHICH WILL RAISE YOUR PUPILS' PERSECUTION AND MISERY LEVELS UP ABOVE THE NATIONAL STANDARD

HEY PRESTO! THE FULLY AUTOMATED BULLY-O-TRON!
OFF
THIS GIANT HYDRAULIC-POWERED STEEL KNUCKLE CAN ADMINISTER A VICIOUS "DEAD ARM" RIGHT ON THE VICTIM'S BCG INJECTION, WITH PINPOINT ACCURACY.

GILBERT'S MACHINE WILL PUT ME OUT OF A JOB.
OFF
BUT I'LL SABOTAGE IT BY LOOSENING A COUPLE OF SCREWS

WE'LL TEST IT OUT ON THIS FIRST-FORMER. STAND BY FOR PRELIMINARY TAUNTING...
PSSSSSSHT
OFF
ON
HISS
HA! THOSE TRAINERS ARE GAY!
I'M GOING TO DO YOU!

CRIKEY! IT MISSED!
SCHOOL GOVERNOR
WHUMP
OFF
SMASH!
..AND THE KNUCKLE HAS COME LOOSE OFF ITS ARM AND GONE THROUGH THE SCHOOL GOVERNOR'S WINDOW!

SPANG!
OOF!

YOU IDIOT, GILBERT!
YOU'VE GONE AND KILLED THE SCHOOL GOVERNOR WITH YOUR BIG KNUCKLE!

WOOOO! WOOOO! I AM THE GHOST OF THE JUST-DEPARTED SCHOOL GOVERNOR!
OO-ER! NOW I'M IN FOR A RIGHT GHOSTLY LEATHERING

NOT AT ALL! I WAS JUST READING THE NOSTALGIC REMINISCENCES OF MY OLD SCHOOLMATES ON THE 'FRIENDS REUNITED' WEBSITE
FRIENDS REUNITED
AND I WAS SO OVERCOME WITH A SENSE OF DEPRESSION AND FUTILITY THAT I DECIDED TO KILL MYSELF ANYWAY!

THANKS GILBERT ~ YOU'VE SAVED ME THE COST OF A BULLET
A-LEVEL CERTIFICATE
PLEASE ACCEPT THESE ASSORTED GRADE 'A' A-LEVELS, AS A REWARD
HEY, GREAT!

AND ≤MUNCH≥ WITH THOSE A-LEVELS I WAS ABLE TO GET INTO OXFORD UNIVERSITY AND DO A DEGREE IN SWEETS STUDIES
OXFORD UNIVERSITY DEPT OF SWEETS AND LOLLIES
GOB STOPPERS
SWEETS
LOLLIES
TOFFEE
HAPPY LEARNING, READERS!

FRU T. BUNN the MASTER BAKER & his GINGERBREAD SEX DOLLS

"...HI... I'M DEBBIE. I'M A 16 YEAR OLD GINGERBREAD GIRL... AND I LOVE HORSE RIDING AND POP MUSIC..."
TAP TAP TAP

HEY! THAT DIDN'T TAKE LONG. SOMEBODY'S ANSWERING!
BLING!
YOU HAVE A REPLY
READ DON'T READ

PHWOOAR! SHE'S FALLEN FOR IT HOOK LINE AND SINKER!
—HI DEBBIE :) ME TOO!!! CAN WE BE FRIENDS? WHAT DO YOU LOOK LIKE? LOVE FROM SOPHIE :)
REPLY?
YES NO

"HI SOPHIE. I'VE GOT BROWN RAISIN EYES AND BLONDE ICING HAIR... WHAT DO YOU LOOK LIKE..?
TAP TAP TAP

BLING!
SHE SOUNDS GORGEOUS! DROOL!
—I'VE GOT BROWN RAISINS TOO BUT MY ICING HAIR IS SHORT AND BLACK :)
REPLY?
YES NO

"...LET'S MEET AND TALK ABOUT HORSES AND POP MUSIC :)..."
BLING!
TAP TAP
TAP TAP

BINGO!
—OKAY!!! I'LL SEE YOU IN THE PRECINCT IN TEN MINUTES!!!
LOVE SOPHIE :)

WA-HEY! THE OLD BUNN CHARM WORKS ITS MAGIC ONCE AGAIN. SHE'LL BE PUTTY IN MY HANDS, THE POOR INNOCENT YOUNG FLOWER.
BUNN & Co
QUALITY BAKERS
I CAN'T WAIT TO DO HER!

TEN MINUTES LATER...
HAIR BY DENISE
NEWSAGENT & RETAIL TOBACCONIST
KEEP

Monthly Bill!

MY PERIODS ARE ALL OVER THE PLACE AT THE MOMENT!

DARLING? WOULD YOU LIKE TO MAKE LOVE TONIGHT?

SORRY, LOVE! I'VE JUST COME ON, I'M AFRAID!

DON'T LOOK AT ME LIKE THAT! I DON'T PLAN IT THIS WAY!!

Paul Palmer

DALTON SPLINTERS TV STAR'S NOSE

Punches thrown at voice-throw Peer

VENTRILOQUIST's dummy *Lord Charles* sensationally announced yesterday how he and Bad Bond *Timothy Dalton* were involved in a bar-room brawl.

The incident occurred following a twelve hour champagne bender that the posh puppet had organised for celebrity chums to celebrate his 400th birthday.

"It was all going rather well." Charles told a press conference held in handler Ray Alan's loft: "We'd all had a bally lot to drink, I lost count after four or five gottles, but the general mood was one of celebration, not violence. At least it was until Mr. Dalton arrived."

Not Going Back in the Box

Liverpudlian golfer Jimmy Tarbuck, a lifelong colleague of the wooden puppet, was present at the party when TV star Dalton made his entrance.

"He (Dalton) spotted Charlie across the room and immediately began hurling drunken abuse at him." Tarbuck explained over his luxury telephone.

"He was ranting about how awful Octopussy was in comparison to The Living Daylights and accusing him of hamming it up in The Spy Who Loved Me."

Not Going Back in the Box

"A few people laughed it off as a joke, but Tim wasn't smiling. He was deadly serious," the celebrity's pal continued. "That's when things started to kick off."

At first the monocled mannequin tried to placate the 57 year-old actor, but it wasn't long before he retaliated:

Not Going Back in the Box

"It's all a bit of a blur, but I do remember calling him a silly ass and explaining that he'd mistaken me for some other poor fellow." Charles told reporters. "It must have been my bowtie, half-scale tuxedo and behaviour as the quintessential English gentleman that confused him."

Eyewitnesses say at this point that boozed-up RSC ship-jumper Dalton:

- ***KNOCKED*** the puppet from his handler's lap
- ***SMASHED*** his dandy monocle and
- ***KICKED*** him in the gollocks

before 'borrowing' a taxi parked outside the club and driving off.

Lord Charles, who has no plans at time of writing to file charges against his high-profile assailant, will be appearing on ITV3 later this year in a new adaptation of the classic 1960s series 'The Saint'.

For your black eyes only - bad boy Bond (above) and (below) the timber aristocrat and his lifelong companion Ray Alan

VIZ 130.

drunken bakers

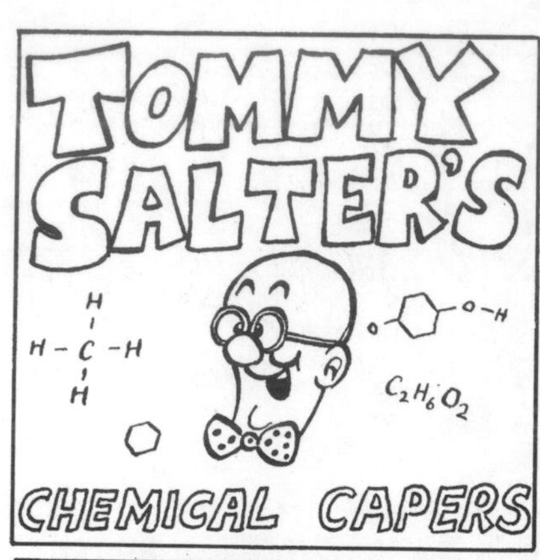
TOMMY SALTER'S
H
H – C – H
H
O–H
$C_2H_6O_2$
CHEMICAL CAPERS

I'VE GOT A SUPER NEW CHEMISTRY SET FOR MY BIRTHDAY
JUNIOR CHEMI SET

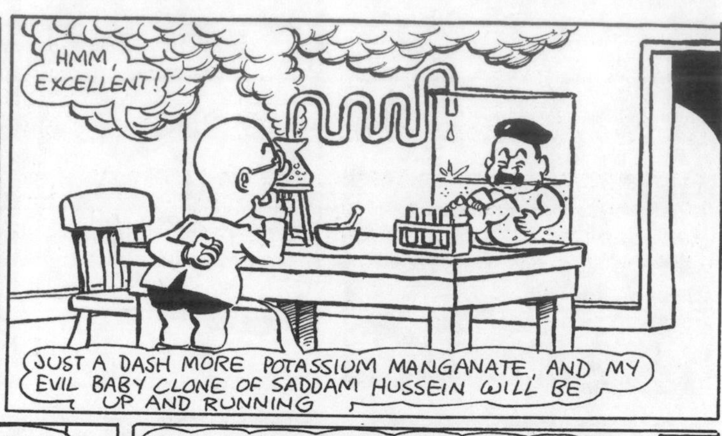
HMM, EXCELLENT!
JUST A DASH MORE POTASSIUM MANGANATE, AND MY EVIL BABY CLONE OF SADDAM HUSSEIN WILL BE UP AND RUNNING

NOT ON MY KITCHEN TABLE, IT'S NOT. CLEAR THAT AWAY WHILE I SET THE TEA THINGS, TOMMY
BUT MUM – THINK OF THE POSSIBLE BENEFITS TO MEDICAL SCIENCE!

I'LL MEDICAL SCIENCE YOU IN A MINUTE, YOUNG MAN. NOW GET RID OF THAT HORRIBLE THING AT ONCE!
BAH!

HOY! YOU'RE NOT DUMPING YOUR EVIL CLONE BABIES IN MY BIN!
OOPS! MR WILSON!
YOU CAN KEEP YOUR BLOODY RUBBISH OFF MY PROPERTY!

MY GOLDFISH POND HAS NEVER BEEN THE SAME SINCE YOU SET UP THIS CHEMICAL WASTE OUTFLOW FROM YOUR BEDROOM WINDOW
HISSS
GURGLE

TSK. THAT'S TYPICAL OF THE GENERAL PUBLIC'S ATTITUDE
THEY WANT TO ENJOY ALL THE ADVANTAGES OF SCIENTIFIC RESEARCH WITHOUT SHOULDERING ANY OF THE RESPONSIBILITY

THE PARK KEEPER WON'T MIND IF I BURY MY CLONE IN HIS FLOWERBED
PARK
HOLD ON A MINUTE, TOMMY

HAVE YOU BEEN FEEDING GENETICALLY MODIFIED CORN TO MY PIGEONS?
THAT'S RIGHT. IT'S AN EXPERIMENTAL NEW STRAIN I INVENTED USING PIGS' GENES

YES. WELL THAT WOULD EXPLAIN THIS, THEN
OINK-COO
OINK-COO
FLAP
SNORT
GREAT SCOTT! THIS IS FASCINATING!

BOOT!
RK
..AND STAY OUT OF MY PARK!

SO
THERE'S NOTHING ELSE FOR IT
FWOOSH!
I'LL JUST HAVE TO DISPOSE OF MY BABY SADDAM HUSSEIN CLONE DOWN THE LAVATORY

TWO WEEKS LATER
WE HAVE REASON TO BELIEVE THAT YOUR SON IS RESPONSIBLE FOR THE TWENTY-FOOT LONG RAT-EATING IRAQI DICTATOR THAT IS RAMPAGING THROUGH FULCHESTER'S SEWER SYSTEM
ARMY
HEY WOW!

GET UP THEM STAIRS WITHOUT ANY SUPPER, YOUNG MAN
BAH! I'M JUST BEING PUNISHED FOR YOUR IRRATIONAL FEAR OF SCIENTIFIC PROGRESS

...AND TIDY YOUR BEDROOM WHILE YOU'RE UP THERE
IT'S AN ABSOLUTE TIP

It Ain't Half Hot Mum!

Tragic Don's Message from the Pits of Hell

PINT SIZE actor Don Estelle, who died earlier this year, has shocked friends and family after revealing that he has been damned to burn in Hell for all eternity. And what makes it worse for the 4'9" corpse is that it's all down to an irregularity in the credits of his 1975 hit single *Whispering Grass.*

SHOWBIZ EXCLUSIVE!

Don, who played bespectacled Lofty in the popular sitcom *It Ain't Half Hot Mum*, believed he had led a blameless life and so was gobsmacked to be refused entry at the Pearly Gates.

He told reporters at a press seance: "St Peter explained that because of *Whispering Grass* I wouldn't be allowed into the kingdom of Heaven. I joked that surely it wasn't that bad a record, but then I noticed he wasn't laughing. He told me the problem was that the vocals on the record had been credited to me and Windsor Davies, although most of Windsor's part was actually sung by session singer Mike Sammes."

commandments

"He told me that I had therefore broken one of the ten commandments, and so I was being sent to Hell," added Estelle, speaking from a lake of eternal fire. "Frankly, I was gutted."

Friends of the actor have organised a petition to protest about his treatment, but according to the Archbishop of Canterbury there is nothing that can be done to save Estelle's soul from perpetual damnation. He told us: "On the surface, this decision may seem quite harsh, but the Bible's very clear on this subject. A lie is a lie and if the Lord were to let Don Estelle off, where would it all end?"

He continued: "Would Don Estelle's family want God to forgive all the other liars of history? What about Hitler, Caligula, Myra Hindley or Milli Vanilli? Somehow, I don't think they would."

green bottles

Speaking from his home next door to Donald Sinden, Windsor Davies expressed his sympathy. "Don was a lovely boy. I know I gave him a rough time as Sergeant Major Williams, but it sounds like Beelzebub's treating him even worse," he joked. "Now I'm going to have to go all religious because I don't fancy joining Lofty in the firey bowels of Hades for five minutes, let alone all eternity!"

Estelle to pay - Don but not forgotten, in happier times

Mike Sammes died in 2001. He declined to comment when we summoned him on a ouija board. "I really don't have time for this sort of thing," he told us via a moving glass.

Too old to ever get out of the bath again?

SAYS TV's MARTIN CLUNES

ORDER NOW and receive your **FREE BUDGERIGAR**

If the advancing years mean you daren't risk getting into a bath in case you never get out again, why not call and arrange to have the new SeniorChoice SpaCentre 200 fitted in the space being wasted by your current bath? For less than the cost of a medium-range tactical fighter aircraft, we can give you back your freedom to wash, and that's something your relatives are sure to appreciate far more than their inheritance. After all, it's only money!

CALL NOW! for a colour brochure and a chat...

08999 455 451

SENIORCHOICE

Regency Custom Shopriders

Dozens of hot mods for your mobility scooter

- CHROME FORKS • "GO-SHOPPING" STRIPES
- PAVEMENT KING ALLOYS • TARTAN PANNIERS
- BING CROSBY "ICE 'N' EASY" I.C.E. SYSTEM
- FRONT-MOUNTED PEDESTRIAN PLOUGH

Call for a catalogue
08999 676000

"It's a real BOON" TV's *Neil Morrissey*

"You know, dear, we blew it..."

STAIRS A PROBLEM?

says TV's LESLIE ASH

"Stiff joints... bad legs... heavy lips... whatever the reason you find climbing the stairs a problem, a Stannard-Rowe stairlift can really make the difference between being downstairs and being upstairs."

Call anytime except during "Countdown" for a free brochure

VISA MasterCard 08999 741741

Pardon?

AS NOT QUITE HEARD ON TV

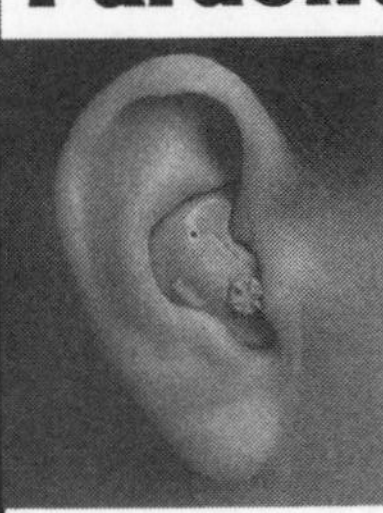

If you're finding it hard to tell the difference between an offer of a cup of tea and a request for help with the washing up, try the new **In-The-Ear** aid from Sexton's

The new Sexton ITE45 enables you to hear up to 80 pre-selected phrases...

- "It's for your own good."
- "They'll be along in a minute with the trolley."
- "It's alright, she can't hear you."

TV's CAROLINE QUENTIN says: *"something something Dundee funnel something"*

Sexton's 08999 588 500

YASSER'S GLASSES
YOUNG YASSER ARAFAT WAS THE LUCKIEST MAN IN PALESTINE - FOR HE OWNED A PAIR OF SUPER X-RAY SPECS - WHICH COULD SEE RIGHT THROUGH LADIES' DRESSES!
I THINK I'LL TAKE A WALK ALONG THE WEST BANK INSTEAD. THAT'S USUALLY HEAVING WITH CRUMPET!

HI READERS! I'M OFF DOWN THE OCCUPIED TERRITORIES WITH MY X-RAY SPECS FOR A BIT OF BIRD WATCHING...
...AND I'M NOT TALKING ABOUT THE FEATHERED VARIETY!

HERE COMES A LADY NOW!

EURGH! THAT'S NOT A LADY - IT'S BBC DIPLOMATIC EDITOR JOHN SIMPSON GOING UNDERCOVER AGAIN!
WHAT A SWIZZ!

NOT SO FAST, YASSER.
OH NO! IT'S THAT PESKY YITSHAK SHAMIR!

HAVE YOU FORGOTTEN?..WE'RE HAVING A MIDDLE EAST SUMMIT TODAY TO DISCUSS THE ROAD MAP FOR PEACE!
AW BUMS! PEACE TALKS ARE BORING. A ROOM FULL OF MEN IN SUITS AND NO LADIES TO GOZZ AT.

SHORTLY...
... DRONE DRONE... ISRAELI SETTLEMENTS... DRONE DRONE... MIDDLE EAST ACCORD... DRONE DRONE... CAMP DAVID AGREEMENT...DRONE DRONE... DRONE...
GOD - THIS IS DULL. I WISH THE QUEEN OF JORDAN WAS HERE SO I COULD OGLE HER BRAS.
YAWN!

...SO THAT'S THE FIRST PART OF THE ROAD MAP SORTED OUT... LET'S ALL HAVE A NICE CUPPA.
SHARON - COULD YOU BRING IN SOME TEA, PLEASE.
SHARON? A LADY! I'LL GET ME SPECS ON!

DROOL! I CAN'T WAIT TO SEE HER GIRDLES AND KNICKERS! I HOPE SHE'S WEARING SUSSIES!

TEA'S UP!
BAH! IT'S AERIAL SHARON!

HANG ON - WHERE ARE THE BISCUITS, AERIAL? WE CAN'T HAVE TEA WITHOUT BICCIES.
DIANE'S JUST BRINGING THEM IN NOW.
DIANE?!
WA-HEY!

HERE'S THE BISCUITS!

HOBNOBS, CHOCOLATE DIGESTIVES OR GYPSY CREAMS, ANYONE?
BAH! IT'S MOSHER DIANE!

12 HOURS LATER...
...SO WE'RE IN UNANIMOUS AGREEMENT THEN - THAT THESE PEACE TALKS HAVE FAILED...
SUMMIT IN PROGRESS
... SAME TIME NEXT WEEK, EVERYONE?

GOD - THAT WAS BORING. STILL, IT'S FINISHED EARLY ENOUGH FOR ME TO GET DOWN THE GAZA STRIP AND LOOK AT LADIES' UNDIES FOR A COUPLE OF HOURS BEFORE BED.

OI, YASSER!
EH!? OH NO. NOT YOU AGAIN.
HAVE YOU FORGOTTEN? YOU'VE GOT A MEETING IN 5 MINUTES.
GROAN!

IT'S THE NEW U.N. GOODWILL AMBASSADOR TO THE MIDDLE EAST. SHE'S WAITING IN HERE FOR YOU.
BAH!

MIND YOU - THESE GOODWILL AMBASSADORS ARE ALWAYS TASTY PIECES. I BET IT'S GINGER SPICE OR S CLUB JO... OR THAT MYLEENE OUT OF HEAR'SAY... HEH-HEH!

AMBASSADOR - ALLOW ME TO INTRODUCE YASSER ARAFAT - AND YASSER, I'D LIKE TO INTRODUCE YOU TO MISS WIDDECOMBE FROM ENGLAND.

FUCK ME!

POSH!
TINKLE!

BLAM! BLAM!
...LERRUZ IN THIS F-FF-FFUCKIN' 'OUSE, YER MISERABLE F-FFUCKIN' B-BB-B-BITCH!
ALL A WANT'S A NICE LIRRUL SIT DAHN...
A CUDD MEK YER A CUP OF TEE, LUV... OR 'ELP TH'BAIRNS WI' THEH 'OMEWORK... OR A'LL PURRA SHELF UP OR SUMMAT. AN' A WAIN'T SHIT CHAIR AGENN, LUV... 'ONEST...
...AN' THAT'S A PROMISE. ON GOD'S OWN F-FFUCKIN' LIFE.
AW, SMASHIN'. YER'LL NOT KNAW A'M EVEN IN, LUV.
TOO REYT A'LL NOT, 'COS YER FUCKIN' STOPPIN' AHT THEER.
EH!?
LOOK AT YERSELF, EIGHT Y'SCRUFFEH CUNT. JUST LOOK AT STATE OF YER.
WOT? EH?
WOT?
YER A FUCKIN' MESS.
WOT? TELLUS ONE THING... ONE FUCKIN' THING.
AN' YER CAN'T CAN YER.
ONE THING? REYT. YER'VE PISSED YER SHELL BOTTOMS, YER'VE GOT SPEW IN YER TASH, YER'VE 'AD THEM UNDER-PANTS ON EIGHT MONTH, YER'VE NEVEH 'AD A BATH, YER REEK OF THE ACE...
AN' YER FUCKIN' LIFTIN' WI' DICKIES, NITS AN' TICKS.
SEE? YER CAN'T, CAN YER.
...AN' ANYWEH, IT'S WOT'S FFUCKIN' INSIDE WOT COUNTS. IT'S EASEH TER PICK F-FF-F-FAULTS, IN'T IT...
'COS NOBODEH'S FFUCKIN' PERFECT.
A MEAN, A COULD SAY THAT YOO WOS A FFUCKIN' UGLEH ROTTON MISERABLE UGLEH F-FF-FFUCKIN' BITCH...
...BUT A WOULDN'T.
BUT WOT CAN A DO, LUV? A WANT TER LOOK AFTEH MESELF... BUT WOT CAN A DO?
Y'CAN START BY 'AVIN' A FUCKIN' 'AIRCUT.
BUT 'AIRCUTS COST MUNNY AN' A'VE GOT FFUCKIN' NOWT.
BURRIF A GIVE YOO MUNNY FER 'AIRCUT, YER'LL JUST SPEND IT ON TH'ACE.
A FFUCKIN' WAIN'T. THAT'S SO UNFAIR. YER'VE 'URT US NOW.
A'LL NOT LET YER DAHN, LUV. A WAIN'T. NOT THIS TIME. A F-FF-FF-FFUCKIN' PROMISE.
ALLREYT. BUT THIS IS YER LAST FUCKIN' CHANCE, EIGHT. 'OW MUCH IS 'AIRCUT?
ONE FORTEH-NINE.
SHORTLY...
...A'VE F-FFUCKIN' LET 'ER DAHN A F-FFUCKIN' 'GENN. SHE WOS REYT... SHE CAN READ US LIKE A F-FF-FFUCKIN' SCRATCHCARD...
A'VE GOT NO F-FFUCKIN' RESPECT FER MESELF... THE ACE 'AS ROBBED US OF IT.
SHE'LL F-FFUCKIN' KILL ME. SHE WILL. A'M DEAD. SHE'LL LOOK AT US AALL FULL OF TH'ACE WI'OUT 'AIRCUT AN' SHE'LL JUMP TER CONCLUSIONS.
SHE'S ALLUS BLAMIN' ME. WELL SHE GIVE US THE MUNNY, AN' THAT CUNT AT THE OFFY SELT IT ME, BURRIT'S ME WOT GETS IT IN THE F-FFUCKIN' NECK. A'M THE FFUCKIN' VICTIM IN THIS.
A'M JUST A PAWN IN A BIG FFUCKIN' GAME OF ACE.
WELL FUCK 'ER. A'LL CUT ME AHN F-FFUCKIN' AIR IN ME SHED. SHE'LL NEVEH KNAW.
REYT..!
SHORTLY...
TAP! TAP! TAP!
DA-DAAA!
WOT D'YER RECKON, LUV? D'YER THINK HE'S TOOK TOO MUCH OFF BACK?
SLAM!
BLAM! BLAM!
WORRISIT, LUV? IS IT ME CLOTHES? TELL YER WOT - A'LL GO GET MESELF A NICE NEW MADE TER MEASURE SUIT, EH?
WI' SPATS AN' A F-FF FFUCKIN' TOP 'AT... 'OW ABOUT THAT?
...ERM... CAN YER LEND US ONE FORTEH-NINE?

Letterbocks

Blitz a mystery

How come my gran survived the horrors of the Blitz, but has been so badly traumatised by the clocks going back that she can't stop banging on about it? The stupid whispy-chinned bitch.

Stuart Duncan, Email

Hats off to the American police. They arrive at Michael Jackson's Neverland ranch to arrest him a mere six months after he admits climbing into bed with young boys on worldwide TV. Perhaps they should get some faster cars.

T Barnham
London

No Soup for Me

On a recent visit to Newcastle I was asked to leave the Popolo restaurant for shouting "Serenity now". I would like to apologose to anyone whose night was spoilt by this, and thank the door staff who were excellent.

Robert Cook
Email

STAR LETTER

"THIS restaurant needs people like you". So said the recruitment poster in my local McDonald's. So I told my identical twin and now he's got a job there.

John Paul O'Kane, Email

The BIG issue

FORGET the War in Iraq, the Crisis in the Health Service, Asylum Seekers coming over here taking all the jobs and Wacko Jacko. There's only one topic on the lips of British people in offices, pubs and clubs the length of the land:

Were REM right to leave Shiny Happy People off their Greatest Hits CD?

We went onto the street, and found the people of Britain very much divided...

YES

...Shiny Happy People was never one of my favourite REM tracks. I think anyone who believes it should have been included on their Greatest Hits CD should be put on the sex offenders' register.

Mrs Tina Whore, costermonger

...I've been a great fan of REM since the early days, but I always hated that song. If it had been included on the new CD I would have put my foot through the stereo and sent Michael Stipe the bill.

Jack Steeple, steeplejack

...The first time I heard Shiny Happy People it was playing on a radio in a Turkish hospital where I was being treated for a septic anal fissure. The song will always remind me of my suffering. Three cheers to REM for leaving it off the album.

Steve Dore, docks worker

...I don't particularly like REM and I have never bought any of their records. However, if I had different tastes I would have liked all their records except Shiny Happy people. As a result I would definitely have bought an album which didn't include it.

Bosco Jancovich, freelance tramp

NO

...I bought that record and I couldn't believe it when it didn't have Shiny Happy People on. I bought another copy but that was the same.

Ray West, tea blender

...Like Mr West, I bought the record, and couldn't believe it when Shiny Happy People wasn't included. I was so incensed I put my foot through the stereo ...and sent Michael Stipe the bill! When his cheque arrived I put my foot through that as well... and sent him the bill!

Emily Nugent, exhaust fitter

...REM have spat in the face of their fans. If they spent less time having an air-rage incident several years ago and more time putting Shiny Happy people on their Greatest Hits CD, they would get my respect back.

Anais Nin, carpet fitter

...I don't particularly like REM and I have never bought any of their records. However, if I had different tastes I would have liked Shiny Happy People. As a result I would certainly not have bought an album which didn't include it.

Bosco Jancovich, freelance tramp

Those speed cameras are useless. Whenever I see one, I just get out and go past it on foot. They haven't caught me yet!

Larry Fist, Lloyton

I would like to thank Darren of Chelsea for not coming to Australia with Jenny. She is a great shag. Thanks again.

Baz
Bondi

It's all very well Meg Ryan getting her kit off for her new film, but why wasn't she doing it twenty years ago before her puppies hit the pan?

Alan Pick
Kingston-upon-Toast

Dream Job

I dreamt I was offered a job at Chanel, selecting their fabrics. I'm concerned, as I think I may have agreed to take it. Is this agreement legally binding? I'm a decorator and have no previous experience in the fashion industry.

Wallace Wainhouse
Email

Fun Lovin' Criminals

Hats off to the witty burglars who stole my entire CD collection with the exception of 'There is Nothing Left to Lose' by the Foo Fighters. I hope that, when sentencing, the judge takes into account their splendid sense of humour.

Chris Scaife, Jesmond

I have just spent three hours making custard using Delia's recipe and it's a triumph, in that it tastes just like Bird's Instant.

A.W. Thompson
Email

Wouldn't it be great if Robert Palmer came back as a zombie.

Paul Gill
Hotmail

** Who would you like to see rise from the dead, and in what form? Perhaps you'd love to see Dame Thora Hird materialise in your bedroom as a bloodsucking bride of Dracula, or maybe you'd prefer Sammy Davis Jnr as a Frankenstein. Write to the Viz Necromancer, PO Box 1PT, Newcastle upon Tyne NE99 1PT.*

The other day I had 9 Mini Kievs, 5 onion rings, Chow Mein Supernoodles and a bag of Walls' Cheesy Balls for my tea. Have any of your readers had a more council house meal than that?

Tim Buck
Newcastle

TOP TIPS

MCDONALD'S. Make your brown carrier bags green in colour so they blend in with the countryside after they've been thrown out of car windows.

Richard Karslake
Oxon

AVOID dogs molesting your leg under the dinner table by coating your trousers below the knee with Ralgex or Firey Jack.

Neil Fortune
Email

A POST-IT note stuck beneath the nose is an ideal deterrent to lip-readers.

Bryn Littleton
Chester-le-Street

GUYS. If your lady's reluctant to swallow, make her eat halloumi cheese to get her used to the taste.

E.C. McG.,
Canterbury

ALCOHOLICS. Don't worry where the next drink is coming from. Go to the pub, where a large selection is available at retail prices.

Ed Freeman
Email

BI-CURIOUS men. Go to a male doctor and complain of rectal bleeding. The resultant erotic anal probe will be a safe way to find out whether gayness is really for you.

Terry Wilson
Wallasey

BOIL an egg to perfection without costly eggtimers by popping the egg into boiling water and driving away from your home at exactly 60mph. After 3 miles, phone your wife and tell her to take the egg out the pan.

James Bell
Email

Arrest warrant issued for Badly Drawn Boy's hat

BADLY DRAWN BOY'S famous woolly hat is being hunted by the police after failing to turn up for a third court hearing.

The hat, which shares a head with the grubby folknik (real name Damon Boy), missed two previous appointments with the law, which led to it being electronically tagged.

When it failed to show up at Oldham Magistrates Court on a health and safety charge on Monday, an arrest warrant was issued.

HAT-SCLUSIVE!

Badly ~ yesterday

However, when police arrived at Boy's head, the hat had fleeed.

Boy, best known for his soundtrack to the film *About A Badly Drawn Boy*, says he is "bladdered" by the disappearance. He last caught sight of his woolly companion more than a week ago when he noticed his reflection in a shop window.

It's as easy as A..B..C!

Theological queries answered by the

Arch Bishop of Canterbury

Dr Rowan Williams

Dear AB of C,

I understand Easter and Christmas are the two most important festivals in the christian calendar, but I often get them mixed up. I know one's about Jesus's birth, and the other is about his death, but which one is which?

Joyce Ollerenshaw, Burnley

* *It's as easy as A...B...C! Easter is the one with the sad ending, where Jesus gets nailed to a cross and dies. The Christmas story is the happy one, where the baby Jesus is born in a stable with no crypt for a bed. In case you're still confused, here's a little rhyme we were taught in theological college.*

Twice a year we celebrate,
Jesus who was really great.
If the two you cannot tell,
Then here's a rhyme to serve you well.

The Xmas Christ born in a shed,
Means we hang socks upon our bed.
While Easter's tale of nails and wood,
Brings choccy eggs that taste so good.

Dear AB of C,

Is there a simple way to remember the 10 commandments? I keep on forgetting one or other of them. Last week I forgot the one about stealing and narrowly avoided being arrested for armed robbery. Last night I couldn't remember the one about adultery and ended up in bed with the woman next door. Talk about being in the doghouse!

Len Plywood, Harlow New Town

* *It's as easy as A...B...C! As Archbishop of Canterbury I have to remember them all. Imagine if I was arrested for robbery or if Mrs Dr Rowan Williams caught me up to my right reverend nuts in the woman next door. The General Synod would never let me hear the end of it! Fortunately, there's a mnemonic to help you remember them all.*

The initial letters of these ten commandments: Do not worship STRANGE GODS, Don't take the Lord's name in VAIN, Keep the SABBATH holy, HONOUR your mum and dad, Don't KILL, Don't do ADULTERY, Don't STEAL, Don't bear FALSE WITNESS, Don't COVET WIVES and Don't COVET GOODS spell out the following easy-to-remember sentence.

Some **G**reeks **V**isit **S**pain, **H**owever, **K**angaroos **A**nd **S**heep **F**art **W**hen **C**harlie **W**illiams **C**hases **G**oats.

See how easy it is? Now you'll never forget the ten commandments.

Dear AB of C,

The bible is always going on about Pharisees and Samaritans. I know that one lot are goodies and the others are baddies, but which is which? Honestly, Dr Williams, it's really, really doing my head in.

Rev. X. Townsend, Arran

* *It's as easy as A...B...C! The Samaritans are the goodies and I always remember that because their name looks a bit like 'Smarties', my favourite sweet. Yum! The Pharisees, on the other hand, are the baddies. Their name reminds me of 'pharmacy' and having to take horrid medicine. Yuk!*

Dear AB of C,

Last month an earthquake in Bogota killed 48,000 people. In August, floods in China killed another 20,000. As I write this letter, a child dies of starvation somewhere in the world every 3 seconds. How could an infinitely powerful God who loves us allow these things to happen?

J. Turner, Pitlochry

* *I must admit, I've never really thought about it. It certainly is a tricky one, now you mention it. But hey, Mr Turner. Lighten up! It's nearly Xmas!*

ROGER MELLIE THE MAN ON THE TELLY...

OH, LORDY... IT'S THE
FAT SLAGS

ON SKEGNESS BEACH...
THAT WAS GREAT, THAT WAS. WHAT D'Y WANT T'DO NOW, TRAY?
DO Y' FANCY CATCHIN' SOME CRABS?
DONKEY RIDES £1

NAH! I GOT SOME LAST NIGHT OFF THAT BLOKE ON THE DODGEMS. FANCY SOME ICE CREAM?
GO ON THEN. NINETY-NINE
I'LL JOIN YER!
ICES
ICE CREAM

D'Y' KNOW... SLURP! I MIGHT GO FOR A 'UNDRED NEXT TIME... SLURP!
ICES
CLOSED

SHORTLY...
HEY, DAVE... FUCK ME! LOOK WHO IT IS!
AYUP, BAZ... DAVE. WHAT YOU TWO DOIN' IN SKEGGY?
WE COME DOWN ON THE PULL LAST NIGHT IN DAVE'S TRANSIT

WELL GUESS WHAT?.. YOU'VE JUST PULLED!
WELL, I COULD 'AVE FUCKED YOU BACK 'OME AN SAVED TEN QUID ON PETROL
AH, C'MON, BAZ! SKEGGY'S A MORE EXOTIC LOCATION. IT MIGHT MAKE IT A BIT MORE EXCITIN' THAN USUAL

HMM... MAYBE YOU'RE RIGHT. SHALL WE DO 'EM ON THE MATTRESS IN THE BACK OF YOUR VAN?
NO! IT'S GOIN' IN FOR M.O.T. NEXT WEEK AN THE SUSPENSION'S 'ELD ON WI DUCT TAPE

WELL 'OW ABOUT WE GO BACK T' YOUR B & B THEN, GIRLS?
CAN'T. WE GOT CHUCKED OUT
WHAT FOR?
DUNNO. WE DIDN'T BREAK ANY RULES OR OWT, DID WE TRAY?

NO. THE LANDLADY SAID RULE ONE WAS 'NO MEN IN THE ROOMS'
AYE! SO WE PICKED THESE BLOKES UP AT THE FAIR, TOOK 'EM BACK AND FUCKED 'EM ON THE STAIRS AND SHE WENT MENTAL.

HEY! WHY DON'T WE DO IT 'ERE ON THE BEACH?
THAT'S A GOOD IDEA. I'VE NEVER DONE IT ON A BEACH!
YOU 'AD THAT BIRD ON A PILE OF SAND, REMEMBER? ...WHEN WE WERE LABOURIN' FOR THAT BRICKIE.

AYE, BUT THAT WERE BUILDERS' SAND... IT'LL BE A DIFFERENT EXPERIENCE DOIN' IT ON A BEACH
EEH, JUST IMAGINE... THE WAVES CRASHIN' ON THE SHORE AS THE PASSION MOUNTS... SO ROMANTIC. IT'LL BE JUST LIKE THAT SCENE IN 'FROM HERE TO ETERNITY'

AYE... RIGHT, I'LL GET US A WINDBREAK, DAVE, YOU GET THE MATTRESS OUT THE VAN
RIGHT
ONLY YOU'LL HAVE TO TURN IT OVER 'COS ONE OF US PISSED IT LAST NIGHT.

SO...
'OLD ON, SAN... ME LID'S COVERED IN SAND
'ERE! I'LL WIPE IT OFF WI' ME KNICKERS

OW! DON'T WIPE IT. YOU'LL CUT ME FUCKIN' BRIM TO RIBBONS... BAT IT OFF!
MOVE OVER, TRAY
OW! FUCK!
WHAT'S UP, DAVE!?!
I'VE JUST KNELT ON SOME GLASS!

OW! GET YER TOE OUT ME ARSE, BAZ
IT'S DAVE... AN' IT'S NOT ME TOE
OW!
SORRY
CLUNK!
EURGH!
WHAT!?

I JUST FOUND A LUMP OF DOG SHIT... LOOK!
CAN I HAVE ME CRICKET BALL BACK, MISTER?
FUCK OFF!
'URRY UP, BAZ... I'M GEDDIN' CRAMP!

TAKE YOUR PHOTO WITH A MONKEY, SIR? TWO POUND
NO! YOU CAN'T TAKE ME PHOTO WITH A FUCKIN' MONKEY
I'M TRYIN' TO 'AVE A ROMANTIC FUCK, FOR FUCK'S SAKE!..

...WHAT THE FUCK!?
SORRY, PAL. ALL WINDBREAKS IN BY 5 O'CLOCK!

WHAT NOW, BAZ?

SQUEAK! SQUEAK! SQUEAK! SQUEAK! SQUEAK! SQUEAK!
UGH! UGH! UGH! UGH! UGH! UGH!

BANG!!
AW, FUCK!
IT'LL NOT GET THROUGH ITS FUCKIN' M.O.T. NOW

DICKIE BEASLEY
YOUNG DICKIE BEASLEY HAD ONE AMBITION... TO BECOME AN ACCOUNT EXECUTIVE AT A TOP LONDON ADVERT-ISING AGENCY...

NOW DON'T EAT ANY OF THIS CAKE, DICKIE. I BAKED IT FOR THE W.I. CAKE STALL TOMORROW... DOESN'T IT LOOK NICE?
HMM?
CORN FLAKES
WELL, YES. IT LOOKS NICE TO ME, MUM, BUT I'M NOT YOUR TARGET CAKE END PRODUCT CONSUMER
THE BAKED CONFECTION MARKET PLACE IS VERY CROWDED. IF YOU WANT TO SHIFT PRODUCT, YOUR CAKE WILL HAVE TO LEAP FROM THE TRESSLE TABLE AND SHOUT BUY ME!
THE AVERAGE CAKE BUYER LOOKS AT EACH CAKE UNIT FOR 1.2 SECONDS... THAT'S ALL THE TIME YOU'VE GOT
I LOOK AT THIS CAKE AND I DON'T SEE ANY REASON TO BUY IT OVER ANY OTHER
BUT IT'S GOT JAM IN THE MIDDLE... IT'S LOVELY!
JAM!? JAM!? HA! HA! HA!
THE CAKE BRAND TENT DOESN'T ENCOMPAS JAM ANY LONGER, MUM... NO!

GET WITH THE PROG-RAMME. LAST YEAR, LEMON CURD WAS THE NEW JAM...
...WHO KNOWS WHAT THIS YEAR'S LEMON CURD IS GOING TO BE

TO MAXIMISE YOUR GROSS MARGINS, IT'S NO GOOD BEING ONE STEP AHEAD OF THE GAME... YOU HAVE TO BE TWO STEPS AHEAD
LEAVE THIS CAKE WITH ME, MUM. I'M GOING TO RUN IT PAST A FOCUS GROUP.

SHORTLY...
OKAY! THANKS FOR COMING ALONG TODAY TO TALK ABOUT THIS PRODUCT. I WANT YOU ALL TO EAT A SLICE AND THEN TELL ME WHAT YOU THINK. NO RIGHT OR WRONG ANSWERS, JUST HONEST COMMENT.
FCUK OFF
OKAY, LET'S FLY THIS KITE

JUST A SMALL PIECE FOR ME, LOVE.
A SMALL PIECE?
YES, PLEASE
SO YOU THINK THE CAKE IS TOO BIG, EH?.. HMM! INTERESTING.

ER... NONE FOR ME, THANKS. I JUST HAD A BIG FRY-UP FOR ME LUNCH
WHAT?.. EGGS, SAUSAGES, THAT SORT OF THING? NICE, WAS IT?
AYE! LOVELY
FCUK OFF
THAT'S VERY INTERESTING

OKAY! WHAT ABOUT YOU?
NO THANKS, SON. I'M DIABETIC
OH! SO YOU'D PREFER CAKE WITHOUT SUGAR?
FCUK OFF
WITHOUT SUGAR?.. NO!.. THAT WOULD BE HORRIB...

"I WOULD PREFER A CAKE MADE WITHOUT SUGAR"
FASCINATING

WELL, I THINK IT'S DELICIOUS, SON... MUNCH! MUNCH!.. I'D LOVE TO STOP AND HAVE SOME MORE... MUNCH!... BUT I'VE GOT A TRAIN TO CATCH

HMM! SO 20% OF THE GROUP CONSIDER TRAINS TO BE MORE IMPORTANT IN THEIR LIVES THAN CAKE!
HMM!
..THIS STUFF IS DYNAMITE!

NEXT DAY...
RIGHT, MUM. I LET THE FOCUS GROUP LOOSE ON YOUR CAKE MOCK-UP
MUM'S CAKE
FOCUS GROUP ANALYSIS 2003
I THINK THESE PULL QUOTES WILL PUT A NEW PERSPECTIVE ON THE W.I. CAKE PROJECT.

"I CAN'T EAT JAM. THE SEEDS GET UNDER MY PLATE"
"CAN I NIP TO YOUR TOILET, SONNY? TEA GOES STRAIGHT THROUGH ME"
FWIP! FWIP!
"SORRY REALLY DO HAVE TO GO AND CATCH MY TRAIN"
"MY JUMPER IS BLUE, MY SOCKS ARE BLUE... GUESS MY FAVOURITE COLOUR IS BLUE"
"SORRY! I REALLY DO HAVE TO GO AND CATCH MY TRAIN"

NOW, I'VE CRUNCHED THE NUBERS, AND I'VE COME UP WITH THIS...
LIKES CAKE
HATES CAKE
LIKES BLUE
PREFERS TRAINS
...YOUR CAKE BRAND TENT TARGET CONSUMER

WHAT DO WE KNOW ABOUT HIM?.. WELL, HE'S A MAN, OR WOMAN, AGED BETWEEN TEN AND NINETY, MARRIED OR SINGLE, WHO LIKES CAKE
THIS IS YOUR HAPPY APPLE, MUM. THIS IS THE PERSON WHO IS GOING TO BUY YOUR CAKE... OR RATHER, HE'S GOING TO BUY...

THIS CAKE!
GASP! IT LOOKS HORRIBLE, DICKIE... IT'S BLUE... AND IT'S COVERED IN FRIED EGGS AND SAUSAGES.
IT MAY LOOK HORRIBLE TO YOU, MUM, BUT TO OUR BRAND CONSUMER, THIS CAKE IS SEX ON A STICK!
LATER...
BARNTON W.I.
CAKE SALE TODAY

I'M SO EMBARRASSED, DICKIE... IT'S THE ONLY CAKE THAT DIDN'T SELL
HMM! PERHAPS WE MISJUDGED THE FOCUS GROUP DEMOGRA-PHIC... OR MAYBE THE MARKET HAS GONE RETRO...

I'LL TAKE IT ON THE STREET AND DO SOME VOX POPS... SEE WHAT OLD JOSEPH PUBLIC THINKS

SO... EXCUSE ME..."THIS CAKE IS TOO RETRO TO FALL WITHIN CURRENT BRAND ACCEPTANCE PARAMETERS". OKAY?
EH!?
DO YOU (A) STRONGLY AGREE (B) AGREE (C) NEITHER AGREE NOR DISAGREE (D) DISAGREE OR (E) STRONGLY DISAGREE?

SPAWNY GET
HEH HEH! I'VE FOUND A RED HOT MUCKY DVD IN THE SEX SHOP DUSTBINS. NOW TO GO AND WATCH IT ON GRANNY'S GREAT BIG TELLY.
I'D BEST PUT IT ON MUTE. I DONT WANT TO WAKE GRANNY UP
HEH! SHE'S WELL UNDER. I THINK ITS SAFE TO RISK A STRUM...
SNORE!
GAW! THAT WAS A GOOD BIT... SHE GOT A RIGHT FACEFULL!
ZZZZZOOP!
...I'LL REWIND IT AND PRESS FREEZE FRAME AND ZOOM IN!
FUCK MY BIG BLACK ASS!
LUMMIE! I MUST HAVE PRESSED THE VOLUME CONTROL!
HEUGH? WOSSAT?
HEUGGGH!!
POP.
GRANNY'S DEAD... HEY GREAT! I HOPE I INHERIT HER BIG TELLY
ROLL!
NEXT DAY...
BAH! SHE LEFT IT ALL TO THE CATS, THE MISERABLE OLD BITCH!
SOLICTOR
SOL
...AND GUESS WHO'S PAYING FOR THE FUNERAL TOO?
CO-OP FUNERAL SERVICES
FUNERALS £100.00
EXCUSE ME - ID LIKE TO GET MY GRANDMOTHER UNDERTAKEN, PLEASE.
CERTAINLY SIR. IF YOU'D BRING HER THIS WAY...
CONGRATULATIONS MR GET! YOUR GRANNY IS OUR ONE MILLIONTH CORPSE! YOU WIN A FREE FUNERAL AND A THREE MINUTE TROLLEY DASH ROUND THE CO-OP!
SO...
READY...STEADY...
GO!!
CO OP
I'M HEADING FOR ELECTRICS! I'M GOING TO GET THE BIGGEST TELLY I CAN FIT IN THE TROLLEY!
ELECTRICALS
GNN!
Puff Pant!
TVs Dept
IT'S NO GOOD! I CANT REACH IT!
TILL
EXCUSE ME, COULD YOU REACH THAT BIG TELLY DOWN FOR ME?
SORRY, IT'S NOT MY DEPARTMENT. I'LL CALL SOMEONE FOR YOU...
TVs Dept
MEMBER OF STAFF FROM ELECTRICALS TO AISLE SIX, PLEASE...
...MEMBER OF STAFF FROM ELECTRICALS TO AISLE SIX...
TILL
TWO MINUTES LEFT, MR GET...
OO..ER!
TAP! TAP! TAP! TAP!
ONE MINUTE TO GO NOW MR GET...
WHIMPER!
HOP HOP HOP!
CLICK!
TIMES UP I'M AFRAID.
...SORRY AUDREY, I WAS HAVIN' A TAB.
BOO!
ALL I GOT WAS THIS DENTED TIN OF BEANS THAT FELL INTO MY TROLLY BY ACCIDENT...
I SAY!!
I COLLECT BEAN TINS, AND THAT TIN YOU'RE HOLDING THERE IS EXTREMELY RARE. THERE WAS ONLY EVER SIX OF THEM EVER MADE TO MARK VICTORIAS CORONATION IN 1837...
57
YOINKS!!
...TO THINK ITS BEEN SITTING ON THE SHELVES OF THE CO-OP FOR MORE THAN 160 YEARS. IT'S QUITE REMARKABLE.
I AM OF COURSE AN ECCENTRIC MILLIONAIRE. HERE'S A MILLION POUND.
57
CHEERS!
£1 MILLION
SO...
WAHEY! I'VE BOUGHT THE BIGGEST TELLY EVER LOADS OF MUCKY DVDS, AN ELEPHANTS SOCK, AND GRANNYS NOT AROUND SO I CAN HAVE IT AS LOUD AS I WANT!
YOU SPAWNY GET!
AC. GPD. ST. DT. SD. VIZ 123 09/03.

How DO you fit 6 HOURS of SEX into the busiest day of the year? Former Police frontman turned arsehole STING reveals his festive tan-trics of the trade

Stingle All the Way

Screw Yule! Sting (right) and wife Trudie Sting (below right) ~ sex sessions go on and on and on, yesterday.

SEXMAS SEXCLUSIVE!

DECEMBER 25th is hectic at the best of times. What with making the dinner, opening your presents and watching the Queen's speech, it often feels like there aren't enough hours in the day. Imagine if you had to fit in a marathon *6-hours of sex* as well!

*It sounds impossible, but that's just what eco-warrior-cum-Jaguar salesman **Sting** manages to do each year. And if you want to live like a star this Christmas, here's his timetable to ensure a successfully stuffed turkey in the kitchen and a successfully stuffed wife in the bedroom.*

Countdown to a Suc-sex-ful XXX-mas

-by Sting

8.00am

"**Christmas** day starts early in the Sting household when the alarm goes off. There's a long busy day ahead of us, and we have to fit 6 hours of sex in somewhere! Me and my wife Trudie Sting squeeze in half an hour of heavy petting before popping downstairs for a breakfast of free-range sausages, fried organic eggs, granary toast and a cup of fairtrade tea.

***Total nookie so far :* 30 minutes**

8.30am

Fully breakfasted, there's just time to check that the turkey has defrosted and turn the Aga up before nipping back upstairs for another quarter hour of cunnilingus.

***Total nookie so far :* 45 minutes**

9.00am

Back downstairs to get the veg ready while the kids open their presents. We only buy organic vegetables because we believe that modern agricultural pesticides can be very detrimental to health. I notch up another 45 minutes rubbing Trudie's breasts, 20 minutes on the left one, 25 on the right, while she's peeling the spuds, chopping the carrots and cutting them crosses in the sprouts.

***Total nookie so far :* 1 hour 30 minutes**

9.45am

The oven's reached 250 F, so it's in with the turkey. It's an opportunity to spend an hour or so opening my presents, but with another four and a half hours of sex to somehow fit in before bed, there's no time to waste. I get on with unwrapping my gifts while Trudie gets on with tickling my nuts.

***Total nookie so far :* 2 hours 30 minutes**

10.45am

Mid-morning, and just time to suck Trudie's nipples while she bastes the turkey. Only 5 minutes, but every little helps.

***Total nookie so far :* 2 hours 35 minutes**

10.50am

With the dinner cooking nicely in the oven most people would take the opportunity to relax. But not in the Sting household. Trudie and I are back upstairs for 20 minutes of mutual masturbation and 5 minutes of her sitting on my face.

***Total nookie so far :* 3 hours**

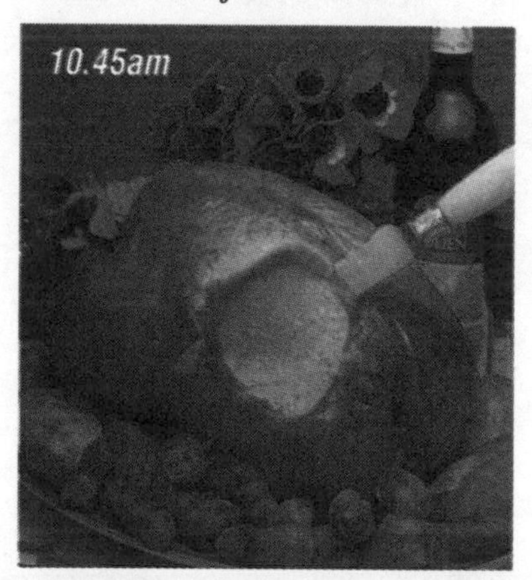

11.15am

We're half way there. With three hours under my belt, I allow myself a small sherry in bed while Trudie pops down to put the sprouts on. But then it's straight back to work, kneading her thighs sensuously for three quarters of an hour until the in-laws turn up.

***Total nookie so far :* 3 hours 45 minutes**

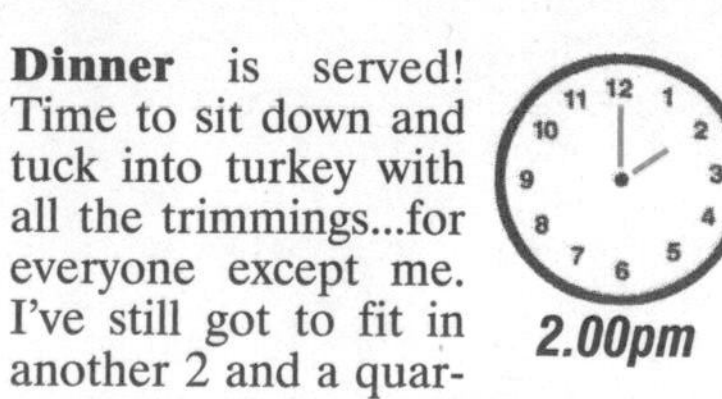

2.00pm

Dinner is served! Time to sit down and tuck into turkey with all the trimmings...for everyone except me. I've still got to fit in another 2 and a quarter hours of sex, so whilst I'm carving the turkey with my right hand I'm giving Trudie's bottom a kinky spank with my left. Then we cover each other in Christmas dinner, and slowly lick it off like in 9 and a Half Weeks. We have to be careful with the pudding, though. It's easy to end up with singed pubes!

***Total nookie so far :* 4 hours 30 minutes**

3.00pm

Everything stops for the Queen's speech. Except me and Trudie's marathon tantric bonk session! It's not that I don't respect the monarchy. Her majesty has her job to do, but I have mine as well. Whilst the Queen tells the nation about her travels and hopes for the coming year, Trudie and I tell each other our most intimate and outrageous sexual fantasies, using explicit language.

***Total nookie so far :* 4 hours 50 minutes**

3.30pm

Time to get our breath back and snooze our way through the Bond film with a box of Matchmakers and a Terry's Chocolate Orange. We might try a bit of oral during a commercial break, but that's about it.

***Total nookie so far :* 4 hours 55 minutes**

It's back into the kitchen, and I sit on the worktop masturbating while Trudie makes the turkey sandwiches.

5.00pm

***Total nookie so far :* 5 hours 25 minutes**

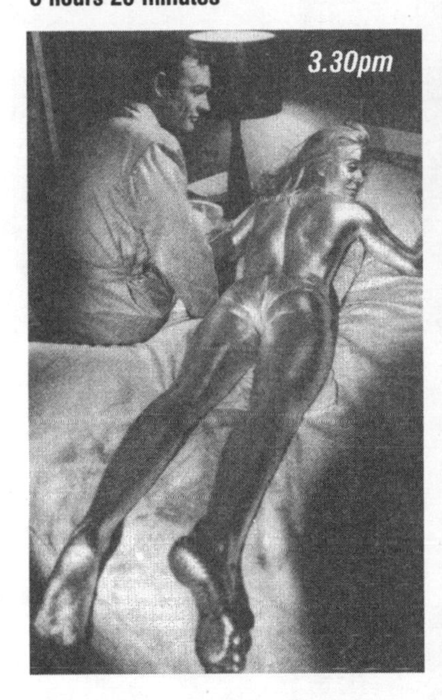

3.30pm

We eat our tea in the sitting room watching Christmas *You've Been Framed.* Trudie and me sit on the sofa and caress each other's genitals with our toes. That's another half hour out of the way. Only another 5 minutes left to go.

5.30pm

***Total nookie so far :* 5 hours 55 minutes**

6.00pm

Nearly there. The end's in sight, so it's upstairs for a 3 minute diddy-ride before the main event.

***Total nookie so far :* 5 hours 58 minutes**

At last. We have penetration. I scuttle Trudie for a good 2 minutes before shooting my bolt.

6.03pm

***Total nookie so far :* 6 hours**

6.05pm

Phew! It's all over and the evening is our own. But we've only got a few hours to get our strength back before starting our next 6 hour sex session... *at bedtime!*

10 things you never knew about... Christmas Dinners

1 As a baby, Christ was brought sprouts by one of the Wise Men as a gift, but he threw up and cried, so the Wise Man gave him some frankincense instead. Since then, sprouts have been a great part of Christian tradition and frankincense has been largely forgotten – a bloody good thing too, since it stinks... *of sprouts!*

2 The eccentric Earl of Crackers *(1770-1825)* invented crackers during a card game. He didn't want to leave his place at the Quantoon table to get his hat, his magnifying glass and his favourite joke, so he famously asked his servant to bring him all three in an exploding toilet roll! The Earl also invented water biscuits and fireworks.

3 Bootylicious bint Beyoncé Knowles loves Xmas Dinner so much that it's the only thing she eats. The independent woman attributes her foxxy figure to a strict diet of THREE Xmas Dinners a day. And at 28,000 calories per meal, it's no wonder she looks so crazy in love!

4 And even Madonna is a Xmas Dinner fan! She first got a taste for them when she visited a traditional East End Xmas Dinner restaurant in 1999 with hubbie Shane Richie.

5 In America, Xmas is called Thanksgiving and starts in November. Americans eat buffalo instead of turkey and shout instead of sing. They listen to Bing Crosby instead of the Queen, and their crackers contain cowboy hats.

6 The now-traditional Xmas Dinner row was introduced by Prince Albert. In a ceremony that continues to this day, the King of Denmark visits the royal family on Xmas Day to start their row for them. Last year's festive punch-up was about the the difference between Cornish Puddings and Yorkshire Pasties.

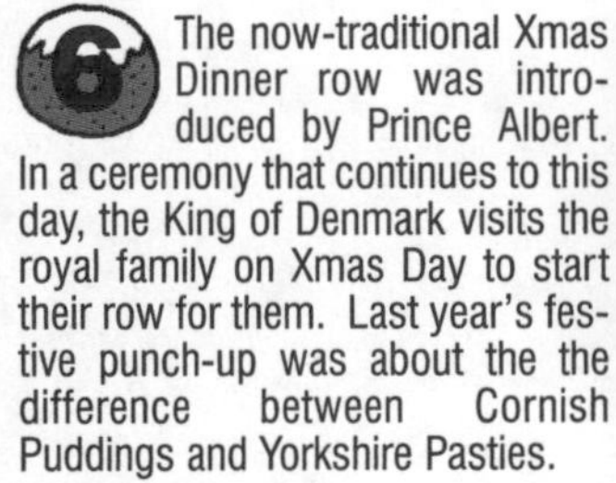

7 In 1976, comedy dancers Morecambe & Wise got the highest ever TV viewing figures for their Xmas Dinner. Eric Morecambe had had two heart attacks that year, and his doctors advised against a big TV special, so the BBC broadcast the duo's Xmas Dinner instead. 26 million people watched them eating turkey and nuts with Robert Dougall, Andrew Preview and Angela Rippon. The next day, the papers were full of stories about Rippon's amazing pair of turkey drumsticks, which had previously been hidden behind the newsdesk. This record stood until 1986, when 68m people watched Delboy falling memorably through his Xmas Dinner.

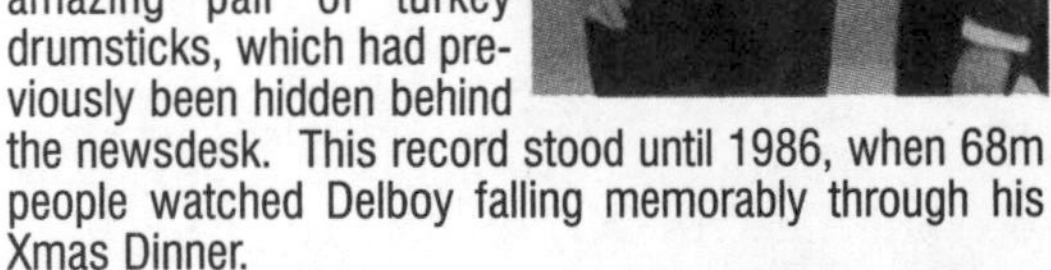

8 For short-haired women, Xmas Dinner is just another day off. Lesbians have not celebrated Xmas Dinner since Queen Victoria declared that she didn't believe it existed.

9 Stuffing used to be made of stuff, but is now usually made of sage and onion. Stuff traditionally included paper, cloth, feathers, stones, owl pellets, twigs, sage and onion.

10 By the year 2000, experts predict that busy space travellers will be able to eat their Xmas Dinner in pill form, as they race towards the moon in time to collect space presents from Moon Santa. We will also have four toes.

TERRY
FUCKWITT
THE UNINTELLIGENT CARTOON CHARACTER

HEY, I LOVE CHRISTMAS. AND THIS YEAR I'VE MANAGED TO PREPARE A CHRISTMAS DINNER FOR MUM AND DAD WITHOUT EVEN BURNING THE TURKEY.
A DRUMSTICK FOR ME PLEASE TERRY

EXCUSE ME. THIS ISN'T YOUR DINING ROOM - IT'S THE OPERATING THEATRE IN THE HOSPITAL
OOPS!
AND THAT IS A PATIENT UPON WHOM WE ARE ATTEMPTING TO PERFORM A HEART BYPASS OPERATION

HONESTLY, TERRY. YOU'VE GOT ABSOLUTE SHIT FOR BRAINS.
HOSPITAL EXIT
FANCY MAKING US SIT AROUND IN A HOSPITAL OPERATING THEATRE ON CHRISTMAS DAY. LET'S GO HOME.

OUTSIDE
WAIT A MINUTE... THIS ISN'T A HOSPITAL...
THIS IS OUR HOUSE AFTER ALL

AND THAT'S NOT A HEART BYPASS PATIENT...
IT'S OUR CHRISTMAS DINNER!

HANG ON - LET'S GET THIS STRAIGHT. IF THIS IS YOUR DINING ROOM, AND THAT'S YOUR CHRISTMAS DINNER...
..THEN WHERE'S OUR PATIENT?

SNIFF SNIFF
OO-ER! SMELLS LIKE SOMETHINGS BURNING IN THE KITCHEN.

FUCK ME! I THINK I'VE OVERCOOKED THE HEART BYPASS PATIENT!
TERRY. YOU'RE A CLUELESS TWAT.

DINING ROOMS, OPERATING THEATRES AND HEART BYPASS PATIENTS INDEED!
SMACK!
TAKE THAT!
OOF!

BUGGER ME. NOT ONLY AM I UTTERLY DENSE, I'VE ALSO GOT A BROKEN FACE
HEY, I'M A TOTAL WASTE OF SPACE

HELLO TERRY. YOU LOOK LIKE YOU NEED A FACE TRANSPLANT. THEY COST TWENTY THOUSAND POUNDS.
FACE TRANSPLAN CLINIC
RIGHT! I'LL HAVE ONE.

NOW, TERRY. WE CAN OFFER YOU A CHOICE OF TWO TYPES OF FACE TRANSPLANT. NUMBER ONE IS THE HANDSOME FEATURES OF A HOLLYWOOD MOVIE STAR...
1
2
..AND NUMBER TWO IS THE DRIBBLY DICK OF A SCABBY OLD TRAMP.

THE CHOICE IS YOURS, TERRY. WHICH ONE WOULD YOU PREFER TO HAVE GRAFTED ONTO YOUR FACE?
ERM... ERM... LET ME SEE...

AND SO
FFFMLLP MMMLLP!
HAVE ANOTHER MINCE PIE TERRY, YOU DAFT CUNT.

TOKEN XMAS SNOW
BIFFA BACON
MERRY XMAS

HOO, MUTHA. WOT'S F' TEA?
SHIT WI' SUGAR ON

WOT'S THAT BIT O' PAPER THERE, BIFFA?
IT'S JUST A NOTE FER YEE FROM SCHOOL
LET'S 'AVE A LOOK THEN

HOO, MUTHA... IT'S FROM THE SCHOOL NORSE! IT SEZ THE BAIRN'S GOT FRIGGIN' NITS!

EURGH! HE HAS AN' ALL! HE'S FUCKIN' LIFTIN' THE LITTLE COMMON CUNT
COMMON?

AS A MATTER O' FACT, NITS AANLY GAN ON CLEAN HEEDS
THAT REET, SON?
AYE! THAT'S FUCKIN' REET!

ARE YEE CAALLIN' ME AN' YER FATHA'S HEEDS DORTY?
ERM..
RECKON YER FUCKIN' POSH THEN, EH?
AYE... WI YER FANCY FUCKIN' HEEDLICE!

THINK YORRA FUCKIN' CUT ABOVE, EH?.. WI' YER DICKIES
LEAVE IT OOT, FATHA. HE'S NOT WORTH IT.

I'LL GET A CURM T' GET THE BASTAADS OOT
A CURM..?
...YUZ'LL NEED MORE THAN A CURM T' GET EM OOT, MUTHA...

...THESE IS GEORDIE NITS...
THEY'RE FUCKIN' ROCK!

HOO, FATHA! I FOOND THIS UNDER THE SINK! THIS'LL KNOCK 'EM OOT!
INSECTO
SUPER STRENGTH INSECTICIDE

CLANK
HNNNG!
OOF!

NAH! THEY'RE STILL AALL CRAALIN' ABOOT!
HMM...
...IT SEZ 'MAY REQUIRE TWO APPLICATIONS'

HNNNG!
CLANG!!

NAH! HE'S STILL LIFTIN... C'MON, WUZ'LL 'AVE T' BORN 'EM OFF!
HEH! HEH! I'LL GAN GET THE PETROL CAN OOT THE CAR BOOT

SO...
DIVVEN'T FORGET T' STRIKE THE MATCH AWAY FROM YERSELL
AYE... SAFETY FORST!

SKRIT
FLOOMF!

AARGH! ME FRIGGIN HEED'S AHAD!
D'YEE WANT T' PUT HIM OOT?
AYE! GIZ THE SHOVEL

SPANG! SPANG! SPANG!
SPANG! SPANG!

LET'S 'AVE A LOOK, SON... AYE!.. DEED AS FUCKIN' DOOR NAILS THEY ARE
Y' FUCKIN' BASTAADS, YUZ

NEXT DAY...
HOO, FATHA! I'VE GOT ANOTHER NURT FROM THE SCHOOL NORSE
EH?..
'S 'AVE A LOOK

FUCKIN' 'ELL! HE'S GOT WARMS NOO!
WARMS!?
WARMS IS NOWT. THEY'RE AS SOFT AS THE SHITE THEY LIVE IN...

...BEND AWA, SON, I'LL KICK THEIR FUCKIN' HEEDS IN F' YUZ
'EAR THAT?
WOT?

THIS UGLY CUNT RECKONS SHE'S GANNA KICK W' HEEDS IN
?
OH, SHE DOES, DOES SHE?
HEH! HEH!
'ER AN' 'OO'S FUCKIN ARMY?

... NEARLY AT THE DAY CENTRE, LADIES. SOON BE HAVING YOUR TEA AND BISCUITS.
I CAN'T HAVE TEA, ME. IT'S LIKE A RED RAG TO A BULL IS TEA...
...TEA, YES.
...TO MY BLADDER.
...BLADDER. YES, THAT'S RIGHT.
DIAL -A- RIDE
GOES STRAIGHT THROUGH ME, TEA DOES. AND ME VAGINAL FLOOR'S AS WEAK AS A KITTEN, SO IF I TRY TO HOLD IT IN, I LEAK.
SHE DOES. SHE LEAKS.
I LEAK.
SHE LEAKS.
THAT REMINDS ME - CAN YOU STOP OFF AT TIMOTHY WHITES FOR SOME NEW RUBBERISED DRAWERS, ONLY THIS IS ME ONLY PAIR AND THE SEALS HAVE PERISHED IN ME URINE FLOW.
... EXTRA LARGE...
WITH THE VULCANISED GUSSET.

DING-A-LING-A-LING-A-LING-A-LING!
BLAM! BLAM!
...AND THEY'LL JEW YOU ON THE TILL IF YOU'RE NOT SHARP AS A PIN.
...PIN, YES.
OPEN
DIAL -A- RIDE
COME ON LEFTY! LET'S GET OUT OF 'ERE!

DRIVE, LEFTY! FACKIN' DRIVE! DRIVE! DRIVE!
BLAM!
...AND I DON'T TRUST THE PAKIS NEITHER.
DIAL -A- RIDE

VROOM!
BANK
!?
TIMOTHY WHITES

THEY'RE NOT GENTLEMEN THESE DAYS THOUGH, ARE THEY?
AYE, WELL. THIS IS IT, ISN'T IT. WE HAD TO MAKE US OWN ENTERTAINMENT IN THEM DAYS, DIDN'T WE.

OOH, NO. NO MANNERS. I BLAME THEM SPACE INVADERS GAMES.
GAMES, YES.
NER! NER!
BLAM!
POLICE

WE DID. I HAD A WHIP AND A TOP AND A DOLLY PEG. NONE OF THIS CROSS PLATFORM CRASH BANDICOOT AND TEKKEN TAG TOURNAMENT VERSION 4.
NER! NER!
BLAM!
BLAM! BLAM!

VROOOM!
NER-NER! NER-NER!
BLAM! BLAM! BLAM! BLAM!
BLAM!
EEH! THE RUDDY NOISE. AND THAT'S SWEARING.
POLICE

EEH, ADA. LOO AT DOLLY'S THROAT.

AND I'VE GOT ME EYE ON THAT LOVELY CHINA TEAPOT. IT WAS HER MAM'S Y'KNOW.
OOH. THE ONE WITH FOURTEEN GRAND IN IT?
AYE.
THAT IS A NICE POT, THAT.

EXCUSE ME DRIVER - COULD YOU STOP OFF AT DOLLY'S ON WELBECK STREET..? ONLY WE'VE GOT SOME BUSINESS NEEDS SORTED.
HUNH!?

... AND DO YOU KNOW ANYBODY WHO'S GOT A VAN..?
SWERVE!
STOP!
... ONLY SHE'S GOT SOME SMASHING EGYPTIAN COTTON BEDSPREADS SHE'LL NOT BE WANTING ANY MORE AND...
DIAL A RIDE